BLOOD in the WATER

BLOOD
in the
WATER

A True Story of
Small-Town Revenge

SILVER DONALD CAMERON

STEER
FORTH
PRESS

First published in Canada in 2020 by Viking, an imprint of Penguin
Canada, a division of Penguin Random House Canada Ltd.

For information about permission to reproduce
selections from this book, write to:
Steerforth Press L. L. C., 31 Hanover Street, Suite 1
Lebanon, New Hampshire 03766

Cataloging-in-Publication Data is available from the Library of Congress

Printed in the United States of America

ISBN 978-1-58642-293-6

1 3 5 7 9 10 8 6 4 2

For the people of Isle Madame—
and, once again, for Marjorie, who always believed

CONTENTS

TIMELINE

June 1, 2013	Phillip Boudreau's death
June 6, 2013	Craig Landry arrested
June 7, 2013	Dwayne and Carla Samson, and James Landry arrested
June 26, 2013	Craig Landry provides the statement that becomes Her Majesty's Story
July 4, 2013	Craig Landry and Carla Samson released on bail
July 22, 2013	Dwayne's first bail hearing: held over for decision
July 29, 2013	Dwayne's second bail hearing: bail denied
Aug 13, 2013	Dwayne's third bail hearing: bail granted with stringent conditions
Oct 16, 2013	James denied bail
Nov 26, 2013	Dwayne's preliminary hearing
Dec 17, 2013	James's preliminary hearing
Nov 10, 12, 2014	James's trial—jury selection

Nov 13, 2014	Trial proper begins—Stephen Drake's opening statement
Nov 17–18, 24–28, 2014	Trial continues
Nov 29, 2014	Verdict: guilty of manslaughter
Jan 29, 2015	James sentenced to fourteen years less time served
May 18, 2015	Dwayne pleads guilty to manslaughter
June 15, 2015	Carla's case dismissed, no prospect of conviction
Sept 11, 2015	Craig sentenced to two years' probation
Sept 22, 2015	Dwayne sentenced to ten years less 103 days served
June 22, 2016	James's appeal against sentencing dismissed
June 12, 2018	James released on parole to halfway house, resumes fishing
June 20, 2018	Dwayne released on parole to halfway house, resumes fishing
Nov 3, 2019	James dies of cancer

CAST OF CHARACTERS

THE FISHING COMMUNITY

Phillip Boudreau, the victim, a poacher and a thief; *Midnight Slider* was his boat

James Landry, fisherman, former owner of the *Twin Maggies'* lobster licence, deckhand

Carla Samson, James's daughter, who acquired the licence from her father

Dwayne Samson, husband of Carla, captain of the *Twin Maggies*

Craig Landry, hired deckhand on the *Twin Maggies*

Margaret Rose Boudreau, Phillip's sister

Gerard Boudreau, Phillip's brother, lobster fisherman and lobster dealer

Linda Boudreau, Gerard's wife, captain of Gerard's boat

Kenneth Boudreau, Phillip's brother

THE LEGAL COMMUNITY

Mr. Justice Simon MacDonald, who presided over Dwayne Samson's hearings

Nash Brogan and T.J. McKeough, attorneys for Dwayne and Carla

Dan MacRury and Diane McGrath, prosecutors in Dwayne's case

Joel Pink, attorney for Craig Landry

Chief Justice Joseph Kennedy, who presided over James Landry's trial

Stephen Drake and Shane Russell, prosecutors in James's case

Luke Craggs, attorney for James Landry

Kevin Patriquin, Nova Scotia Legal Aid Society

Corporal Denzil George Fraser Firth, RCMP, chief investigator of Phillip Boudreau's death

Stephen White, genealogist, Centre d'études acadiennes, Université de Moncton

Raymond LeBlanc, paralegal assistant, returning officer, co-proprietor of Shamrock Store

Pearl LeBlanc, Raymond's wife and co-proprietor of Shamrock Store

Ronnie LeBlanc, their son, who circulated the petition and is married to Dwayne's sister Janet

Edgar Samson, proprietor, Premium Seafoods

Staff Sergeant Daniel Parent, RCMP (retired)

Hubert David, contractor, Phillip's neighbour

Betty David, his wife

Tony Veinot, crab-boat skipper, friend, and occasional employer of Phillip

Thilmond Landry, Phillip's neighbour

PROLOGUE

IT WAS IN 2013 that Phillip Boudreau was dropped—allegedly—to the bottom of the sea, but his neighbours would not be entirely surprised if he walked out of the ocean tomorrow, coated in seaweed and dripping with brine, smiling.

After all, Phillip had often vanished for long periods during his forty-three years, and he always came back to where he'd grown up—Alderney Point, at the edge of the Acadian village of Petit de Grat on Isle Madame, Nova Scotia. Afterwards it would turn out that he had been in prison, or out West, or hiding in the woods. Perhaps the police had been looking for him and he'd have tucked himself away in other people's boats or trailers, or curled up and gone to sleep in the bushes of the moorland near his family's home, his face coated with droplets of fog. He and his dog often slept in a rickety shed outside his parents' home, where the narrow dirt road ends at the rocky shore of Chedabucto Bay. He'd even been known to hollow out a snowbank and shelter himself from the bitter night in the cold white cavern he'd created.

He was a small man, perhaps five-five, with a goatee and a ready smile. He usually dressed in jeans, sneakers, a windbreaker, a baseball cap. Whenever he was released from prison, word would go around Isle Madame: *Phillip's out.* Lock the shed, the barn, the garage. *Phillip's out.* If your boat's missing, or your four-wheeler, talk to Phillip. Maybe you can buy it back from him. *Phillip's out.* If you want a good deal on a marine GPS, an outboard motor, a dozen lobsters, check out the Corner Bridge Store and Bakery. Phillip likes to hang out there. He ties up his speedboat, *Midnight Slider*, at a little dock nearby.

Some people loved Phillip. He could be funny, helpful, kind. He was generous to old people, good with animals, gentle with children. Other people hated and feared him, though they tended to conceal their feelings. If you crossed him he might threaten to sink your boat, shoot you, burn down your house. He could make you fearful for the safety of your daughter. Would he actually do anything violent? Hard to say.

If you went to the Royal Canadian Mounted Police detachment in nearby Arichat, they would tell you they couldn't do much until he actually committed an offence. Perhaps they'd tell you that you could get a peace bond, a court order directing Phillip to stay away from you and your family and your property. From time to time the Mounties would arrest Phillip for "uttering threats"—or for any of a dozen other offences—and send him back to prison. But he'd be out again soon enough, and if you'd helped put him inside, watch out.

So most people quietly avoided Phillip, carefully steering around him the way a lobster boat navigates a rocky shoal.

He did a tidy little business in hallucinogens and was available as a vandal for hire, particularly with respect to lobster traps. An Isle Madame lobster trap is a baited wooden cage weighted with rocks and lying on the sea floor. It's tied by a long slender rope to a buoy that floats at the surface. The fisherman hooks the buoy, hauls up the trap, and removes his catch; then he rebaits the trap and drops it overboard again. The trap is worth about $100, but the value of the lobster it catches can be in the thousands of dollars.

Nothing prevents a poacher from hauling someone else's traps in the middle of the night and selling the lobsters as his own. And if the buoy rope is cut off, the owner can't even find the trap. If I have a grudge against you, what better way to harm you than to slide out at midnight and cut a bunch of your traps? But if you catch me at it the outcome won't be pretty. So if I don't want to take a chance on doing it myself, I can always hire Phillip.

Phillip Boudreau was by no means the only man who ever cut traps in Petit de Grat, but he was the dominant figure in that line of work. He would also take credit for things he hadn't done, just to bolster his reputation as a crafty rascal operating by stealth and beyond the reach of the law. A Fisheries officer who confronted him had the tires of his car slashed. When he bought new tires, those were slashed too. Phillip? Try to prove it. If you confronted him, he'd just smile.

Phillip could make your life a misery—but if he was your friend and thought you needed something he would provide it, whether or not he owned it. So you had to be careful about idly voicing your desires.

And then, from time to time, he would disappear—for days, or weeks, or months. But he always cropped up again.

There had been attempts to kill him—conspiracies, even. But on June 1, 2013, he was said to have been drowned—and not by thugs or druggies but by highly respected local fishermen. A lot of people thought the very idea was ridiculous. Phillip was wily and resilient and he swam like a seal. Trying to drown him would be like trying to drown a football. No doubt he was hiding out somewhere.

But he was never seen again.

I

HER MAJESTY'S STORY

JUNE 1, 2013, was a brilliant, sunny morning on the south coast of Isle Madame, just off the southeastern coast of Cape Breton Island. Lobster boats were slipping through the calm water all around the rocky shore off Petit de Grat and Arichat, diesel engines muttering as fishermen hauled up traps, removed lobsters, rebaited and reset the traps. The thirty-six-foot *Twin Maggies*, skippered by Dwayne Samson, was working in a dimple on the coast known as l'Anse aux Maquereaux, Mackerel Cove. The fishing licence had been given to Dwayne's wife, Carla, by her father, James Landry, when he turned sixty. She also owned the boat. James, now sixty-five, was working that morning as an employee, a deckhand. The second deckhand was Craig Landry, forty, a third cousin to James.

At about 7:00 a.m. Craig spotted a fourteen-foot speedboat, *Midnight Slider*, moving among their traps. The crew knew it well. It belonged to Phillip Boudreau, who had bedevilled and taunted the *Twin Maggies* for years. *Midnight Slider*'s speed made it easy for Phillip to elude slow, heavy fishing boats like the *Twin Maggies*.

On that fateful June morning, however, shots were fired and *Midnight Slider* stalled. The two boats collided. Shortly afterwards another fisherman found *Midnight Slider*'s battered hull floating awash. Its outboard motor was gone. A gas can was floating nearby. Phillip Boudreau had vanished. Meanwhile, the *Twin Maggies* had continued to tend her traps, unloading her lobsters at the end of the morning at the Premium Seafoods wharf in Arichat.

The next day, the three crew members were questioned closely by the Royal Canadian Mounted Police. Five days later, on June 6, the RCMP charged Craig Landry with second degree murder. The next day they arrested Dwayne Samson and James Landry and charged them with murder as well. Carla Samson was charged as accessory after the fact. The *Twin Maggies* was impounded. It was now an alleged murder weapon.

The accused were interrogated separately and intensively. Dwayne and Craig said nothing, but after fifteen continuous hours of questioning James made a statement. He said that when the *Twin Maggies* found Phillip Boudreau cutting their traps that morning, he got Craig to bring him his rifle. Then he fired four shots. He thought one of the shots might have wounded Phillip and one might have stopped his speedboat by disabling its motor. James then seized the wheel of the fishing boat from Dwayne and rammed *Midnight Slider*. He was so mad he was "seeing black." He swung around and rammed the smaller boat again, capsizing it. He wanted to destroy it. After that they didn't see Phillip anymore, and they went on hauling their traps.

It was a powerful story. But three weeks later, on June 26, Craig Landry told the Mounties a very different story, and later directed a videotaped re-enactment out on the water. On July 4 he was released on $50,000 bail, subject to stringent conditions about where he could live and who he could see. Carla Samson was also released on $25,000 bail. She had to surrender her passport and observe a curfew from midnight to 6:00 a.m.

On July 22 her husband applied for bail. The prosecution was strongly opposed. Dwayne Samson was allegedly the perpetrator of a vicious murder, as Craig Landry's testimony had revealed. Buttressed by additional information from the RCMP investigation, that testimony had become, in effect, Her Majesty's Story, the core of the Crown's official version of events.

Her Majesty's Story begins with a ringing telephone at Gerard Boudreau's ramshackle house around 7:00 in the evening of May 31, 2013.

Gerard Boudreau, Phillip's oldest brother, lives at Alderney Point, not far from his parents' home, at the very end of a twisting road that winds down the rocky eastern shore of Petit de Grat Harbour. Gerard owns a wharf, a lobster pound, and a lobster licence. His traps are set around the mouth of the harbour; some are in Mackerel Cove, directly across the harbour mouth, within sight of his home. Gerard doesn't actually tend the traps himself anymore. He is a diabetic, spectacularly obese, at least three hundred pounds. His diabetes has caused the amputation of his left leg and his right thumb. In 2013, when Gerard's brother was killed, his fishing boat was skippered by his wife, Linda.

On that May evening, it was Linda who answered the phone. The caller was James Landry, a longtime friend of Gerard's. She passed the phone to Gerard. James told Gerard that the *Twin Maggies* had lost about thirty lobster traps in the previous couple of weeks, and asked whether Gerard had seen Phillip around the harbour. Yes, said Gerard, Phillip had indeed been cruising around the harbour in *Midnight Slider*.

As Gerard tells it, James then said, "Well, it's his last night on the water. He won't be playing on the water tomorrow night." Gerard and Linda shrugged it off; people often threatened Phillip, but nothing much ever came of it. James, however, describes the call very differently. He says that he was returning an earlier call from Gerard, and that once he confirmed that it was probably Phillip who'd been cutting the traps, he asked Gerard, "What am I gonna do?"

"There's only one thing you can do," Gerard replied. "Get rid of him."

At that moment, Phillip was at the Corner Bridge store, next to the bridge that crosses Petit de Grat Harbour. He was selling stolen lobsters.

Craig Landry's wife worked at the store, and Craig often saw Phillip there. A few days earlier, Phillip had told Craig quite candidly that he had indeed been cutting the *Twin Maggies*' traps. He didn't like Carla Samson, he said. Carla had called the Department of Fisheries and Oceans on him, and the local DFO officers had in turn told Phillip that Carla wanted his theft and vandalism stopped. The episode had simply goaded Phillip. Whenever someone called Fisheries on him, said Phillip, "I go out and cut their traps. I cut Carla's traps three times this year, and I'm not finished." This was no surprise to Craig, who had fished the previous year with another fisherman, John Martell. Martell had also called Fisheries about Phillip, and had lost twenty-five traps as a result.

"It doesn't matter to me," Craig said to Phillip now. "It doesn't change anything for me." As a deckhand, a waged employee rather than an owner, he got paid no matter how much lobster the *Twin Maggies* caught or didn't catch.

Late that evening, Phillip went home to his parents' small, single-storey home. He had no bedroom; he slept on a mattress on the kitchen floor. He woke early, talked briefly with his sister Maggie, and left the house around 5:45 a.m. Wearing new green rubber boots, jeans, a sweater, and a black baseball cap, he was heading for the floating wharf behind the Corner Bridge store. On his way he also saw his brother Kenneth, who was going to work at the Premium Seafoods crab processing plant nearby. Kenneth asked where he was off to so early in the morning, and Phillip said he was heading to his boat.

Fifteen kilometres away, on the north side of Isle Madame, Dwayne Samson was up and on the road just after 4:00. He drove his grey four-door Chev pickup truck from D'Escousse to Petit de Grat and picked up Craig Landry. Talking about sports—the Toronto Blue Jays had lost the previous night—the two drove on to the nearby hamlet of Little Anse to collect James, who didn't own a vehicle and had never held a driver's licence.

Petit de Grat and Little Anse constitute the least assimilated corner of Isle Madame, and the usual language of daily life there is Acadian French. Speaking French, the trio drove back through Petit de Grat to nearby Arichat, where the *Twin Maggies* was tied to the wharf at Premium Seafoods' main plant. They loaded their gear aboard and motored off. By 5:00, just before daybreak, they were hauling their first traps on the eastern side of Arichat Harbour. Arriving at each trap, they flipped the buoy lines over powered sheaves—grooved pulleys attached to small steel-pipe cranes—and then reeled in line until the traps rose dripping from the water.

Traps are laid out in groups, or "strings," with the buoy on each one identifying the owner. At the height of the season the inshore waters of Nova Scotia are heavily speckled with these colourful buoys; the boats pick their way among them like birds foraging for grain in a recently harvested field.

In Petit de Grat, meanwhile, Phillip had called Gerard on his cell phone at 6:25 to ask whether he should go to Mackerel Cove and pick up two of Gerard's traps that had been driven by a storm into water too shallow for Gerard's big boat to reach. Yes, said Gerard, who took the call on his deck overlooking the harbour. Five or six minutes after the call he saw *Midnight Slider* heading for Mackerel Cove.

By now the *Twin Maggies'* crew had finished hauling their first string of 125 traps in Arichat Harbour and were motoring around Cape Hogan, the headland that separates the harbours of Arichat and Petit de Grat. As they rounded the cape Alderney Point came into view and they could see a boat fishing near the green navigational buoy nearby.

They knew the boat; it was *Pete and Julie*, owned by Venard "Pigou" Samson. Farther on, they could see Mackerel Cove and the adjoining indentation in the rocks known as L'Anse à Richard, Richard's Cove.

"There's a boat in by the shore," Craig said in French.

"It's probably Phillip," said Dwayne, also in French. "Just keep an eye on him, see what he's doing."

They kept watching Phillip as they hauled their traps. They saw *Midnight Slider* head for Mackerel Point, where their traps had previously been cut.

"He must be playing with our traps again," said Dwayne. "We're going over there. James, tie a knot on this trap so we can find it again."

Phillip watched the bigger boat's approach without apparent alarm. *Midnight Slider* was far faster than the *Twin Maggies* or any of the other fishing boats. In fact he'd often race across their bows, swerving right in front of them, sometimes waving a knife or holding up a lobster to let them know he'd been robbing or vandalizing their traps. Taunting them, reminding them that he was invulnerable.

At the wheel of the fishing boat, Dwayne gave an order.

"Charger le fusil." *Load the rifle.*

Nobody moved.

"Craig, met trois shells en fusil," said Dwayne. *Put three shells in the gun.*

Craig went below, took the Winchester .30-30 out from under the bunk, and loaded it with three rounds. He came back up and told Dwayne that he'd put in the three rounds but hadn't chambered any and hadn't cocked the rifle, so it wasn't ready to fire.

"He's going to get a scare this time," said Dwayne.

Craig returned to his position behind the wheelhouse. Then, as *Twin Maggies* approached *Midnight Slider*, Dwayne turned to his father-in-law.

"James, are you going to shoot?"

James ducked below and came back with the gun. At this point Phillip started his Evinrude outboard and headed for shore. When the two boats were perhaps forty yards apart, James dropped to one knee and fired. The bullet hit the water alongside the speedboat. Frightened, Phillip turned towards *Twin Maggies*, shouting "I didn't do anything, I didn't cut any traps! Don't shoot!" But James was taking aim again and Phillip steered away, speeding up the harbour towards Petit de Grat.

James shot again. Phillip's outboard stalled. James shot a third time, and Phillip fell, shouting "Tu m'as cassé la jambe!" *You've broken my leg!* Craig turned away. "It scared the shit out of me," he said later. He meant it literally: much later, he testified in court that he had soiled himself.

"Shoot again," said Dwayne.

"I got no more shells," said James. "Get me a shell."

Craig, still looking away, heard someone fetch another shell and load it into the rifle. Then he heard the crack of another shot. Phillip was shouting, "Stop, James, stop!"

Dwayne said, "Fire again."

"I got no more shells," James repeated.

"That's enough!" cried Craig. "Don't shoot anymore! No more shooting!"

Everyone fell silent for a moment or two. Then James grabbed the gaff—a long fiberglass rod with a hook at the end—and told Dwayne to steer around the bow of Phillip's boat so that he could snag its bow line. Once he hooked it he passed the line to Craig while Dwayne gunned the engine and headed out to sea with *Midnight Slider* in tow. Phillip was slumped now beside the engine. Craig let the line slip through his hands, which angered James.

Twin Maggies circled and picked up the bow line again, and this time James tied it to the spar on the stern. Dwayne gunned the engine once more. Looking astern, Craig saw why *Midnight Slider*'s engine had stalled: the propeller had wrapped up the lines from a couple of lobster traps; the traps were skidding along the surface behind *Midnight Slider*. Now Phillip crawled forward with a small knife, like a steak knife, and cut the bow line, further enraging James.

"Turn around and run over him!" James cried. "Sink the boat!"

Dwayne rammed the speedboat. Then he circled and rammed it again. *Midnight Slider* had filled with water and Phillip was clinging to it. Dwayne circled again, and *Twin Maggies* ran right over the speedboat. Now Phillip was in the water, clinging to the red plastic gas can, shouting, "Stop, James!"

"You won't cut any more of our traps," said James grimly.

"You're done with cutting traps," said Dwayne. Now James hooked Phillip with the gaff and told Dwayne to drive. But Dwayne drove a little too fast, and Phillip slipped off the gaff. Dwayne circled around and James hooked the gaff in Phillip's sweater. As they drove seaward, Phillip wriggled out of his sweater.

"Go round again," said James. This time when James caught Phillip he held him close to the boat—and this time, Craig thought, Phillip drowned. When Dwayne stopped, Craig saw white foam coming from Phillip's mouth, and when James released him, Phillip rolled face down in the water.

"Get the anchor," said Dwayne. Nobody moved. "Craig, get the anchor." Craig tried to lift the small cockpit anchor off its bracket, but he couldn't. Dwayne strode into the wheelhouse and brought out a big four-pronged grapnel made of stainless steel. He and James ran a line under Phillip's arms and a couple of times around his neck, and tied it off. Dwayne went back to the controls.

"Is this far enough?" he asked.

"How deep are you?" James asked.

"Twelve point two fathom."

"Yes, you're deep enough," said James. He let the grapnel go. Phillip Boudreau's body drifted down out of sight.

Dwayne spun the wheel. The *Twin Maggies* headed towards shore, and the crew continued hauling their traps as though nothing had happened.

2

COURTROOM 3:
APPLICATION FOR BAIL

THAT'S HER MAJESTY'S STORY, as delivered by Crown prosecutors Dan MacRury and Diane McGrath. It relies heavily on the testimony of Craig Landry. The Crown has chosen to charge the four accused separately. Evidently, the prosecution sees James Landry, Dwayne Samson's father-in-law, as the driving force in the attack on Phillip Boudreau, and the easiest of the four to convict. They will try James first, and then—having convicted him, they hope—they will easily be able to convict his son-in-law. So it will be many months until Dwayne's trial, and he is in court today to ask to be let out on bail while he waits.

Nash Brogan has been listening intently to Her Majesty's Story. It is now his task to undermine it, blow it up, destroy it.

Before anyone was even arrested, Carla Samson and the three crewmen from the *Twin Maggies* conferred with Brogan, a noted criminal lawyer practising in Sydney, 130 kilometres from Petit de Grat. Brogan agreed to act for all four. Nash Brogan is described within the legal profession as bright, imaginative, voluble, and volatile. A native of the port city of North Sydney, he belongs to a large and affluent Irish family whose interests have included coal mining, real estate, and fishing, specifically buying and selling lobsters. Brogan himself earned his way through university and law school by working summers as a seaman on the Great Lakes.

He loves being in court, loves appearing before a jury, and, at the age of sixty-three, he accepts mainly what he calls "profile" cases—cases that interest him and that satisfy his taste for the dramatic. His first advice to his new clients was to say absolutely nothing to the police. He warned them that it would not be easy.

"The RCMP are very, very good at what they do," he said. "When the police arrest you, they probably won't question you until they let you sit for fourteen or fifteen hours. While you wait, they may or may not have the heat turned way up. If it's not going to be hot, it's going to be cold. They may or may not feed you; they usually don't. When they start questioning you, they will tell you that one of the other parties—or both parties—gave statements and incriminated you, and so you might as well give a statement too."

Then, he said, they'll appeal to your emotions: you come from a good family; don't prolong the misery you've brought upon them. You're a good person, but you had a bad moment. Tell us about it. Think about your little girl. You don't want to be in prison while she's growing up, do you? Tell me what happened and let me see what I can do for you.

In criminal cases, Brogan explained later, "We don't look at moral guilt. We look at legal guilt, okay? We look at, what can they prove?" With no body, and with no statement from any of the four accused, it would be extremely difficult for the Crown to prove anything at all.

But James made a statement, and then Craig made the statement that became Her Majesty's Story, so both of them had to find other lawyers. Brogan was still acting for Dwayne and Carla Samson, however, and although Carla was free on bail, Dwayne was still behind bars.

So now Nash Brogan, draped in black robes, is shuffling papers at a table in Courtroom 3 of the Justice Centre in Port Hawkesbury, Nova Scotia, fifty kilometres from Petit de Grat, preparing to argue that Dwayne should also be released on bail for the months he will be awaiting his trial. The visitors' gallery is full of rural working people wearing windbreakers, jeans, plaid shirts, down vests, heavy sneakers—the same garb that Phillip Boudreau wore. The media are here in force, crowding the front row of the gallery: the Canadian Broadcasting Corporation, the Canadian Press, CTV Television, *The Globe and Mail*, *The Chronicle Herald*, *The Cape Breton Post*, the local Port Hawkesbury paper *The Reporter*, and the local radio station, 101.5 The Hawk. Two freelance writers are also present. One is novelist Linden MacIntyre, until recently the host of CBC-TV's *The Fifth Estate*, who grew up here. The other freelancer is me; I've lived on Isle Madame since 1971.

Standing around in the courtroom before the bail hearing begins, I find myself chatting with Joel Pink of Halifax, who now represents Craig Landry. Bald, wry, and genial, Pink is a legendary criminal lawyer. In the most celebrated of his sixty-odd murder trials, he defended John Alexander MacKenzie of Antigonish, the killer of three people who had been tormenting him for years. The Crown's evidence was overwhelming, and MacKenzie had even confessed. Pink took the case all the way to the Supreme Court of Canada, where he won MacKenzie an acquittal.

Pink is the co-author of *From Crime to Punishment*, currently in its eighth edition, "the most comprehensive and up-to-date introduction to criminal law and criminal procedure now available in Canada." He is the son of a noted lawyer, a father of lawyers, the brother of the executive director of the Nova Scotia Barristers' Society, of which Joel himself has been the president. In all, there are nine lawyers in his immediate family. Joel Pink is probably the only criminal lawyer whom many Nova Scotians would instantly recognize on TV.

It was Joel Pink who advised Craig Landry to give his vivid account of Phillip Boudreau's murder, and Joel now tells me that Phillip's body has still not been found. As we speak, a flotilla of search boats is out looking for it with underwater cameras, divers, sonar—everything in the floating forensic toolbox. But so far, no body.

Dwayne Samson seats himself in the front bench of the gallery. He is no gnarled, pipe-smoking, horny-handed old salt. He's forty-three years old and perhaps six feet tall with steely grey hair. He looks composed, respectful, attentive. Carla, thirty-seven, is seated a few rows behind him. They've been together for fourteen years, since 1999. At that time they both worked for an Isle Madame oil company, Greg's Fuels, Carla as a clerk and Dwayne as a truck driver delivering the fuel. When Greg's Fuels was sold and its operations moved to the Halifax area, they moved as well. The two bought a house in the suburbs in 2001, got married in 2003, and became the parents of twin daughters in 2005. The next year, Carla's father, James Landry, approached them about taking over his lobster licence. Dwayne and Carla took the necessary training, put in the sea time, and moved home to Isle Madame. They built a spacious new house in 2009. Trim and youthful, they are an attractive, successful couple.

Mr. Justice Simon MacDonald enters. Everyone rises, and the hearing begins.

A bail hearing differs from a trial in several ways. The rules of evidence are more relaxed, and some degree of hearsay is admissible. But the big difference is that the burden of proof falls on the applicant. The Crown doesn't have to prove anything today. Instead, Nash Brogan must convince the judge that Dwayne Samson *should* be released.

Brogan has filed two briefs with the court, arguing that granting bail is totally in harmony with case law and the Criminal Code. The other documents already filed with the court include Craig Landry's statement and an affidavit from Corporal Denzil Firth, the lead investigator for the Royal Canadian Mounted Police. Their affidavits outline Her Majesty's Story, and both men will be appearing as witnesses at this hearing, so both are excluded from the courtroom. Right now, Nash Brogan is arguing for the admission of another document, namely the late Phillip Boudreau's criminal record.

Phillip's record runs to twenty-eight pages, the first eleven of which list his convictions. The remaining pages set forth additional charges that were withdrawn or dismissed. The actual convictions date back to 1987, when Phillip was seventeen. He presumably had a juvenile record as well, but that remains sealed. His adult record shows multiple convictions on numerous offences. Mischief. Possession of narcotics. Theft under $5000. Theft over $5000. Motor vehicle theft. Breach of probation. Break and enter. Break and enter with intent to commit an indictable offence. Possession of stolen property. Escaping lawful custody. Resisting arrest. Harassment. Assault. Uttering threats to cause death or bodily harm.

Dan MacRury, the prosecutor, does not think the record is relevant to Dwayne Samson's bail hearing—and if it is, only the actual convictions should be admitted. Tall, heavy, dark-haired, arrayed in billowing black robes, MacRury might be described as a mountain of a man, or at the least a very substantial hill. He is an equally substantial figure in the legal system. A prosecutor for nineteen years, he is currently the chief Crown attorney for Cape Breton. He is also a vice-president of the Canadian Bar Association and a member of various working groups—federal, provincial, even international—on cyber crime. Within a few months he will be named a judge of Nova Scotia's provincial and family courts.

With respect to Phillip Boudreau's criminal record, MacRury takes the view that the person on trial here is Dwayne Samson, not Phillip Boudreau, and the charge is not a trivial one; it is murder.

Brogan counters by arguing vigorously that the law tilts towards allowing bail to any accused, even one charged with an offence as grave as murder. He cites Section 515(10) of the Criminal Code, which says that bail should only be refused on one of three grounds: if the accused is likely not to show up for trial, if the accused would be a danger to the public, or if detention is necessary to preserve public confidence in the administration of justice.

None of these three grounds applies, says Brogan. Whatever the outcome of his trial, Dwayne is eager to get through the legal process, deal with the consequences, and resume his life. He is a responsible citizen, husband, and father who has had to deal with relentless pressure from a lifelong criminal. Craig Landry's affidavit describes how Phillip was constantly threatening, robbing, and harassing Dwayne and his family. Nor was Dwayne alone in this. Phillip's last actual conviction was in 2010, Brogan concedes, but just two days before his death he was threatening a fisherman named Clarence David, warning him that if he didn't stop keeping company with a particular woman his employer's traps would be cut. Phillip, says Brogan, had been "instilling fear into the community, and he had a record that indicates that he was quite capable of fulfilling any threats that he made."

Justice MacDonald still has his doubts about admitting Phillip's record—but this is a bail hearing, so he allows the first eleven pages, the list of actual convictions.

Brogan calls Dwayne Samson to the stand. Dwayne confirms that he has driven trucks and done other jobs for several local companies. He has letters of reference and offers of employment from Premium Seafoods, AFL Tank Manufacturing, Boudreau's Fuels, and Superior Contracting. This is almost a roll call of the larger businesses on Isle Madame, and they all portray Dwayne as honest and trustworthy, an excellent employee, someone that any of them would be happy to hire. He also has an offer of employment from Chet Boudreau, an Isle Madame man who runs a home construction company in Halifax, and a dozen letters of reference about his voluntary work in community organizations. He'd like to be released into employment in Isle Madame so that he can see his children regularly. Failing that, he'd like to be released into the custody of his sister Ramona Boudreau in Halifax, who is prepared to sign a bond for him.

In cross-examination, Dan MacRury walks Dwayne through each of the options that have been presented. What hours would he work? Who would monitor his activities? Do the employers have any weapons on their premises? Dwayne is forbidden to talk to his wife—but if he were released into his sister Ramona's custody, does he think Ramona would really enforce that prohibition?

Yes, he does—and Ramona Boudreau thinks so too. She is thirty-one, a grade one teacher in Halifax. She has agreed that her brother can stay with her. Ramona has a statement from TD Canada Trust showing that she will have no difficulty putting up a bond of $50,000 to guarantee that Dwayne will follow whatever conditions the court imposes. Her husband has also agreed. She confirms that Chet Boudreau, who is her brother-in-law, would be happy to hire Dwayne to work building houses with him. No, she tells MacRury, there are no firearms in her home.

Ronnie LeBlanc takes the stand. His parents run Shamrock Store, a convenience store in D'Escousse, on the north side of Isle Madame, which is also where Carla and Dwayne live. Ronnie grew up in the store and now lives across the road from it. He's worked for the Nova Scotia Liquor Commission since 1987, and currently manages the liquor store in nearby St. Peter's.

Ronnie's wife is Dwayne's sister Janet, and he knew that, contrary to some rumours, Dwayne had a great deal of support in the community. So, after Dwayne's arrest, he got up a petition and made it available in several locations in Isle Madame. At Brogan's request, he reads the text aloud.

"Whereas Dwayne Samson has been charged with the murder of Phillip Boudreau," says Ronnie, "and whereas the Crown is opposing Dwayne Samson's release from jail prior to trial, we the undersigned residents of Isle Madame hereby support the interim release of Dwayne Samson."

What did the people of the island know about the allegations against Dwayne?

"Well," says Ronnie, "there was a lot in the paper, from press stories that James Landry had shot Phillip Boudreau, there was talk about the boat being rammed, there were rumours that he was missing and tied to the motor of the boat. Between Facebook, the local media, and general conversation, people were certainly aware of the circumstances."

Brogan introduces Exhibit 2, a CBC news story. MacRury objects, saying that Brogan should rely on the evidence, not on news stories. He questions the relevance of the CBC report.

Brogan is visibly pleased by this challenge. The story is, he says, "very germane to the issue at hand." Dated June 24, it was written by CBC reporter Phonse Jessome, and "it outlines in detail the police allegations." (Joel Pink has told me that he didn't know who leaked the information to Jessome, but that the reporting was absolutely accurate.) The fact that the story had been broadcast, says Brogan, strongly suggests that the people who signed the petition knew Phillip had been killed and that Dwayne was accused of murdering him. It follows that people in the community knew what had happened and understood what they were signing. The judge agrees.

Brogan returns to Ronnie LeBlanc, and establishes that the population of Isle Madame is around 4300 and that more than 700 voters have signed the petition, giving their addresses and phone numbers. Ronnie testifies that Isle Madame has roughly 2800 qualified electors, and that about 1800 voted in the last provincial election. And where did he get that information?

"The returning officer of Richmond County," says Ronnie.

Who is—?

"My father. Raymond LeBlanc." And did Ronnie have conversations with those who signed the petition?

"Certainly. They were very sad to hear what happened, and they wanted to support Dwayne in any way."

And what would Ronnie himself say about the general character of Dwayne Samson?

"Well, I've been married to his sister for twenty-six years now. I've known him since he was very small. I've never known him to have an angry bone in his body, actually."

In cross-examination, MacRury establishes that the petition includes a few names from off Isle Madame, and that Ronnie doesn't know whether any of the signatories have a criminal record. Ronnie also agrees that he hasn't read Craig Landry's statement, and that he didn't share Craig's statement with those who signed the petition.

Next up is Venard Samson, Dwayne's father, also from D'Escousse, who is more than willing to have Dwayne stay at his home. He and his wife, Susan, have no mortgage, and they would put up $50,000 bail.

Venard is followed by Pearl LeBlanc, Ronnie's mother, proprietor of Shamrock Store. She has lived in D'Escousse since 1940. She and her husband, Raymond, own two corporations, with assets well in excess of $100,000. Pearl has known Dwayne since he was born, and is confident that he won't breach any bail conditions. She and her husband are willing to post $50,000 bail for him. Yes, she knows what Dwayne is charged with, and she understands her responsibilities. Dan MacRury wants to be clear about her role.

"Are you suggesting that he will come and live with you?" he asks.

Pearl looks puzzled, but she is not fazed.

"Well, he can if he likes," she says.

The Crown has a witness to call, but it's noon. The court adjourns till 1:15.

Reeves Street in Port Hawkesbury is that part of any Canadian town where golden arches jostle with buckets of chicken while Tim Horton scores big time, boasting two coffee shops in three blocks. Mayor Billy Joe MacLean owns the largest tavern here, The Carriage House. On the opposite side of the street, in a fading strip mall called the Causeway Shopping Centre, is the town's best restaurant, a homey little place specializing in Acadian food. The Fleur-de-Lis Tea Room is owned by Brenda Chisholm Beaton, a charming and savvy woman who will eventually replace MacLean as mayor. Every day that the Phillip Boudreau hearings, trials, and appearances continue, her restaurant will fill up with lawyers, reporters, and observers and she'll do a brisk business in Acadian fish cakes, seafood chowder, and the Petit de Grat Sampler (fish cake, haddock, home fries, and coleslaw).

I find myself thinking about lawyers, and about something I learned from my friend Antonio Oposa, Jr., a brilliantly inventive environmental lawyer in the Philippines. For Tony Oposa, legal cases are stories, and lawyers are storytellers. People learn from stories; that's how Jesus taught. The courtroom is a grave, dignified theatre; or, if you like, it's a fierce battleground for warring stories. Tony himself specializes in highly original lawsuits—stories about the rights of future generations, about the rights of nature, about equity and fairness in environmental matters.

What stories are jousting in Courtroom 3, just down the hill? Nash Brogan is shaping a story about a fine, industrious couple, good parents and citizens, who find themselves enmeshed in intolerable circumstances that impel them into actions completely contrary to their basic character. Brogan is arguing for Dwayne's release, but he is also carefully placing artillery for the assault he will launch in Dwayne's subsequent murder trial, many months in the future. Meanwhile Dan MacRury—who's eating his lunch over there by the wall— is forging a true crime drama about stone-faced unrepentant killers who need to remain behind bars, a story he will advance vigorously at trial. And Joel Pink is a stage manager coaching Craig Landry, who portrays himself as an innocent bystander swept up in an emotional hurricane, improvising as necessary until the storm blew through.

The stories here reflect the central paradox of this saga. As one visiting journalist has noted, in murder cases the public tends to "canonize" the victims. The deceased was—always—a wonderful young husband and father who died far too early, or a long-suffering abused woman in middle age, or a noble priest who forgave his attackers even as his life ebbed away.

In this case, however, the public is remarkably sympathetic to the killers, as Nash Brogan's story has skilfully demonstrated. Who ever heard of a murder trial where hundreds of people petition the court to release the accused murderer on bail? Where respectable business people line up to offer him employment? Where neighbours are willing to mortgage their homes and businesses to bail him out? Admittedly, not everyone sees Dwayne Samson that way. For some people on Isle Madame, those who commit monstrous acts are by definition monsters, and nobody thinks murder is an acceptable problem-solving technique. But clearly a lot of well-informed people believe that Dwayne Samson is a good man in a bad spot.

I am also musing over the fact that all the legal talent in this case is from far away. Brogan and MacRury are from Sydney, nearly two hours to the east, while Pink is from Halifax, more than three hours to the west. I have just learned that James Landry will be represented by Luke Craggs, who is also from Halifax. Port Hawkesbury has no shortage of lawyers, so why are no local barristers involved? The answer, says Kevin Patriquin, who runs the legal aid service in Port Hawkesbury, lies in Phillip Boudreau's long criminal record. Every lawyer practising in this part of Nova Scotia has had a previous relationship with Phillip. Every single one.

The lawyers and reporters pay for their lunches. Back in Courtroom 3, the hearing resumes.

Dan MacRury, for the prosecution, calls Corporal Denzil George Fraser Firth. Corporal Firth is with the Northeast Nova Major Crime

Unit of the RCMP. He's based in Bible Hill, two and a half hours' drive away. Firth is the lead investigator into the death of Phillip Boudreau, and his testimony is mainly contained in the affidavit he has already filed with the court. That affidavit, in turn, rests on statements the police have gathered from three major sources: James Landry, Craig Landry, and Gerard Boudreau, the victim's diabetic brother. Firth's role is to corroborate and amplify Craig Landry's testimony, to drive home the truth of Her Majesty's Story.

Nash Brogan's mission, as defence counsel, is to sap the strength of Firth's testimony, which has included a good many additional details, notably the crew's disposal of the rifle (they concealed it in a blanket, then took it to Dwayne and Carla's home and cleaned it) and the conference they held later that day at the Samson house. At that meeting they concocted what we might call the Cock-amamie Story: Phillip had come roaring out of the fog a day earlier and run into them, leaving marks on the hull of the *Twin Maggies*. That would account for the paint scrapings and scuff marks from *Midnight Slider*, which Dwayne had vainly attempted to scrub off.

Corporal Firth's testimony has also touched on the remarkable substory of Gerard Boudreau's observations. Gerard has said that he watched the whole episode from his deck, with binoculars. He heard the rifle shots, saw *Twin Maggies* circling and *Midnight Slider* disappearing, and watched the fishing boat tow something out to sea. But although he had seen this dramatic altercation and knew that it involved his brother, he had said nothing to the police when they visited him at 7:30 that morning and then didn't call them until noon. By that time Venard "Pigou" Samson, who'd been fishing off Alderney Point, had found *Midnight Slider* floating awash, called Search and Rescue, and towed the speedboat to the fishermen's wharf in Petit de Grat. The Fisheries officer had come to the wharf, then the Mounties. Isle Madame was crackling with rumours. The police were taking statements and seizing evidence.

Why had Gerard not called the Mounties right away? Because he didn't have the phone number, he told the police later, and he didn't have a phone book.

"Did you find that shocking?" Nash Brogan asks Corporal Firth. "Your brother's being killed and you don't even call the police?"

"It's an odd statement, there's no doubt about that," Firth says, nodding. "And in fact we discussed that at our daily briefing."

Gerard never appears in court. The official explanation is that he's run off, gone into hiding, can't be found. Sitting in a wheelchair in his crooked little house in Alderney Point, Gerard scoffs at this story. Lifting a fold of his vast belly off his lap and re-settling it, he says he was here at home the whole time. "Three hundred pounds and an artificial leg, how far can I run?" Instead, he claims, the police twice came down to get him, and the second time they were halfway to Port Hawkesbury when they told him his presence wouldn't be required after all, and sent him home again.

In countering Her Majesty's Story, Brogan's basic strategy is to portray Craig as self-serving and Firth as a purveyor of secondhand information, particularly about the community. Firth's affidavit mostly summarized the findings of others who did the interrogations; he himself has had very little hands-on engagement with the evidence, or with Isle Madame and its people. Since the bail hearing is all about releasing Dwayne back into the community without shaking the community's confidence in the administration of justice, community opinion is crucial, and Firth can't really speak to that. Brogan, however, has brought powerful evidence that the community sees the accused as "hardworking, decent people whose emotions got out of control, and then the situation spun out of control." James Landry has told the police, ruefully, that "it only takes five minutes to change your life." Moreover, Brogan concludes, both the statutes and the case law strongly assert that bail should be granted unless there are powerful reasons to refuse it.

Firth's appearance wraps up the presentation of evidence. Now

Diane McGrath, Dan MacRury's associate, delivers the Crown's final arguments against releasing Dwayne on bail. A former legal aid lawyer with a special interest in domestic violence and sexual assault, McGrath is on her way to the bench along with MacRury; in 2017 she too will be appointed a judge of the provincial and family courts.

McGrath clinically dissects Brogan's arguments. Brogan has portrayed Dwayne very sympathetically, but the accused is charged with a horrible crime, and he has already tried to interfere with the administration of justice by disposing of the body and the gun, trying to clean the boat, and conspiring to create a false story. She thinks Ronnie LeBlanc's petition is irrelevant; this is not a trial by public opinion. She does not believe that Brogan's plan offers adequate supervision. Indeed, she can't see that there actually *is* a plan. What Brogan has offered is only a smorgasbord of possibilities: different residences, different employers, different jobs.

In truth, she says, Dwayne doesn't know where he'd be working, or what hours, or even whether he'd be working entirely within Nova Scotia. And yes, Craig Landry has been released on bail, but Craig was a minor player; Dwayne, as the skipper, could have ended the whole thing. McGrath argues that a "reasonable person"—that hoary legal concept—"would be appalled" at Dwayne's release. And that in itself is sufficient grounds to deny bail. She cites *R. v. Hall* (2002), a leading decision on the subject of bail from the Supreme Court of Canada.

"When justice is not seen to be done by the public," she reads, "confidence in the bail system and more generally the entire justice system may falter. When the public's confidence has reasonably been called into question, dangers such as public unrest and vigilantism may emerge." For her, the heart of the matter is the preservation of public confidence in the administration of justice.

Justice MacDonald is not prepared to decide on the spot. He adjourns the hearing.

———

A week later, on July 29, Justice MacDonald reveals his decision.

He carefully reviews the law and the Crown's case, starting with the police testimony—the discovery of Phillip's ruined boat, the paint and scuff marks on the *Twin Maggies*, the identities of the crew, the first interrogations of the crew members, Craig's subsequent revised statement and video re-enactment of the events. He notes that Carla had told police she was not aboard the boat that day, but that Phillip had been aggressive with her crew and their fishing gear and had threatened to destroy their gear, burn down their houses, and kill her crew. He describes the enigmatic phone call between James Landry and Gerard Boudreau, the phone call the next morning between Gerard and Phillip, and Gerard's observation of the collision of the two boats. He discusses in chilling detail Firth's account of James Landry's long and confusing statement to the police, during which James declared that he should have taken action against Phillip ten years earlier, and that he hoped the body would never be found: "Let the crabs eat him."

Corporal Firth, says the judge, "stated that the victim was disliked by many people in the community who expressed the opinion that he got what he deserved. Another portion of the community felt the matter went too far, and a small number of those people are thought to pose a risk to the accused if provided with the opportunity." He dismisses Ronnie LeBlanc's petition, remarking acerbically that "the court is not to decide the granting of the interim release on the results of a poll or popularity contest."

The key issue is whether there's a substantial likelihood that Dwayne Samson will interfere with witnesses or otherwise throw sand in the gears of justice. Justice MacDonald notes that the evidence of Dwayne's prior attempts to frustrate the investigation comes from Craig Landry via Corporal Firth—but none of that is confirmed by the testimony of James Landry, who says simply that after *Twin Maggies* rammed *Midnight Slider*, "the only thing they saw come up was the boat and they never saw—or as he said, they never seen—Mr. Boudreau after that. Two different stories from two different co-accuseds."

He then cites an influential opinion by Chief Justice Beverley McLachlin declaring that "At the heart of a free and democratic society is the liberty of its subjects. Liberty lost is never regained, and can never be fully compensated for." McLachlin further noted the fundamental imbalance between the two sides in criminal law, "where the vast resources of the state and very often the weight of public opinion are stacked against the individual accused."

So Justice MacDonald doesn't think it wise to allow Dwayne to return to Isle Madame, but he's impressed with Ramona Boudreau's willingness to post bail and to supervise her brother's activities in Halifax, and he is "also impressed with the material supplied by the applicant with respect to his stature and reputation in the community."

In the end, Justice MacDonald's only real misgivings about granting bail are that he is "not satisfied with the proposal put forward for his release, and therefore he is denied bail at this time. If the applicant comes up with a better supervisory plan I would be prepared to re-entertain the matter. Mr. Brogan, any questions?"

"No," says Brogan. "Thank you very much, My Lord." And Dwayne Samson is remanded back to jail.

Later, Nash Brogan will say that he was very disappointed with this decision. Right now, though, he seems quite satisfied. He has known from the outset that the court wouldn't discharge Dwayne back into his own community. By asking for that, however, he has been able to get into the record the remarkable evidence attesting to Dwayne's character—the petition, the job offers, the friends and relatives willing to risk big money on him. Brogan has clearly shown that Dwayne Samson is not, in a general way, a criminal. The only crime he ever committed—probably the only crime he and his co-accused ever *would* commit—was killing Phillip Boudreau.

It's all about Phillip Boudreau. So who was Phillip Boudreau?

3

A RUSTIC ROBIN HOOD

ISLAND VOICES

"Look, I know Phillip since he was five years old—and even then you'd have thought he was six foot four and bulletproof, he was that mouthy. And bad? My Jesus Christ. But bad as he was, he never hurt nobody. He never deserved what happened to him."

"Phillip would steal the beads off Christ's moccasins. But then if you needed them, he'd turn around and give them to you."

"My uncle Remy was dying of cancer, and Phillip came to see him. 'I'm sorry you're sick,' he said. 'You like ducks?' 'Yeah,' said Remy. 'Yeah, I like ducks.' Next day here's Phillip with a pair of plump ducks. 'That's a nice thing for you to do,' said Remy, 'thank you kindly.' Few days later, Remy meets his friend Paul. 'You know a funny thing,' says Paul, 'I'm raising ducks but they *seem to be disappearing.' 'Uh-oh,' says Remy. 'I think maybe I ate a couple of your ducks.' (PAUSE) 'They were some good.'"*

"Yeah, that's Phillip. He'd steal it, but if you needed it, he'd give it to you. I used to call him Robin Hood."

Lots of people are happy to talk about Phillip, but few want their names used. Isle Madame is a small place. More importantly, it's an Acadian community, originally settled by ten French families after the fall of Louisbourg in 1759 erased the French colony of Île Royale and created a British colony of Cape Breton Island. "We're all a family here," a friend of mine once said. That's almost literally true, and like most families, islanders will be very frank among themselves—Henri's a hopeless drunk, Henrietta is thick as a brick—but if an outsider notes that Henri reeks of rum and Henrietta generally seems to miss the punchline, the whole family will fiercely deny it.

So I will tell you things that were said within the family. I heard them. But telling you who said them? Sometimes, yeah. But mostly not.

ISLAND VOICES

"Phillip didn't mind jail, you know. Oh, no. Sometimes in the fall of the year he'd call some poor person and say, 'I'm gonna do a break and enter at such-and-such a place. You call the cops on me, and you'll get a $500 reward and I'll go to jail for the winter.' And then he'd send a thank-you card to the cop who arrested him."

"He didn't send me a card. But he did thank me for it the next time I saw him."

"I talked to Phillip once at his office—you know, at the store where he hung out. He said to me, 'What's not to like about prison? Three square meals a day, you're warm, you're dry, and you get all the sex and drugs you want.' For Phillip it was a vacation."

"One year he slept all winter in Hubert David's travel trailer. He was hiding from the cops. Hubert never knew till Phillip came around in the spring to thank him. True story. Go ask Hubert—he'll tell you."

So I went to see Hubert, who lives at Alderney Point. Phillip was his neighbour.

The section of road entering the village of Petit de Grat is called "the Stretch." It passes the baseball field, the cemetery, the public library, the Acadian cultural centre, and the Petit de Grat campus of Université Sainte-Anne. After rising over a low hill the road slopes down to the rocky shore of Petit de Grat Inlet, which separates Isle Madame proper from Petit de Grat Island. The inlet is the village's harbour.

Most of the homes and buildings of Petit de Grat lie strewn along the two banks of the inlet. The settlement is laid out like a capital letter H, with a bridge over the inlet forming the crossbar of the H. The core of the village is at the bridge, on both sides of the inlet. If you continue down the Isle Madame side you pass St. Joseph's Credit Union, St. Joseph's Catholic Church, the fishermen's wharves, the Samson Enterprises shipyard, and the community hall. Farther down that shore of the inlet—the lower left leg of the H—is a district known as Boudreauville. Beyond Boudreauville is a lovely seaside hike, the Cape Auget Eco Trail, and some distance beyond the end of that trail, inaccessible by road, is Mackerel Cove, where the *Twin Maggies* caught up with Phillip Boudreau.

Across the bridge, on the opposite shore, is the Corner Bridge Store and Bakery, which also serves as the post office. This is where Phillip Boudreau hung out, with *Midnight Slider* at a little dock nearby. If you turn right after the store, past the crab-processing plant, and drive two and a half kilometres to the end of the road— the tip of the lower right leg of the H—you arrive in Alderney Point, often referred to by locals as just "the Point." If you look across the inlet from the Point, you're looking at Mackerel Cove.

The cramped little house where Phillip Boudreau grew up is the very last home on that shore. It stands at the end of a spur road called the Joshua Road. It belongs to his parents, Gerald and Marie-Louise Joshua Boudreau.

You might say that Alderney Point is Phillip's home, but it would be more accurate to call it his habitat. This is moorland, rock and swamp and water. It's dotted with ponds and covered in low bushes. The few trees that persist in this naked, wind-scoured landscape are tough little black spruce.

A dirt track off the Joshua Road is called David's Lane. And here, a stone's throw from Phillip's home, lives Hubert David. Hubert is a short, bright, genial man—a description that would fit many of the Acadians of Isle Madame. He is a busy and well-regarded building contractor. When you ask him about Phillip and the trailer, he laughs and shakes his head and looks at his wife, Betty.

One spring, Betty tells me, she came back in after opening up the trailer and said, "Hubert, why did you take the covers off my cushions in the camper?"

"She blasted me!" Hubert grins. "I said, 'Betty, I didn't even go to your camper!' 'Well,' she said, 'all the covers are off of the cushions.' So a couple of weeks later we're going for a walk down here by the lake, and the cops are looking for Phillip. The cop goes up that way, and then he comes back going the other way, and that's when Phillip hollered to us. He was hiding in the bushes."

"Phillip said, 'I just want to say thank you very much,'" Betty remembers. "He said, 'I slept in your trailer the last three months, it's the only safe place for me, but I leave at 6:00 in the morning, so nobody ever seen me leave. It's me that took the covers off the cushions.' I said, 'Well, why didn't you open the cupboards? There's pillows, there's blankets, there's everything to keep you warm instead of taking the covers off the cushions. The blankets and pillows were there all winter.' He said, 'No, no, no, I don't touch the cupboards.'"

Phillip had his own code of conduct, his own loyalties, his own eccentric sense of morality. Hubert was on his good side. But even a cordial relationship with Phillip had its complexities, says Hubert, because if you mentioned something that you'd like, "he would go steal it and give it to you. I don't think he had the learning ability to think that he was doing anything wrong."

But he wouldn't steal from Hubert. Or so he said. But Hubert wondered.

"He always said to me, 'Hubert, I will never ever steal from you,'" says Hubert reflectively. "So one day the cops were looking for him, and my dog barked." Hubert went to the window. Phillip was walking past the back of the house. He didn't see Hubert watching.

"There was a piece of rubber at my shed," Hubert recalls. "He looked at the rubber, and I said to myself, 'Today I'm gonna find out if he's telling me the truth, that he'll never steal from me.' He stood the rubber up beside the shed there and took off. A little later, my phone rang.

"He said, 'Hey, Hubert, I just came from behind your house there. Could I buy that piece of rubber that's beside your shed? I wanna make a flap door so that when my father and mother lock me out of the house, me and my dog can stay in the shed.' That's what he wanted the rubber for. You see that shed over there, the little rotten shed, the one that's falling apart? That's where he used to sleep, him and the dog."

Which brings us to "the Bowsers," the local nickname for Phillip's family. The original Bowser is Phillip's father, Gerald Boudreau, now in his nineties, who displays what *BuzzFeed* reporter Peter Smith described as "unrelenting wiliness." Gerard, the oldest son, is sometimes called "Big Bowser." Phillip was "Little Bowser" or "Phillip à Bowser." A daughter, Margaret Rose, or "Maggie," lives with her parents. A third brother, Kenneth, lives in a basement nearby. A basement? Yes: the big banks have traditionally been sniffy about lending in small Maritime communities like Isle Madame; that's why Petit de Grat people bank mainly at their own credit union. And one clever solution to the absence of mortgages has been to pour a concrete basement, put a waterproof deck over it, finish it, and then live in the basement while you save the money to build a house on top of it.

Families are complex organisms, with their own characteristics and identities. It would be startling, for example, if someone in the Pink family chose to be a poet or a plumber rather than a lawyer. Thus Gerard told *BuzzFeed*'s Peter Smith that "Bowsers were always in mischief. They had nothing. They poach year-round to get what they want to live to eat, and we grew up still doing the same thing."

Families also have bitter quarrels. Phillip in particular was often isolated within his family, more like an appendage than an integral part of it. At the time of his death he was enjoying the relative luxury of a mattress on his parents' kitchen floor. Things might have been worse; in 1990, he was under a one-year probation order to "refrain from contacting or attempting to contact, at any time with your parents for any reason, whether directly or indirectly, unless specifically authorized in writing by your probation officer or the court." Why? A neighbour says, "Phillip threatened to burn their house down or some other crazy thing like that. They got freaked and called the cops."

"That kid, when he was young," says Hubert David, "you could ask him to pack five cords of wood. If he was all alone, he'd pack every bit of it, and you'd pay him after he was finished. But if Kenneth came up, his brother, they couldn't get along. I couldn't hire both of them. I could only hire one. And him and Gerard, they had more than one fight too."

One of Phillip's teachers remembers that Phillip struggled in school right from the beginning. Other incoming pupils sometimes could read a bit, or at least knew a few letters of the alphabet. Not Phillip. She gave him a little extra help when she could. He treated her with warmth and respect all the rest of his life.

His frustrations, she says, tended to emerge as aggression.

"He had a hard time working with other children. He was very frustrated a lot of the time, and the frustration came out in, you know, the elbow, or the teasing or the pulling of the hair—because he was that kind of child way back then.

"So at one point I did contact the parents for a meeting fairly early on in the school year. A couple of times they couldn't make it, but finally they arrived at the school. The principal was there, and Phillip's other teachers were there. We talked about his behaviour and his discipline, and we talked about his lack of a lot of the skills and abilities that he should have had. And I remember the father turning to me and saying, 'We're going to talk to him when we get home. Wait till I get home. He's going to get punished, and if you ever have any more problems with him, you call me. I have a nice two-by-four in the shed . . .'

"Those words still ring in my head, because I never called the parents after that. Never once—and I told the principal, 'You can call them, all of you can—but I will never call them again.'"

Teachers remember Phillip coming to school with cuts and bruises on his face. One bitter winter day he kept falling asleep at his desk. A teacher asked if he wasn't feeling well. Phillip explained that it had been his turn to stoke the wood stove the previous night, so he hadn't had much sleep. He was about eight years old.

"*They used to beat Phillip with sticks when he was little. Oh yeah. Oh, that was known. They treated him a little bit worse than the family dog.*"

"*He could be comical. There's a woman here used to be a nun. Her and Phillip liked each other. Not long before he died he went in front of her car and sprinkled 'holy water' over it, on the hood, just like a priest would do at Mass.*"

"*He took my four-wheeler one time, went for a joyride, left it with $350 of damage. No point going after him, and no point calling the cops. I just got it fixed; I was glad to have it back. Two years later he meets my daughter-in-law in the store. 'Hey,' he says, 'who's your father-in-law?' She told him. 'I thought so,' says Phillip. 'That's a nice man. I gotta bring him a feed of lobsters.' He never did, though.*"

"*Well, certainly he'd hunt out of season. Are you kidding me? I do it too, me. I never go hunting during the season. Oh no, never. The woods are full of fools. It's way too dangerous.*"

Tony Veinot is an offshore crab-fishing captain who lives in Halifax but spends three months of the year fishing out of Petit de Grat. After twenty summers in Isle Madame he knows the place intimately, and loves it. If he had to move from Halifax, he says, he would move to Isle Madame. He and his crew are at sea for a week or so, and then back into Petit de Grat to land their catch at the crab-processing plant, which usually takes three or four days. The crew, who are often from nearby Mi'kmaw communities, aren't needed when the boat is at the wharf and generally opt to go home.

So Tony is left alone aboard *No Pain No Gain*, a $750,000 vessel—meaning that if he wants to go anywhere, he needs a watchman. His favourite watchman was Phillip Boudreau. As it happened, on the morning of Phillip's death Tony was coming in to unload his catch and looking forward to seeing him.

"We were actually really good friends," he says, "and every time I come in from snow crabbin', he would come aboard the boat. We hung around all the time. He'd give me the shirt off his back. His parents were great to me. His family was super to me. Like, they took me in and they would wash my clothes and cook meals for me and treat me like gold."

Tony admired the simplicity of Phillip's life and his lack of concern for possessions. "Some people don't necessarily like to have a regular 8:00 to 5:00 job," he reflects. "Phillip never had any wants for any money. He didn't need a nice vehicle or a nice house or a nice boat or anything, and he was pretty happy, right? He was just one of those guys that never really wanted much in life."

Was Tony troubled by Phillip's reputation?

"I never judge people by what other people say about them." He shrugs. "I judge people about how I interpret them. Phillip had a hard upbringing, but overall he had a heart of gold. Two months before he got killed, I seen him with half a crate of lobsters—I don't know where he got them—and he gave them to old people. It was almost like he would rob from the rich and give to the poor, you know what I mean? At his funeral there was lots of old people that loved Phillip.

"I actually took the wreath out and laid it for him in the harbour. There was two boats went out, *No Pain No Gain* and *Irish Mist*. I took a bunch of his friends and people from the community, and we laid the wreath off the mouth of the harbour roughly where he got murdered, and they sang and stuff.

"It's a shame it happened. I try and feel for the other family, too. I don't know the other people—I just know what I heard—but I'm just a normal person, I work hard, I've got a wife and two young kids. And if somebody threatens me or my family, I might do something too. You know what I mean?

"His mouth always got him in more trouble than anything else, just saying stupid stuff. Like, if the fishermen were fighting out there, cutting each other's gear, and somebody's gear went missing, Phillip wouldn't even have done it, but he'd still take the blame for it—like, 'Oh I did that.' Why would you even say something like that? He used to piss me off sometimes with the stupid stuff he'd say.

"I know he's done some bad stuff. But there's definitely two sides to Phillip."

One neighbour told me that Phillip even stole from his brother Gerard, and that at the time of Phillip's death, he and Gerard hadn't been on speaking terms for more than a year. A former police officer confirmed that the two never got along personally, but that "they cooperated on business matters."

However that may be, the two of them were speaking on the morning of June 1, 2013—or so Gerard says. Gerard talks about Phillip fairly warmly. He doesn't think Phillip was any worse than a number of other young men with no skills and no job, who support themselves with a little poaching, some petty theft, and a dab of drug dealing. People often wonder why Gerard didn't hire Phillip to work with him as a lobsterman. Gerard says you couldn't count on him. He'd work for a few days, and then he'd get paid—and once he was paid, he was gone.

Gerard, too, sees Phillip as a Robin Hood figure, poaching or stealing from the rich to give to the poor. Once, when a neighbour needed meat, Phillip borrowed a gun from Thilmond Landry, another neighbour, and went off to Gros Nez, at the opposite end of Petit de Grat Island. There he shot a deer and cleaned it. He brought it home, gave it to the neighbour, and returned the gun to Thilmond.

Gerard shrugs. Everybody was happy, aside from the deer and the game warden.

If Phillip was Robin Hood, then the Mounties played the hapless Sheriff of Nottingham in this long-running farce. (Actually, if Phillip was Robin Hood, we might want to reconsider our view of the original Robin Hood.) On one occasion, Phillip was running away from the police. His favourite escape route was the water, and he swam like an eel. He jumped off the wharf and swam down the harbour. Gerard, who was nearby in a boat, picked him up and put him ashore at a distant wharf. The Mounties berated him for letting Phillip go. "Look," Gerard told them, "I'm not going to do your work for you. You could borrow a boat and go after him yourself. But he's my brother, and I'm not going to sit there and watch him drown."

Phillip's escapes are the stuff of folklore and legend. The Mounties come after him, and Phillip plunges into the water and swims across the narrow harbour. The police have to drive up to the bridge and back down the opposite shore. When they get there, Phillip dives into the water and swims back.

One time he swam out to what was once Mouse Island before it eroded; it supported an important navigational light, so it was preserved as a massive vertical steel tube just offshore. It looks like a huge bucket filled with rocks and topped by the rusty skeleton of the now-disused light. Phillip climbed up on the rock pile and taunted the cops, yelling and capering and laughing. The cops ranged around the shore, commandeered a small boat, and rowed out to the island. No Phillip. The whole rock pile is only about ten metres in diameter, but they couldn't find him. They gave up and rowed ashore—at which point Phillip reappeared on the rock pile, laughing and jeering at them.

Robin Hood 1, Sheriff of Nottingham 0.

Jessica Boudreau—no near relation—is a dental hygienist. Slender and fit, she likes to run, do yoga, work out, and paddle the waters around Petit de Grat in her sea kayak. She was out at sea one afternoon when Phillip roared up beside her in *Midnight Slider.*

"Jessica, what are you doing out here?" he said. "This is way too far out for kayaking. Get in closer to shore." And he hovered protectively till he was satisfied that she was safe.

Another time he told her, "I was at your place last night." Why didn't he come in?

"You were asleep," he said. It turned out he was being chased by the police. So he'd driven a little four-wheel ATV down through their yard to the shore, where she and her husband have a wooden deck with some Adirondack chairs. Settling himself comfortably, Phillip watched the cops flying back and forth across the bridge looking for him. Eventually they gave up and he went home.

One day Phillip hurried into his brother Gerard's house saying, "The cops are after me. Keep a lookout, I need a shower." He had a very quick shower and then vanished into the woods again. He would sleep anywhere, in any weather—in a shed, under a boat, in Betty David's trailer, under the trees, on the open moor. The stories seemed to say that he would sleep rough even when he wasn't being pursued. No, said Gerard, only when the cops were after him.

Thilmond Landry's house stands atop a steep little drumlin in the centre of Alderney Point. The view commands all the territory from the Bowser family home to Gerard's establishment: home, wharf, breakwater, lobster pound. Thilmond knew Phillip well. He would often hear Phillip out on the water just below his home, singing while he hauled up lobster pots—and not only at night. On one occasion, Thilmond walked down the hill and found Phillip sleeping in his truck.

"I woke him up—I'm tellin' you, he had a bag of weed, I could buy your car it was that big," Thilmond remembered. "I mean it was half the size of a pillow. I said, 'Phillip, get away from here with that.' Not that I cared about the weed. I said 'Go hide that somewheres else. Cops happen along here, you're fucked.' He didn't even know where he was at. I'm sure it was for somebody else. You *know* it's not his, not a bag of weed that size."

Thilmond often found Phillip in strange places. One time, when he knew Phillip was on the run, he was out on the moor training a young dog to hunt birds when the dog slipped away and then returned with a packet of egg sandwiches wrapped in foil.

"Right away it hit me: Phillip's got a camp here somewheres. So I grabbed my gun and I walked—hey, I almost stepped on him. He was sleeping in the fog, Phillip. He had a brown leather jacket and hip rubber boots. It was that foggy he was fuzzy on his face. I really thought he was dead. He had a .22 right alongside of him. I touched the barrel of my shotgun to his face. And right away he reached for his gun. I said, 'You're too late.' He had smoked a bunch of dope and fell asleep there. And he said, 'I had some sandwiches here.' I said, 'Yeah, my dog took them, they're down there. They're all fuckin' squish.'

"He was one of the toughest fellows—I've seen him jump off the breakwater here. Four cops were after him. He jumped off the breakwater in the water. Well, I was sure they had him. They looked, they searched. They searched Gerard's boat. And Phillip was on the backside of the breakwater, and it was just as cold as today. And he waited them out."

Robin Hood 2, Sheriff of Nottingham 0.

"Another time I saw four cop cars over there at his mom's and I had seen Phillip outside not too long before that," Thilmond said. "I said to Norma, 'Phillip's fucked. Look at that. Four cop cars.'"

But Phillip had seen the police before they saw him. He slipped down to the shore below the low bluff behind Thilmond's house. Thilmond watched while a couple of Mounties set off in that direction.

"There's a cross there now, across from Bowser's house." Thilmond pointed. "I don't know if you've seen it, a cross with Phillip's name on it. Anyway, two cops went down the shore there. Well, I said to Norma, 'They got him, he's fucked.' And after a while the two cops come up by the ball field down there, and they were alone. I said to Norma, 'Phillip's gotta have a hole dug in the bank somewhere.' And the two cops walked the ball field till they come to the cape here. One of them had binoculars. And then they walked the road back to Bowser's, and the four cop cars left.

"'Well,' I said to Norma, 'I can't fucking believe this. There's no way the cops—I mean, how could they miss him?' So I walked around there, it was low tide, and Phillip was walking the shore this way, towards me. We met there. I said 'Holy fuck, Phillip, I thought you were going to be on your way to Dorchester Penitentiary.' He said, 'They walked by me half a dozen times.' He said, 'Thilmond, I buried myself in the seaweed, in the kelp. They walked by me back and forth talking away on the radio, saying, 'There's no sign of him'—and they never seen me.'"

The Sheriff of Nottingham, hoodwinked again.

In all these stories, Phillip never seems to get rattled or frightened. He doesn't come off as a grown man jousting with the law. He's more like a child playing mischievous games, and most people don't seem unduly alarmed by his hijinks. They regard him as a fact of life, and rather an amusing one.

ISLAND VOICES

"There was another time the cops were after Phillip, and he rolled himself up in the seaweed on the beach—and the Mountie was talking on the phone sayin' he couldn't find Phillip and takin' a

leak at the same time. And he was pissin' on Phillip. Phillip was right at his feet."

"And my GPS was gone. And I said, 'Jesus Christ, if I get ahold of that little bastard I'm going to take a hammer and break all his fucking fingers.'"

"I put Phillip in the back of my truck with a long plank. I backed up the truck till the plank could just reach from the tailgate to the loft of the barn. He'd go up the plank and I'd drive away. No footprints, see? If anyone would come, they'd say, 'Well, he can't be there. No tracks in the snow, and the door was never opened.'"

Phillip repeatedly eluded custody. One time the RCMP came after him in force, using dogs and a helicopter, among other things—and they still couldn't find him. The moorland in Alderney Point is dotted with ponds and small lakes, so as Phillip saw his pursuers approaching, he plunged into a pond and sank to the bottom. He lay there while his breath lasted, then put his head out and took a quick breath as he looked around. After a bit he could see that the search had moved on, but he stayed underwater till he was absolutely confident they were gone.

Take that, Sheriff.

On June 1, 2013, a lot of people in Isle Madame didn't really believe Phillip was dead. They thought he had swum ashore. They expected him to show up after a while, just as he'd done so many times before. They thought he was probably hiding in the woods. But this time he never came back.

4

COURTROOM 3:
BAIL GRANTED

AUGUST 13, 2013

SAME THEATRE, SAME CAST OF CHARACTERS. Mr. Justice
Simon MacDonald opens the proceedings.

Prosecutor Dan MacRury rises, bulking large in his black robes.
He reminds the court that on the previous occasion it had ruled that
Dwayne Samson could in principle be released on bail—but only
under more precise and stringent supervisory conditions than the
defence was proposing at that time.

The defence has now proposed new release conditions, says
MacRury. The Crown agrees that these would meet the court's
requirements, "and therefore we consent." One of the crucial things
is that the accused, except for coming to court, will not be in
Richmond County, which includes Isle Madame, but in the Halifax
area, and he'll be under house arrest unless he's at work or is in the
company of Ramona or Weldon Boudreau.

The judge has a question. The proposed conditions stipulate that
Dwayne is to have no contact with a list of individuals connected
with the case. These include witnesses, members of Phillip Boudreau's

family, and his co-accused, including Carla Samson. Carla, however, is not only his co-accused but also his wife, with whom his children are living. Justice MacDonald is concerned about whether there is some provision whereby an intermediary can be involved for the sake of the children—"or is that out completely?"

It's out completely, says MacRury, and a flurry of discussion ensues. It turns out that the conditions do forbid Dwayne and Carla from talking together about anything at all—but that Dwayne can certainly talk directly to the children.

With that settled, MacRury sets out the conditions of Dwayne's release. First, Ramona Boudreau will put up $60,000 bail—$50,000 from a mortgage and $10,000 in cash. Dwayne will live with her twenty-four hours a day except between 7:00 a.m. and 5:00 p.m., when he's working on Chet Boudreau's construction projects. If he leaves the house at any other time, he's to be accompanied by either Weldon or Ramona. He will remain in the Halifax Regional Municipality at all times, unless he's attending court—and in that case he has to notify the RCMP twenty-four hours in advance. In addition, he's to report to the nearest RCMP detachment every Friday between the hours of 9:00 a.m. and 7:00 p.m.

Dwayne may not under any circumstances be in the County of Richmond, nor may he possess any firearms, ammunition, or explosive substances. He's not to possess any cell phone or mobile device. He is to surrender his passport, if any, to the RCMP, and he may not apply for another. He must present himself at the door of Ramona Boudreau's house within two minutes of a request to determine compliance with the terms of the release—and if he fails to do so, it will be deemed that he's not home.

Nash Brogan is concerned that Dwayne should specifically be allowed to leave Halifax in order to attend court or meet with his legal counsel. Justice MacDonald says that's understood—but he thinks that if Dwayne is leaving Halifax, he should not only have to notify the RCMP but also to state where he's going—"because if they go knock on his door and he doesn't answer in two minutes, he's in trouble."

Justice MacDonald pauses. "Okay, Mr. Brogan, have you got the cash?" Yes, says Brogan, he has a certified cheque. The judge asks Dwayne to stand.

"Mr. Samson," he says, "I have a judicial interim release application on your behalf from Mr. Brogan. Mr. MacRury has looked it over and is satisfied that it has sufficient restrictions and containment to ensure that the provisions of Section 515 of the Criminal Code are covered."

He reads out the restrictions so that the record will show that Dwayne has heard them and accepted them. He notes that if Dwayne wished to communicate in any way with any of the listed individuals, he would need a court order. He's allowed to go to work, but "when I say you're released to go to work, that means directly to work and directly home, and not to be hanging around Tim Hortons or restaurants like that.

"Finally, I want to say to you, Mr. Samson, that if you breach any of these terms of release you could end up back in jail until the matter is over with. Do you understand?"

Dwayne does understand, and he also accepts the terms of the release.

"Okay," says MacDonald. "I'm going to adjourn this matter to your court appearance on November 25, 2013, at 9:30 a.m. in Courtroom Number One."

And after the necessary papers are signed, Dwayne Samson walks out into the sunny warmth of an August afternoon.

5

THE ADMINISTRATION
OF JUSTICE

WITH DWAYNE SAMSON SAFELY stored away in Halifax, three
of the four accused are out on bail. The fourth is James Landry, and
the Crown is not letting him out of custody at all. The next move
will be a full-scale murder trial starring James. Apparently the prosecution hopes to convict him so conclusively that Dwayne will per-
ceive his own position as hopeless and will plead guilty without
going to trial.

The strategy makes sense: try your strongest case first, and use
the result against the secondary defendants. But James's trial won't
begin till mid-November of 2014, which creates a fifteen-month
pause in the legal process. It's an opportunity to reflect on what just
happened with Dwayne, and to view the hearing and the whole
legal apparatus in its local context.

As Nash Brogan reminded the court, there are only three reasons
to deny bail, and two of them clearly did not apply to Dwayne
Samson, who was neither a flight risk nor a danger to the public.
The only legitimate reason to deny him bail was the need to preserve

"public confidence in the administration of justice"—which assumes that the public actually does have confidence in the administration of justice in the first place.

Is that true?

Laws are made by those who have the power to enforce them. It is impossible to understand Cape Bretoners' attitudes to the law without some understanding of the interplay of power and law in the long, violent history of Cape Breton Island. Since this is an Acadian story, we can start with the Acadians.

"Noah à Gilles à Henry à Simide à Henri à Georges à René à René à René à Louis," said ten-year-old Noah Saulnier.

"Bon! And that's who you are," said his father, Gilles.

Noah is a tenth-generation Acadian, descended ultimately from Louis Sonier. Louis was a sailor, born about 1663 in Vitre, Brittany. In 1684 he married Louise Bastineau in Grand Pré, in what is now Nova Scotia. The couple had ten children, and every Saulnier (or Sonier, or Sonnier) in North America descends from their union.

In Acadia, the same name may have morphed into numerous spellings over the centuries. I am a member by marriage of the Thériault family; my late wife, Lulu, was a Terrio. That's how her family spells their surname, but I can provide you with sixty-one different spellings. That's right: sixty-one variants. Voici: the Terrieux all derive from a plowman named Jehan Terriau, born in Poitou, France, in 1601, when Queen Elizabeth I ruled England and the hottest ticket on the London stage was a new play called *Hamlet*. Jehan married Perrine Rau around 1635, and in 1637 the couple were living in Port Royal, in what later became Nova Scotia, where she gave birth to Claude Terriot, the first of their eight children. Marie-Louise Terrio—Lulu—arrived after eleven more generations. When we married, her son Mark became my beloved son Mark Terrio-Cameron. He belongs to the thirteenth generation of Tereyaus in

Nova Scotia: Mark à Lulu à Arthur à Miller à Aimé à Honoré à Louis à Simon à René à Joseph à Germain à Claude à Jehan.

The very approximate boundaries of "Acadia" expanded, shifted, and shrank repeatedly during the turbulent early period of European settlement in northeastern North America. At their greatest extent, they roughly matched the boundaries of Mi'kma'ki, the territory of the Mi'kmaw people which includes all three Maritime provinces, plus portions of Quebec and Maine. Today there is no territory of "Acadia" at all; the term refers to all the areas once occupied by Acadians and particularly to regions still characterized by Acadian history, language, and culture.

The story of Acadia begins in 1604, when Samuel de Champlain and his crew spent a terrible winter on an island in New Brunswick's Schoodiac River, which Champlain blithely renamed the St. Croix. After nearly half the party died, the settlement moved across the Bay of Fundy to Nme'juaqnek, the place of bountiful fish, which was renamed Port Royal. Building productive farms by diking the tidal meadows, cultivating the rich bottomland of the Annapolis Valley, remaining on cordial terms with the Mi'kmaw people—the Acadian settlers seem to have lived prosperous and happy lives. At the time of Acadia's first census, in 1671, Port Royal boasted 392 people, 482 cattle, and 524 sheep. The forty-seven family names in that first census included Babin, Richard, Petitpas, Gaudet, and Poirier—names of my neighbours today. They also included Boudreau and Landry, the distant ancestors of Phillip, James, Craig, and Carla.

From Port Royal, the Acadians slowly expanded along the Bay of Fundy and beyond, establishing settlements along the shore of the Gulf of St. Lawrence and as far afield as Epekwitk and Unama'ki—which the French called Île Saint-Jean and Île Royale, respectively, and which are now known as Prince Edward Island and Cape Breton. Throughout this time France and England battled continually for control of North America. The British seized Acadia in 1654 but returned it in the Treaty of Breda in 1667. In all, the British made six attempts to take Acadia before they finally captured and kept it in 1710. Over the next fifty years, the French made six attempts to take it back.

Despite this clash of empires, during their first century the Acadians prospered under a benign canopy of neglect. Acadia was a long way from Europe, and neither France nor England paid much attention to its people, no matter which monarch ostensibly ruled them. As the nineteenth-century American historian Francis Parkman says, in his patrician manner,

> They were contented with their lot, and asked only to be let alone. Their intercourse was unceremonious to such a point that they never addressed each other, or, it is said, even strangers, as *monsieur*. They had the social equality which can exist only in the humblest conditions of society, and presented the phenomenon of a primitive little democracy, hatched under the wing of an absolute monarchy.

These qualities characterize the Acadians to this day. Egalitarian and democratic to the bone, they also treat one another like members of one immense family—because, to a large extent, they are. Most belong to the same few dozen families that arrived before 1700, although that fact is sometimes disguised by names resulting from intermarriage (Bond, Skinner, Dingwall, McDonald) and anglicization (White, Gould, and Perry for LeBlanc, Doiron, and Poirier). In addition, different Acadian communities often have quite different clusters of family names. Chéticamp, for example, in northwestern Cape Breton, boasts scores of Aucoins, Larades, and Cormiers, but those names don't even appear in the telephone directory of Isle Madame, 160 kilometres away. Climb back up the family tree far enough, however, and almost any Acadian can uncover a relationship with almost any other Acadian.

So Acadians still do not call one another "monsieur." In fact, they almost invariably call one another by the familial pronoun "tu" rather than the more formal "vous."

Parkman further notes that, "while one observer represents them as living in a state of primeval innocence, another describes both men and women as extremely foul of speech." And that's still true, too. I think of Acadian cussing as a form of bilingual folk poetry. I take a powerless battery from my boat to the local garage, and Claude Poirier shakes his head sadly as he announces his diagnosis: "C'est tout fucké, ça."

"He's so goddamn cute!" says an Acadian grandmother adoringly, cradling her baby grandson. "I could just squeeze the fuckin' shit right outta him." Perhaps my favourite line of all is a disgusted Acadian's declaration that "That fuckin' t'ing is fuckin' well fucked."

But the fact that the European governments ostensibly ruling Acadia were barely aware of its existence doesn't mean the Acadians were without law. English-speaking Canadians tend to think of "law" in the form of British common law—as a set of written requirements, permits, and prohibitions embodied in a complex apparatus of statutes, police, lawyers, courts, and prisons and deriving its authority from the Crown. Common law, however, is only one of three great legal traditions in Canada, the others being French civil law, which applies in Quebec, and the many legal traditions of the First Nations. All three are recognized in the Canadian constitution.

So what do these traditions have in common? What *is* law, in its essence? The brilliant Indigenous legal scholar John Borrows says that law is that which guides our behaviour and directs our interaction with one another and with the world around us. Sometimes these laws are sacred in character, like dietary rules, prescribed ceremonies, or the Ten Commandments. Sometimes they are rooted in biology, like the obligation of parents to care for their offspring. Sometimes they are bodies of written statutes and regulations. Sometimes they are customary, or symbolic—unwritten conventions understood by all who use them, like the long-standing tradition whereby a government that loses a confidence motion in Parliament must resign.

When disputes arose in the rustic democracy of the early Acadians, writes journalist and author John Demont, "they worked them out themselves, often with the clergy serving as unofficial judges." Community rules and decisions were often made by a vote of the heads of the local households and enforced by consensus. Specific legal practices varied from place to place and from one period to another, notes Stephen White, the legendary Acadian genealogist at the Université de Moncton. Procedures also varied according to the seriousness of the issue. Major crimes—matters of "high justice"— might be referred to the formal colonial government, but "low justice" issues might be decided by the local seigneur or by a council of elders.

"In a colony of 450 people, very little could be done without everyone knowing about it," White tells me, smiling. "So you couldn't get away with much, or there'd be serious consequences." That's still true; when I comment on the Acadian habit of leaving the doors unlocked, White reminds me that it's not very risky because "you know the old lady across the street is always watching." And he tells me a story about the Forgeron family of Isle Madame.

The original Forgeron lived in eighteenth-century Louisbourg when Cape Breton was still Île Royale, a French colony. His name was Thomas Lesauvage, a medieval French name meaning "wild" or "native" more than "savage." "Bleuets sauvages" are wild blueberries, for instance, but native people were also "sauvages." Thomas, a locksmith, made most of the locks in Louisbourg; he shrewdly kept copies of the keys, which he later used in a series of robberies. He was caught and jailed—but, says White, "he had also made the locks for the jail, so he picked the locks, let himself out, and fled to Acadia."

At this point, "Acadia" was the mainland of Nova Scotia, which was in British hands, so Thomas was safe. But there were always plenty of Mi'kmaq in and around the Acadian communities, so "Thomas Lesauvage" fell on Acadian ears as "Thomas the Native," which was confusing. In addition—note this—the Acadians even then had no locks, so Thomas's trade was worthless. Instead, he became a blacksmith, a "forgeron," and his original surname gradually atrophied. His descendants were Forgerons, and many of them eventually moved to Isle Madame, where they became a distinguished family of sea captains and traders.

In matters of "low justice," the Acadians typically relied less on written rules than on shared understanding of what was proper and fair, and good for the community. Their attitude, says White, was "'If that young man is stealing, there's something wrong in our community. We need to do something, find something to occupy his time. How can we fix the problem?' The approach was never destructive; it was always constructive."

One deeply respected Acadian law says—silently—that since we all rely on one another for our well-being, everyone must do what he or she can for the general welfare of the community. You come out to work at the village hall, provide meals for the sick and transportation for the elderly. You volunteer at community functions such as dances, assist at Mass, serve on the cemetery committee and on the board of the co-op or credit union. The economy of an Acadian community is commonly dominated by co-ops; visiting Tignish, PEI, one time, I was amused to discover that every single business in town, including the gas station, the fish plant, and the funeral parlour, was a co-op.

In goods, cash, or time, you give what you can to help others through life's inevitable emergencies. By the same token, when your own time of need arrives, you have the support of your whole community. One example: when a home burns down, or a family faces a serious illness or loses its breadwinner, the community often organizes a "day" for the family. From morning to night, the community hall hosts bake sales and raffles, games and silent auctions. At suppertime volunteers provide a meal, and in the evening there's a dance with a well-patronized bar. Everything is donated by community members and delivered by volunteers—the pies and cakes, the pots of stew and chowder, the door prizes, the tools and teapots and CDs, the live music. The proceeds, including admission to the dance and the earnings from the bar, are simply given to the afflicted family.

In a parish of 1500 people, on an island of only 4300, such a "day" routinely raises $5000 to $15,000. After the death of one particularly beloved volunteer, the community of Louisdale, just off Isle Madame, raised $50,000—enough to send the deceased woman's daughter to university.

This is a system of mutual aid that's been operating long before the phrase "social safety net" was coined. It also represents the deepest level of security you can have: a web of community relations that ensures you won't be hurt because nobody wants to hurt you. This is the close mesh of civility that makes Acadians—and Maritimers in general—so reluctant to move away, and so homesick when they do.

But mark this: the amount that will be raised in a "day" closely reflects the support you've provided to others. On one such occasion, I found the hall virtually deserted; the day's proceeds couldn't have amounted to more than a couple of hundred dollars. I asked someone why.

"Well, look who it's for," he said. "What'd that guy ever do for the community?"

That's the nature of Acadian law: the Golden Rule, with teeth. It's a system of rewards and responsibilities, developed by the community, that shapes individual behaviour.

Customary practices governed the Acadians for a century or more. And although the imperial struggle between French and English went on like a thunderstorm over their heads, they generally strove, with considerable success, to remain neutral. Some joined in sorties with the Mi'kmaq against the English. Most, however, resisted their French priests' pressure to take up arms against the English, just as they made it clear to the English that they would affirm allegiance to the British Crown only if they would not be required to take up arms against the French. That policy served them well for 150 years, during which, writes Isle Madame historian Don Boudrot, "new customs and traditions arose, a distinct culture emerged, and these people came to consider themselves Acadians, not Frenchmen." By then, even their language had become distinctive, preserving medieval words and expressions that had disappeared in France and incorporating English and Mi'kmaw terms to describe North American realities. Quite recently my friend Edwin DeWolf and I were stripping shingles off my old house. Underneath we found not tarpaper but birchbark.

"Ah," said Edwin. "Muskwee!" That's the pronunciation of "maskwi"—the Mik'maw word for birchbark.

By the 1750s, the British, now firmly in control of Acadia, were mobilizing for the final assault against the remaining French colonies in Île Royale and Quebec—and were demanding that the Acadians swear an unconditional oath of allegiance to the British Crown. When the Acadians adamantly refused, the British commenced the brutal process of ethnic cleansing known as the Expulsion of the Acadians—in French, Le Grand Dérangement, the Great Disruption. In September 1755, after seizing the Acadians' boats and weapons, British troops herded the men of Grand Pré into their church and read out a royal proclamation declaring that all the Acadians' possessions, including lands, homes, and livestock, were "forfeited to the Crown, except for money and household goods, and that you yourselves are to be removed from this his province."

This was a legal proclamation, issued by the British colonial government, no doubt designed to strengthen public confidence in the administration of justice.

At the end of October a fleet of four decrepit ships carried eleven hundred Acadians away to the Thirteen Colonies. After clearing the Annapolis Valley and the isthmus of Chignecto, British troops marched into what is now New Brunswick, destroying Acadian communities on the St. John River and along the Gulf of St. Lawrence. Wherever they went families were separated, farms and villages burned, wells poisoned, livestock slaughtered. Families were deliberately divided; this is the background to Henry Wadsworth Longfellow's famous epic poem, *Evangeline, A Tale of Acadie*. One shipload after another carried deportees to the English colonies all down the Atlantic seaboard, where they were entirely unwelcome and often treated with astonishing contempt and cruelty. Eventually the English colonists refused to accept any more detested and destitute French Catholics, so later waves of deportees were sent to France and England. Many later made their way to Louisiana, becoming the Cajuns of today.

During the first few years of the Expulsion, numerous Acadians eluded the troops by hiding in the woods, often with their Mi'kmaw allies, or by escaping to Île Royale or Île Saint-Jean, which were still in French hands. Some fought back, notably Joseph Broussard, or "Beausoleil," whom John Demont calls "the Acadian Ché Guevara" (and who is, Demont notes, an ancestor of the pop singer Beyoncé). But in 1756 the Seven Years' War broke out, and two years later the English captured the massive French fortress at Louisbourg. Île Royale and Île Saint-Jean passed into English hands, and the Expulsion continued in the newly ceded territories. Once again, disease and malnutrition killed hundreds, while innumerable others drowned. Don Boudrot reports that in Île Saint-Jean, 3450 Acadians were put aboard nine leaky ships, several of which sank; in the end, only 700 arrived in England. Overall, between 10,000 and 18,000 Acadians were deported. Thousands more died or were killed.

Stories of the Expulsion remain part of Acadian family lore and legend. For example, because there are so few Acadian family names,

Acadian families are often subdivided into clans with nicknames. In Petit de Grat, the descendants of a prosperous man named Sylvère Samson are known as "Catou," a distillation of "qui a tout," meaning "who have everything." One family of Landrys (or Landries, or Londerees) are the "Ouiskins" (pronounced Wishkin), the "Chinwhiskers." Another Landry family descends from three brothers who played cards at a local store and had to take their winnings in groceries; the brothers chose lard, and their descendants are known as the Landrys Saindoux—the Lard Landrys. One of these is Thilmond Landry, Phillip Boudreau's neighbour; another is James Landry, Phillip's nemesis.

The large numbers of Boudreaus (or Boudrots, or Budros) are also divided into clans, including the Tucks, the Gurlins, the Cakes (who took their winnings in cake instead of lard), the Tocs (whose fishing boat engine went "toc-toc-toc"), and les Oiseaux (the Birds, descendants of Zéphyre Boudreau, an extraordinarily proficient duck hunter). The Bowsers—Phillip's family—are Boudraults Oiseau.

Another clan of Boudreaults are les Madouesses, the Porcupines, whose nickname goes right back to the Expulsion, when Charles Boudreau was hiding out in the woods, feeding his family by trapping animals for the pot. One day, says Stephen White, he'd caught a porcupine—a "madouesse," a Mi'kmaw word adopted by the Acadians—and was removing it from the trap when he heard someone coming. Fearing it might be an English soldier, he hid. He had no weapon, so when the man came close, he smacked him in the face with the porcupine. But the man was an Acadian, a friend, who ever afterwards called him "mon maudit madouesse"—my goddamn porcupine.

The Seven Years' War ended with the Treaty of Paris in 1763, and by 1764 the Acadians were gradually returning from exile. In 1766, says Don Boudrot, 800 Acadians gathered in Boston and began the journey home—on foot. After sixteen weeks they arrived at the St. John River, and many weeks later they reached the Acadian homelands in and around the Annapolis Valley. By now their farms had been "granted" to English-speaking settlers, chiefly from New England, but the following year the returnees were awarded a large wooded area on St. Mary's Bay. They'd walked a thousand miles—and 250 years later, they're still there. That's the home of Noah Saulnier—Noah à Gilles à Henry à Simide . . .

This is the stuff of myth and legend, with which the Acadians were very familiar. A similar walk back to Acadia, but starting in Georgia, is the narrative core of the internationally celebrated novel *Pélagie-la-Charrette*. As its brilliant Acadian author Antonine Maillet once told me, few Acadians were literate, but they had—and have—a phenomenal storehouse of oral history and literature. Maillet herself once interviewed a very old woman named Primeau who lived far up a Louisiana bayou and spoke only French. She asked Madame Primeau to tell her an old story. Madame Primeau promptly recited a version of a medieval French poem called the *Roman de Renart*, the Fable of Reynard—but she was delivering a version earlier than the first written version, which itself dates from 1174 AD. The *Roman* is full of classical references—Homer, Ulysses, Hector, Helen—all of which are common first names on Isle Madame. Indeed, the very rocks in the sea nearby have classical names: Castor, Pollux, Cerberus. The Acadians may not have been literate, but they were neither uncultured nor unsophisticated.

The returned Acadians were not allowed to create large towns, but instead were settled in widely scattered and somewhat inhospitable spots around the coast—Chéticamp, Chezzetcook, Pubnico, Bouctouche, Escuminac, Caraquet, Tignish. They had been farmers, but henceforth they would be fishermen and, later, shipwrights and traders. For the next 200 years they would be second-class citizens—but after 1967 they'd share in the general resurgence of French language and culture in Canada. Fifty years later, in 2017, Nova Scotia welcomed its first Acadian lieutenant governor. The Queen's new representative in what was once Acadia was former Supreme Court Justice Arthur LeBlanc, an Acadian from West Arichat, Isle

Madame. In 1971, when I first bought property in Isle Madame, Arthur LeBlanc managed the transaction for me.

The Expulsion and return constitute the national saga of the Acadians, probably the greatest national story in all of Canada. It's a story of blood, treachery, and endurance that continues to shape Acadian families and communities today. It's a story about British law and government and the vigorous administration of injustice. I recount it here partly because it is such a fascinating and dramatic epic, but also to bring home the point that for Acadians, the story is more like memory than history.

And now, I hope, you will feel the weight of a few simple sentences:

"Every Acadian sleeps with a suitcase packed."

"People in Petit de Grat really don't like to call the cops."

"To an Acadian, the phrase 'English justice' is an oxymoron."

"I was gonna kill Phillip Boudreau. I mean it, I was gonna *kill* that son of a bitch. It wouldn't have mattered to me about the Queen or King George or the cops, not one bit."

King George? King *George*? Maybe George VI, who died in 1952—or might this be an echo of George II, in whose name the Acadians were deported?

In the clash of the empires, the Mi'kmaq were closely aligned with the Acadians; both were Catholic, both were deeply rooted in the territory, and neither was happy about the incursions of the British. More importantly, as Mi'kmaw historian Daniel Paul notes, the Mi'kmaq and the Acadians shared a whole suite of values, including "mutual respect for neighbours, democratic practices, welfare of the community before oneself, and a desire to be left in peace, to name a few." The Acadian practice of a fundraising "day," for example, closely resembles the Mi'kmaw custom of "salite," an auction to raise money at a funeral.

And if Acadian and Mi'kmaw values were similar, so too was their attitude to law. Mi'kmaw law reflects the Mi'kmaw view of the world, Mi'kmaw spirituality, and the Mi'kmaw language, all of which derive from deep consideration of the natural world. For the Mi'kmaq, say Trudy Sable and Bernie Francis in their stunning little book *Mi'kma'ki, The Language of This Land,* the landscape is "sentient, ever-changing, and in a continual process of becoming." Because reality is in constant flux, the Mi'kmaw language, unlike English, is centred on verbs—actions, relationships, states of being. Mi'kmaw legal principles, writes John Borrows in *Canada's Indigenous Constitution,* are similarly dynamic, customary, and deliberative; they require extensive consultations so as to reflect the people's changing experiences and evolving understanding of the world. All of which seems deeply sane, profound, and responsive to reality.

And the Mi'kmaq, too, have no reason to feel confidence in the administration of British justice. For the Mi'kmaq, British legal practices include signing treaties that you flagrantly disregard, appropriating land that was never yours, "granting" it to your own people, generously giving blankets infected with smallpox to the real owners and stewards of the territory, and herding them into "reserves" which cut them off from the resources of land and sea that have always sustained them. These "reserves" become steadily smaller as your "Indian agents" slice off pieces and sell them. You deny the residents adequate sanitation, housing, and water. Then you seize their children and hold them captive in schools where they're beaten and raped and forbidden to speak their own language. All this is done under the cover of "laws" the Mi'kmaq played no role in creating and to which they have never consented.

To an Acadian or a Mi'kmaw, then, English common law presents itself as rigid, insensitive, hostile, and unrealistic—an artificial set of rules that don't resonate with the nature of reality, or with authentic lived experience, or even with basic principles of equity and fairness.

Highland Scots are the other large group of European settlers in Cape Breton—and their experience of the administration of British justice is no sweeter. After defeating the Scottish Jacobite army at the Battle of Culloden in 1746, the English did to the Highlanders exactly what they would do to the Acadians ten years later: hunted them down and murdered them, burned their houses and expelled them from their territories, drove them onto leaky ships bound for America and Australia, and "granted" their clan land to English noble families, whose descendants and successors own it to this day.

The grand tradition of British justice in Cape Breton continued right into the early twentieth century, when heavy industry was establishing itself 130 kilometres away from Petit de Grat around the harbour of L'sipuktuk—renamed Sydney in honour of a British baron. American interests established a steel mill there in 1901, fed by iron ore from the mines of Bell Island, Newfoundland, and fuelled by local coal from the vast coal fields around Sydney Harbour. These coal fields, which extend under the sea all the way to Newfoundland, were owned by the Dominion Coal Company, which by 1912 was operating sixteen collieries and producing 40 percent of Canada's coal. A decade later, Sydney—which had previously been much smaller than Arichat—had surpassed it to become a city of about twenty thousand, ringed by mining towns clustered around the pitheads.

Coal and steel ultimately employed more than sixteen thousand men in Cape Breton. They came from all over the world—from the British Isles, of course, but also from European countries like Poland, Ukraine, Italy, and Greece and from the West Indies, the Middle East, East Asia, and elsewhere. Many of them came from Cape Breton's scattered Acadian villages and other rural communities. The miners and steelworkers made industrial Cape Breton the only multicultural community in the Maritimes—but they were little better than slaves. They worked twelve-hour shifts, seven days a week; at shift changes they worked twenty-four hours straight.

And when the demand for coal or steel slackened, the workers' hours were cut or they were laid off completely. They rented their houses from the company, bought their supplies at "pluck-me stores" owned by the company, had their illnesses treated by company doctors. The prices of these services were set by the companies, and the costs were deducted from the workers' paycheques. By the time the amounts were totted up, a miner or steelworker might find he owed money to the company. One miner named MacDonald once opened a pay envelope to find just a single penny inside. His family is known to this day as the "Big-Pay MacDonalds."

The exploitation was all perfectly legal; laws are made by those who have the power to enforce them, after all. The workers' only effective defence was union organization and mass action—strikes and slowdowns, demonstrations and picket lines. And since all of that was perfectly illegal, it was met with armed resistance by the companies, abetted by government. When the miners went on strike in 1922 the provincial government called out the militia, dispatching twelve hundred cavalrymen to the coal fields, erecting machine-gun nests with searchlights and barbed-wire barriers at the pitheads, and placing bombing planes on the alert. During the steelworkers' strike of 1923, a force of mounted company police armed with baseball bats and whips rode into a Sunday morning crowd in Whitney Pier, indiscriminately beating everyone within reach. One policeman rode his horse up three flights of stairs in a boarding house, doing his best to fortify public confidence in the administration of justice by clubbing everyone he met.

In the great miners' strike of 1925, the company's negotiating techniques included cutting off credit at the company store and then, three months later, cutting off electricity and drinking water from the miners' houses in New Waterford. On June 11 thousands of miners, determined to restore the water, marched on the pumping station at Waterford Lake. The company police charged the crowd, firing more than three hundred shots. One of them went through the heart of a miner named Bill Davis, a father of ten. The crowd captured the policemen but didn't harm them; instead, it jailed the officers. Bill Davis had the largest funeral in the history of Nova Scotia. June 11 is still a public holiday in Cape Breton.

The administration of justice was equally robust in the outports, where the fishermen were economic vassals of the fish plant owners, who sold them food and supplies and then bought their fish, unilaterally setting the prices for both transactions. Later, when the offshore fishery adopted big steel draggers, the crews were forbidden to form unions. The law regarded them as "co-adventurers," working not as employees but as partners in the fishing voyages. That made some sense when the fishermen owned their own boats, or built big offshore schooners together and operated them on shares. By the 1960s, however, catches were declining, the inshore fleet was shrinking, and the offshore fleet was owned by transnational corporations whose draggers went to sea for twelve days at a time, summer and winter, in blizzards, in hurricanes, in howling gales with mountainous seas. When they were bringing in a lot of fish, the draggermen often worked twenty hours straight. Plenty of them died.

Working as much as five thousand hours a year, triple the hours of the average industrial worker, the draggermen were lucky to average a dollar an hour. It was, of course, the company that did the calculations. On one bitter midwinter trip in 1959, a fisherman named Everett Richardson and his mates sailed January 17, landed February 4, and made $2.01 each.

"And the one cent was in the envelope too," Everett grunted, "just with the two dollars."

Everett Richardson was a leader in the landmark fishermen's strike of 1970–71, the story that first brought me to Isle Madame. Two hundred and fifty fishermen had gone on strike, not for better pay or working conditions, but simply for the right to form a union. I eventually wrote a book about the strike, *The Education of Everett Richardson*. The striking fishermen were from Petit de Grat and

Canso, which face each other across Chedabucto Bay. They found themselves confronting not only the companies and the government but also the police, the clergy, the media, and the courts—the whole ruling elite of the province.

At one point the administration of justice required that Everett Richardson be sentenced to nine months in jail for picketing in defiance of an anti-picketing injunction. The labour movement exploded right across the province, shutting down shops and job sites everywhere. The court backed down. Ultimately, the fishermen won the right to unionize.

And now, I hope, you will feel the weight of a few more simple sentences:

> "In the war, Lefty and me, we were in the trenches in Italy, and then we realized who the regiment next to us was. 'Jesus, Lefty,' I says, 'these are the same bastards that had the machine-gun nest on top of the nail mill in Sydney during the big steel strike. Keep facin' 'em. You don't want them sons of bitches behind you.'"
>
> —World War II veteran in Isle Madame

> "CONTEMPT FOR THE LAW: WHAT ELSE COULD AN HONEST MAN HAVE?"
>
> —Headline in *The Fourth Estate*, Halifax,
> after Everett Richardson's sentencing

> "[The courts] can send free men to jail for refusing to allow the law-machine to rob them of their natural and constitutional rights, but they cannot make justice out of injustice."
>
> —Editorial in *The Cape Breton Highlander*,
> Sydney, on the same occasion

> "DOWN WITH CAPITALISM!"
>
> —Sign in the May Day parade in Glace Bay in the 1920s

"When justice is not seen to be done by the public," read Diane McGrath, opposing bail for Dwayne Samson, "confidence in the bail system and more generally the entire justice system may falter."

Confidence in the justice system. Really? Among the Acadians and the Mi'kmaq and the Scots, the miners and steelworkers and fishermen of Cape Breton Island? *Really?*

The world economy changed. Users of coal switched to natural gas and oil. An increasingly global economy made it cheaper to buy railway track from Asia than from Sydney. Cape Breton's steel mill and its only remaining colliery were closed in 2001. The pulp and paper industry shrank and the fishery all but vanished. The codfish, once so numerous that John Cabot said they "stayed the passage" of his ships, were becoming small and scarce. By the early 1990s one of the world's greatest food resources had become commercially extinct, and the federal government—having regulated it into oblivion—declared a moratorium on the cod fishery. A quarter of a century later, the stocks have still not recovered. The cod collapse was an ecological and economic catastrophe that cost forty thousand jobs and gutted entire communities. A disaster of these proportions in Ontario would have been considered a national trauma. But there was no soul-searching about the cod. No heads rolled. There was no Royal Commission.

The animals at the bottom of the ocean food chain are crustaceans: shrimp, crab, lobster. That is mainly what is left in the sea. A few communities survive and even thrive on these fisheries. A licence to fish lobsters now sells for the best part of a million dollars, and a lobster fisher's annual earnings are well into six figures. One of the communities still thriving is Petit de Grat, now almost the only active fishing village in southeastern Cape Breton. Its prosperity is a testament to the shrewdness and energy of its people.

Overall, however, the communities of Cape Breton are shrinking as the young people emigrate. The children of the miners, the paper-makers, the fishermen, and the steelworkers are in Ontario, on the West Coast, and, above all, in Alberta. Those who remain have had to find other work to do.

Stephen Drake was the last president of the once-powerful District 26 of the United Mine Workers of America. He had grown up in the coal town of New Waterford and had become a miner, like his father and both his grandfathers. In 2000, the mines closed and union laid him off. He wrote a graceful elegy for the brave men who had shared his vocation.

"There is no finer person on this planet than the working man who carries his lunch can deep into the bowels of the earth," Drake wrote. "Far beneath the ocean he works the black seam; an endless ribbon of steel his only link to the fresh air and blue skies. The steel rails symbolize a miner's life, half buried underground, half reaching toward his final reward."

Flash forward now to Courtroom 3, on November 13, 2014. The murder trial of James Landry is just beginning. The black-robed prosecutor rises to address the judge and the jury.

"This case is about murder for lobster," he says.

The phrase "murder for lobster" will stick to this case like a burr to a sheepskin. It will be in headlines and stories all over the world. And—although I haven't seen him for years—I know the prosecutor who coined the phrase, the man who's up there to present Her Majesty's Story again.

It's Brother Drake—Steve Drake, late of the United Mine Workers.

6

COURTROOM 3:
MURDER FOR LOBSTER

NOVEMBER 13, 2014

"THIS CASE IS ABOUT murder for lobster," declares Steve Drake, beginning the prosecution's opening argument. "The Crown will present evidence to show that the case is not about a momentary lapse of reason, where the accused suddenly and temporarily lost control." Instead, the Crown proposes to show that Joseph James Landry carried out a sustained attack on Phillip Boudreau. It will use James's own words: "Get rid of him."

Right now James Landry is sitting against the left wall between two sheriffs, exactly where Dwayne Samson once sat. He wears thick spectacles, jeans, and a striped shirt. A short, husky man, he has greying hair and dark, bushy eyebrows. He watches the proceedings intently.

The story is attracting national and even international attention. Once again, the whole front row of the gallery is occupied by the media—all three Canadian TV networks, The Canadian Press, *The Globe and Mail*, provincial and local newspapers and radio stations, *BuzzFeed* from the United States, and so on.

A jury of twelve local people sits to Steve Drake's right. They have been painstakingly chosen, not just from Isle Madame, but from the whole of southern Cape Breton Island. All the same, the region is so interconnected that it's not easy to find people who don't have linkages or strong prejudices for or against the accused. Jury selection took place behind closed doors, but I'm told that one juror asked the judge to be excused, admitting voluntarily that he had a prejudice that might be a problem. A prejudice?

"I taught your kids," the potential juror told the judge. Yes, and—?

"I have a prejudice against *you*." The honest citizen was excused.

The judge is His Lordship Joseph Kennedy, chief justice of the Nova Scotia Supreme Court. His Lordship grew up near Halifax and practised law in Bridgewater, but he's been a judge for most of his career. He loves his job and particularly loves jury trials, and he treats the jury with impeccable respect, repeatedly referring to them as "a good jury." When explanations are needed, he is patient and clear. He's both realistic and patriotic: Canada, he says, "bad as it is, is as good as it gets." In keeping with Nova Scotia tradition, he is a dedicated fan of the Boston Red Sox.

His Lordship imposes a publication ban. The media cannot identify jurors or potential jurors, and during the trial nothing can be communicated except evidence brought forward in the presence of the jury.

"As to Twitter," he says, "that is at the discretion of the court—and you may tweet."

Steve Drake continues. The evidence, he says, is like a large jigsaw puzzle composed of witness testimony and physical exhibits. The Crown will put those pieces before the jury. In this case the Crown's evidence will include sixteen exhibits, twenty-four witnesses, and an agreed statement of facts. His case will be a more detailed edition of Her Majesty's Story, amplified and buttressed by witness testimony, photographs, and physical objects.

The witnesses will include several RCMP officers, and some experts—on ballistics, for example—as well as a number of minor players, like the people who were on the wharf when *Twin Maggies* came in from fishing on that fateful day. They will also include members of Phillip's family, officers from the Department of Fisheries and Oceans, and several local fishermen. In addition, we will hear Craig Landry's account in his own words, and we will hear from James Landry via video recordings of his statements to the RCMP after his arrest.

Drake asks the jurors to be understanding towards the witnesses, who have been brought to court under subpoena to discuss, in public, difficult things that happened almost a year and a half ago. He reminds them that in most criminal cases there's a complainant, a person against whom the crime was committed. The complainant usually has a lot to say about the events—but in a murder case, the complainant is dead and can't testify. In this case even the body is missing, which leaves a further gap in the jigsaw puzzle of evidence. But nothing prevents the jury from putting the puzzle together despite that missing piece and seeing the big picture.

The prosecution's first submission is the agreed statement of facts—facts that the prosecution and the defence have both accepted and mutually agreed not to challenge. This will shorten the trial significantly. Justice Kennedy explains that the operative word is "facts." The Crown and defence have agreed that certain things won't have to be proven by witnesses. Both sides accept that what's in the agreed statement of facts "is reality, is the truth, is proof beyond a reasonable doubt."

Steve Drake's colleague Shane Russell reads out the statement of facts. Like Nash Brogan, Russell is a native of North Sydney. He's been a Crown prosecutor since 2004, just a year after he finished law school. He sits on the Council of the Nova Scotia Barristers' Society, and his charitable interests include Loaves and Fishes, which provides meals, clothing, and food to Sydney's neediest people.

Lobster is not among his favourite foods. In fact, he has a severe allergy to it.

The agreed statement of facts includes a map of the Petit de Grat area with all the relevant points marked on it. The statement confirms who the players were, including their dates of birth. It describes the two boats and also their condition when they were seized as evidence. It records the precise latitude and longitude of the spot where Phillip's boat was found. It states that Phillip's body was not recovered and that he has not been seen since June 1, 2013. It confirms that a Winchester model Ranger .30-30 calibre rifle, serial #5596251, was seized by the RCMP on June 7 at the Samson residence, and asserts that four bullets fired from that rifle had penetrated *Midnight Slider*. It affirms that the police recovered two green rubber boots and a teal and black baseball cap from Mackerel Cove.

The prosecution's first witness is Corporal Denzil George Fraser Firth, the lead investigator in Phillip Boudreau's disappearance, a familiar figure from Dwayne Samson's bail hearing. He's a big man, bald and bullet-headed. He's wearing a dark business suit with a blue shirt and green tie, but he somehow makes the suit look like a uniform. The work of the Major Crime Unit he belongs to, he says, is "90 percent homicide investigations." He recounts how he was called to Petit de Grat on June 1, 2013, and presents the physical evidence the police have collected—the photos, rubber boots, baseball cap, bullets, rifle, and so on. The Major Crime Unit prepared the map showing all the key locations. They also took three statements provided by James Landry in June 2013.

James Landry's defence counsel, Luke Craggs, rises to cross-examine Corporal Firth. A fit-looking sandy-haired man of forty-one, Craggs favours lighter-coloured suits—sage, medium blue—which make him stand out, even in his robes, among the coal-black dramatis personae of the courtroom. Raised in Edmonton, where his father taught engineering at the University of Alberta, Craggs applied in

1997 to the law schools of both McGill and Dalhousie Universities, then got in his car and started driving east without knowing whether either had accepted him. En route he learned that McGill had turned him down, so he bypassed Montreal and drove on to Halifax, where he discovered that Dalhousie had accepted him. He married a Nova Scotian woman and never left.

Craggs loves the human drama, the passion and fury, of criminal law. He'd be bored stiff doing more sedate forms of law. His email address is lcraggs@notguilty.ns.ca. With a practice focused on criminal defence, he has more than a passing acquaintance with the gruesome and the macabre—for example, the case of a young man who was being abused and stalked. One day the young fellow walked up to the door of his tormentor and knocked. When the man opened the door he blew the man's head off with a shotgun. The body was discovered a month later, when the neighbours investigated the smell and the flies.

Such matters are Craggs's daily work. He takes them more or less in stride, and originally assumed that other lawyers would have similarly unflappable sensibilities. At a Christmas party for the Halifax Regional Municipality's legal staff, however, he was talking with someone about his work when he suddenly realized that nobody else was speaking. Everyone was listening, aghast. He was never invited back, which did not distress him unduly.

Now he leads Corporal Firth through a review of Craig Landry's encounters with the RCMP. All the accused were questioned on June 1. Craig was arrested and interviewed again on June 6, Dwayne and James on June 7. All three were charged with second degree murder. They had the right to remain silent, and Craig did remain silent for the next couple of weeks, at which point either he or his lawyer—Joel Pink—let the police know that he had new information he was willing to share. On June 26, in the presence of his lawyer and with audio and video recorders running, he told them what became Her Majesty's Story. On the following day, in and around Mackerel Cove, with the cameras running, he led them in a re-enactment of the killing.

Firth agrees: that's what happened. After that, however, the charges against Craig Landry were reduced from second degree murder to accessory after the fact. With the Crown's consent, he was released on bail and never locked up again. Craggs doesn't ask whether a deal had been negotiated, but the question hangs almost audibly in the air.

Next, Craggs leads Firth in some detail through the search for Phillip's body. Both the Nova Scotia and New Brunswick RCMP dive teams searched extensively for it. In September, a sophisticated Navy dive team with advanced equipment also searched the area. Nobody found any sign of Phillip. Now another question hangs in the air: if you don't have his body, how do you prove that Phillip Boudreau is actually dead?

The court adjourns for lunch.

That afternoon, the Crown calls a stream of witnesses. Phillip's sister, Margaret Rose Boudreau; his brother Kenneth; and his brother Gerard's wife, Linda, establish Phillip's habits and movements. Linda confirms that James Landry called Gerard about Phillip the previous night, though she didn't hear what was said. Three Premium Seafoods workers attest that the *Twin Maggies* was a little late getting back to the wharf that day to sell its lobsters. It bore some red paint scrapes on its bow, and the crew unloaded something wrapped in a camouflage blanket that was the size and shape of a rifle.

"Pigou" Samson, a fisherman for fifty-two years, testifies that he saw what he thought was a dead deer in the water that morning, but found on investigation that the object was a half-sunk speedboat. He searched the area and found a gas can and an anchor, but no sign of any occupant. He radioed the Coast Guard and dropped a lobster trap to mark the spot where he had found the speedboat. The boat's orange bow line had been cut, so he tied on a blue rope of his own and towed the boat to the Petit de Grat fishermen's wharf. There he left it in the care of two other fishermen, Huntley David and Louis Boudreau, and went back out to continue the search.

Huntley David reports that he watched over the boat till the RCMP arrived. A small man with a short grey beard and dark hair, he has been a fisherman for forty-eight years. He knows James Landry well; the two fished together in the 1970s. *Midnight Slider* showed cracks and other damage. Its outboard motor was missing, and its orange polypropylene bow line had been cut. When the police took possession of the boat, he went back out and spent the rest of the day searching for Phillip.

Fisheries Officer Grant Timmons will attest the next morning that he saw red scuff marks on the bow and the bottom of the *Twin Maggies*, both when she was in the water on June 1 and when she was hauled out of the water the following Monday. His superior, Field Supervisor Norman Fougère, will follow him onto the stand. Isle Madame opinion considers these two—especially Fougère, as the senior officer—to be at least partly responsible for Phillip's death, along with the RCMP. If they had been doing their jobs, the argument runs, they would have put an end to Phillip's antics, and the fatal confrontation in Mackerel Cove would never have occurred.

But none of that emerges in this morning's testimony. Under questioning by Steve Drake, Norman Fougère identifies various locations on the map, recognizes photos of the wharf where Phillip kept his boat, and notes that the headland officially called Cape Hogan—near Mackerel Cove, where the *Twin Maggies* encountered *Midnight Slider*—is locally known as "the wreck" or "the wreck shore" because there used to be a wrecked ship in that location. This is a ragged, violent coast, and it has actually known a phenomenal number of wrecks. (In fact, less than four nautical miles westward from the wreck shore itself is Cerberus Rock, where the tanker *Arrow* broke up in 1970 and created the worst marine oil spill in

Canadian history.) Nobody knows just how many ships have been wrecked on the coast of Nova Scotia, but author Jack Zinck believes it may be as many as five thousand. Isle Madame has seen more than its share of them.

On June 1, 2013, however, as Norman Fougère testifies, the water was what fishermen often describe as "flat oily ca'm." Fougère was on his days off when the Joint Rescue Centre asked him to go to Petit de Grat to identify a half-sunk boat that was being towed to the wharf. He went, and saw that the badly damaged boat was Phillip Boudreau's *Midnight Slider*. He didn't think the orange bow line had been cut. He had seen Phillip in the boat the previous day, when "I was doing some snow crab work, and Phillip came zooming by with the boat and made his usual comments to us." Phillip was sitting in the stern and steering with the tiller on the fifteen-horsepower Evinrude outboard motor. Nobody asks Fougère about the "usual comments."

After seeing the battered boat, Fougère went to another wharf to meet two incoming crab boats, whose skippers were friends with Phillip, to check whether they had seen him. One of those skippers was Tony Veinot. But neither skipper had seen Phillip. Fougère then drove to Alderney Point and made a series of phone calls. He answers questions about electronic charts and about the equipment normally found on a lobster boat—including whether it has one or several anchors. He remembers seeing the *Twin Maggies* with scuff marks on the bow. He enumerates the boats that normally fish in Mackerel Cove. And then he stands down.

Steven Dorey, who works at the Rona building supplies store, testifies that he expected to buy some lobsters from Dwayne at the wharf, but when the boat was late getting in he bought them later from Dwayne at his home. Constable Jim Wilson reports taking charge of *Midnight Slider* and then going out the next day with the police dive team, who recovered a fifteen-horsepower Evinrude in about twenty feet of water.

This is Friday noon, and the Crown's case has moved faster than expected. Their next witnesses will be experts who have been told to attend on Monday, and then Craig Landry. After that they will play the video of James Landry's three statements to police. In the meantime the jury is released and the trial stands adjourned.

On Monday morning prosecutor Shane Russell gives the court a map of the next few days. Today he will present evidence from RCMP Sergeant Kevin Mallay, an expert in the recovery of electronic information; Constable Tom MacLeod of the Underwater Recovery Team; and Joseph Prendergast, a ballistics expert, who will testify about the impact and trajectory of the bullets that hit *Midnight Slider*. The *Twin Maggies* is being brought to the courthouse basement, where the jury will be taken to see it as part of Prendergast's testimony.

Mallay testifies for forty minutes about the chart plotter that was seized from the boat. The plotter is a navigational computer with a built-in Global Positioning System (GPS) receiver that pinpoints the boat's position as calculated from satellites. It stores information internally and on either of two magnetic storage cards. This plotter has only one card, and neither the card nor the internal storage contains any information at all except a couple of routes apparently entered into memory when the unit was installed in 2007. This is unsurprising; a lobsterman travels exactly the same route every day, so there's no reason to record his track. What he mainly wants from the computer is guidance in the fog: Where am I now, exactly? Which way to my next trap?

It's hard to see how this testimony serves the prosecution. Right after the killing, a rumour percolated through Isle Madame to the effect that Carla Samson had gone to the *Twin Maggies* before it was seized and erased data that would have shown exactly where the boat had been that day—but Mallay's testimony contains no hint of anything like that, and it appears the boat was under close observation from the moment it docked. So what was the point of the last forty minutes?

Constable Tom MacLeod is tall and dark: dark suit, dark shirt, dark tie, bushy eyebrows, and greying temples. He's been a diver for thirty-seven years, commander of the Underwater Recovery Team since 2009. He presents the official record of seven days of underwater searches by the dive team, starting with six divers going underwater the day after Phillip Boudreau's disappearance. The weather was still calm and the divers had sixty feet of visibility in the water. It was an "extremely beautiful place to dive because of the clarity of the water." The divers went down in pairs, each on a "sled"—a short, wide surfboard-like device towed by a Zodiac inflatable boat, a system that allows divers to scan enormous swaths of the sea floor very quickly without running out of oxygen or strength. In principle, two divers on sleds in such clear water could scan a track 240 feet wide—almost as wide as the length of a football field.

In four dives, the divers covered a very large area of the bottom just outside Mackerel Cove. Close to their starting point, at the location that Pigou had marked with his lobster trap, they found an outboard motor upside down with two ropes wrapped around its cowling, leg, and propeller. The two lines led to two nearby lobster traps that were still in place on the bottom. The engine was one of two targets of their search, and they had found it. Their other target was Phillip Boudreau, and despite several more large sweeps, they did not find him.

MacLeod provides some information about the behaviour of bodies underwater. A current of half a knot—about as fast as a decent average swimmer can swim—will tumble a victim along on a flat bottom. If the victim is clothed, perhaps in a Ski-Doo suit, the garments will provide some buoyancy, lifting the body slightly off the bottom; it will move unimpeded in the current. A jacket often captures a pocket of air at the shoulders so that the body will stand upright in the water, on tiptoe in the pale green light. When it moves, the toes leave a shallow furrow in the sand.

In cross-examination, MacLeod says he never wants to stop a search. He always hopes to find a body and give closure to the family. That, he says, is "why I do what I do." But the decision to quit is sometimes dictated by sea and weather conditions and sometimes by "upper management," who have to weigh the cost of expensive specialized equipment like side-scan sonar or magnetometers. And sometimes the areas to be searched are "just too vast." Phillip's body is said to be in twelve fathoms of water—seventy-two feet—so MacLeod could, in principle, have his divers trace the twelve-fathom contour line that snakes across the chart. At the mouth of Petit de Grat Harbour, however, that line covers more than two miles of open sea. In addition, MacLeod's thirteen-foot Zodiac has a horrible GPS and no depth sounder to measure the depth of the water. So that approach won't work.

Luke Craggs wants to know when a body floats or sinks.

"It's a guessing game," says MacLeod. "We're all unique. We're all individuals. Body fat. Content. Did he have a beer and pizza before he died? Temperature of the water. Depth of the water. Thin, muscular people very rarely come up. Body fat of people who are normal, maybe overweight ten or twenty pounds, give them five to nine days in water that's not below thirty-seven degrees. Gases— your body breaks down the enzymes to create the gas. If you don't have a hole in you, you will come up. And you'll stay up until the gas is exposed—mouth, anus, birds poking at you. Once that gas is exposed, you'll go down, and you'll never come up again."

Craggs wants to know whether it's "fair to say that it would be easier to find somebody tied to an anchor and dropped in the water than someone who's just drowned and floated off without an anchor tied to them."

"If we have the correct information, yes."

On redirect, Steve Drake asks about the effect of tying an anchor to a body.

It would "never come up," MacLeod says. The gases might lift it a bit, but when the gases escaped, the corpse would settle back down. "We've had jumpers off bridges who decomposed inside their sweaters and pants and never came up."

On which appetizing note the court rises for lunch.

Over fish cakes and beans, I reflect on the progress of the trial. The Phillip Boudreau killing is essentially one single event, though the Crown has chosen to prosecute it as four separate cases. In the beginning, the prosecutors in charge of all four cases were Dan MacRury and Diane McGrath, who conducted Dwayne Samson's bail hearing. James Landry's trial, however, is being prosecuted by Shane Russell and Steve Drake. Why?

During the fifteen months since Dwayne Samson's bail hearing, MacRury has been elevated to the bench as judge of the provincial court. Before that he had often discussed the Boudreau case with Russell, who was particularly familiar with key issues like the admissibility of evidence, and so, when MacRury was promoted, he asked Russell to take over the case. In a homicide case the Crown traditionally appoints two prosecutors, and Russell asked for Drake as a partner.

Drake had been laid off permanently by the United Mine Workers in 2002. Not wanting to emigrate to Alberta, he had gone back to law school, joining the prosecution service in 2006. His union experience prompted the Crown Attorneys' Association to elect him president in 2012, when the association opened negotiations with the provincial government for their very first collective agreement. Russell, meanwhile, had gone straight from high school to university and law school, becoming a prosecutor in 2004. He was twenty years younger than Drake, born a year after Drake went to work in the mines, but he was nevertheless the senior counsel. In this trial, however, the two regarded themselves as co-counsel.

One observer called them "Mutt and Jeff"—Russell short, bald, and stocky, Drake tall, lean, and angular. In court they performed like tennis players in a doubles match. Traditionally, the senior counsel—Russell—would open and close the case, but Drake thought he'd figured out a particularly powerful opening statement, so they agreed that he would open and Russell would close. They divided the examination of the witnesses more or less arbitrarily, with a couple of exceptions. Since Drake had a better knowledge of boats and fishing and knew Isle Madame as a motorcyclist, he would examine both Craig Landry and the police diver, Tom MacLeod.

It was Drake who wanted Phillip Boudreau's boat, *Midnight Slider*, presented to the jury, but Russell knows ballistics and trajectories. So the prosecution will suggest that ballistics expert Joseph Prendergast examine the boat in the presence of the jury, and Russell will examine Prendergast. They'll make this suggestion to the court now, right after lunch.

Back in the courtroom, before the jury enters, Russell raises the practical issues. Prendergast will testify about the shots that were fired at Phillip Boudreau's boat. Prendergast has all the resources one might expect—photos, sketches, diagrams—but the Crown also wants the jury to see the battered hull of *Midnight Slider*. The boat is now in a loading bay in the basement of the courthouse. Russell wants to take the whole jury down there so that Prendergast can actually show them the physical evidence—points where the bullets entered and exited, trajectories, the location of the only actual bullet the police recovered.

Chief Justice Kennedy sees the merits of the plan, but it poses a couple of difficulties. For one, everything that takes place in the presence of the jury must be recorded. How will that be accomplished? Second, as defence lawyer Luke Craggs points out, trials are public events, and it's obviously impossible to jam the crowd of spectators into a loading bay. Justice Kennedy decides that inviting the media into the loading bay will suffice. He suggests that Russell proceed right now with the rest of Prendergast's testimony—his qualifications, his actual written report, and so forth. The court will adjourn early, and the judge and the lawyers will go to the basement and figure out how to deal with these problems. The jurors can see the boat in the morning.

Joseph Prendergast takes the stand. A natty little man in a chalk-stripe suit, he's a firearms and toolmark examiner. (Toolmarks are the marks made by tools, like the dimples produced by a hammer.) He's been employed with the RCMP since 1991. His qualifications become Exhibit 17. He has studied bullet-path analysis, muzzle-to-target distance determination, range determination, and similar esoterica. The Crown wants him qualified as an expert in such matters. Luke Craggs is fine with that. A statement of Prendergast's qualifications becomes Exhibit 19.

Prendergast was called in a couple of days after Phillip's disappearance to examine *Midnight Slider* at the RCMP detachment in Arichat. He submitted his report on June 12. Shane Russell gets him to review some nautical terms: the front of the boat is the bow, the back is the stern, the left side as you face forward is the port side, the right side is the starboard side. The central spine of the boat is the keel, and the top edges of its sides are the gunwales, pronounced "gunnels."

Rain patters rhythmically on the skylight as Russell leads Prendergast through his report in minute, soporific detail. Looking across the courtroom, I see a sheriff's officer yawning uncontrollably; glancing at the jury box, I see at least one juror nodding off while others look glazed. I don't blame them. I would love to slump down and close my eyes myself.

Prendergast testifies that four bullets struck the boat, all of them between the bottom and the gunwale. Two of these entered from forward on the port side. Another pierced the starboard side. The fourth bullet penetrated the stern and lodged itself under a plywood floorboard—the only bullet to be recovered. This pattern,

Prendergast confirms, is consistent with the boat having been in motion when the shooting took place, or with the shooter having been in motion, or both.

The jury is excused an hour early. His Lordship Joseph Kennedy, James Landry, and the lawyers head downstairs to look at the boat. The trial will resume in the morning.

Midnight Slider sits on the floor of an anonymous concrete room—concrete floor, concrete block walls painted cream, black folding chairs, plastic folding tables. The journalists are ushered in first; the jurors are admitted later, along with James Landry.

"Even though we're in a garage, we're still in a courtroom," Chief Justice Kennedy told the jury before we moved downstairs. "I think you should be able to wander around the boat, take the opportunity to see the boat and to see what the witness is testifying to. There should not be any conversation either among yourselves or with anybody down there. You should function as you would in the courtroom, except that you will be downstairs in the basement, wandering around the boat."

Prendergast identifies the boat, which becomes Exhibit 20.

Midnight Slider is white with a red stripe and an aluminum rub rail along the gunwale. The red deck and interior are faded, and a bit of orange rope hangs from the bow ring. The rub rail is buckled inward adjacent to the rear seat on the starboard side, where the *Twin Maggies* must have struck it. That seat would normally be sealed to provide flotation, but its top stands open and a rectangular hole gapes through the hull. That's the point of impact—the seat where Phillip Boudreau was presumably sitting in his disabled boat as the larger vessel bore down on him, its bow looming over him like a diesel-powered image of doom.

The boat looks battered and sad, a scruffy visual testament to violence. Joseph Prendergast points out the bullet holes, the points of entry and exit, the different directions from which they came. He lifts a fiberglass floorboard, under which he found the only bullet he recovered. The relatively flat trajectories of the bullets show that they would have been fired from some distance away.

Back in the courtroom, Prendergast again takes the stand. Shane Russell asks that a sketch of the boat drawn by Prendergast be entered into evidence, and turns the witness over to defence lawyer Luke Craggs. Craggs asks Prendergast to describe the rifle seized by the police at Dwayne Samson's home. Prendergast identifies it as a lever-action Winchester .30-30 with a scope and a tubular magazine that probably holds nine cartridges. The range is about three hundred yards, and the only bullet found in the boat is of the same calibre. Prendergast steps down.

Shane Russell tells the court that there are issues about the forth-coming evidence that need to be settled before the Crown presents Craig Landry's testimony to the jury. The Crown and the defence have been discussing these issues, but sorting them definitively will require a "voir dire" (Latin for "to speak the truth"), a trial-within-a-trial held in the absence of the jury. The evidence in a voir dire might be called meta-evidence: evidence about evidence. In this case, the Crown considers certain alleged "facts" to be both impor-tant and believable, but under the rules of evidence they could not normally be presented to the jury. The Crown is asking Chief Justice Kennedy to make an exception and allow them. The defence will resist that argument. Kennedy will decide.

So now the judge sends the jurors back to the jury room. He instructs the media that whatever transpires in a voir dire cannot be reported until the jury is sequestered at the end of the trial. Indeed, the evidence in a voir dire is not supposed to influence the larger trial at all; case law dictates that even a presiding judge like Kennedy himself must ignore what he hears in a voir dire. Juridical brains are evidently built with watertight compartments and the ability to un-know things they have learned.

The issue in this voir dire is the hearsay rule. In essence, the hearsay rule exists to prevent the acceptance of gossip or misunderstanding as fact. If I tell you that Phillip Boudreau was a poacher, that doesn't prove that Phillip *was* a poacher. All you actually *know* is that I said he was. In his opening statement at this trial, for instance, Steve Drake told the jury that at one point Phillip Boudreau yelled "You broke my leg!" That "fact" is reported only by Craig Landry. The broken leg has not been confirmed by any other evidence—for example, medical evidence. In the absence of the body, however, no such evidence is possible. Another way to test the truth of that utterance would be to bring Phillip to court and have him cross-examined, but that's impossible too.

Yet the fact of Phillip's broken leg, if true, is important. Can it be believed? One of the exceptions to the hearsay rule is called "res gestae," pronounced "rez jest-ay." Res gestae (Latin for "things done") recognizes that people say things naturally, spontaneously, and without deliberation in the middle of an event. Those statements can be highly credible because there's little opportunity or motivation for the speaker to concoct lies or for the witness to have misunderstood them. There's nothing ambiguous about "You broke my leg!"

The hearsay rule would normally bar some statements purportedly made by Dwayne Samson, too. If no other evidence confirms it, Craig's report that Dwayne said "James, are you going to shoot?" is pure hearsay, and can't be allowed into evidence—unless the Crown can show that res gestae or some other exception applies.

Another exception, known as "adoptive admission," occurs when an accused admits guilt either explicitly or implicitly, sometimes even by silence. For example, the police often plant an informer in a cell with an accused, trying to induce the accused to admit guilt, either explicitly or implicitly or even by silence. "Boy, you really took care of that bastard, didn't you?" says the informer. The accused replies, "Yeah, he didn't know who he was messing with." That's an admission of guilt; it becomes stronger as an adoptive admission when the accused further confirms it. So the informer says, "You shot him four times?" and the accused says, "Three." Normally the admission would be hearsay and wouldn't be allowed as evidence. In this case, however, the defendant, knowing the content of an accusation against him, confirms or "adopts" the truth of the accusation by his words or conduct.

The court recesses so that Shane Russell and Luke Craggs can confer about the list of thirty-three statements in Craig's testimony that Craggs might challenge as hearsay. I fall into conversation with Joel Pink, Craig Landry's lawyer, who is wondering how Craggs will handle his client. He thinks Craggs should treat him sympathetically "because he's telling the truth. There's no point attacking him, he's not lying." Pink muses that if he were in Craggs's shoes, defending James Landry, he'd try to build up a defence of provocation, "because that brings in manslaughter as a possibility. I'd offer the Crown manslaughter and ten years, and then your client is out in three years." At this point, neither of us knows that Nash Brogan offered that exact deal at the beginning of the case and that the Crown rejected it out of hand.

"Your case is only as good as your facts," Pink says. "The decisions as to how to treat them are the things that keep you awake at night. But what happened out there with these guys is, they lost it. They just *lost* it."

When the court reconvenes, the list of thirty-three possible hearsay statements has been reduced to fourteen, but it's become clear that the voir dire will take all afternoon, and may not be concluded today. Justice Kennedy isn't available for the remaining three business days of the week, so he sends the jury home until the following Monday, six days hence. By now it's lunchtime, and he adjourns the court till 1:30.

———

After lunch, with the jury absent, the trial-within-a-trial begins. Craig Landry is sworn in and prosecutor Steve Drake leads him in exhaustive detail through Her Majesty's Story once again, starting with the first sighting of something moving on the water some distance away in Mackerel Cove. Craig's testimony covers the shooting, the rammings, the gaffing and towing and drowning of Phillip, and finally the process of tying the body to an anchor and sinking it.

Because the voir dire is all about the credibility of Craig's report of the words actually spoken by Dwayne, James, and Phillip, Drake is particularly attentive to the exact phrasing of the speakers—which is difficult, because Craig is reporting, in English, sentences that were actually spoken in French. During Dwayne's bail hearing fifteen months earlier, for example, Craig testified that Dwayne stopped the boat and asked "Is this far enough?," after which James asked "How deep are you?" and Dwayne said "Twelve point two fathom." James replied, "Yes, you're deep enough." But this time Craig says that James replied "That's it."

It turns out that what James actually said was "C'est bien ici," and that what Craig is reporting are differing translations of that phrase. The essential meaning is certainly the same, but the need for Craig to translate introduces an element of uncertainty about the very thing the procedure is trying to establish. What was actually said, and can the court rely on Craig's account of the dialogue? And even if the dialogue is being accurately reported, is it admissible as evidence or must it be rejected as hearsay?

On cross-examination, Luke Craggs also inquires in minute detail about the actual sequence of speech and action that fateful morning. When he gets to the third shot that James fired, and Phillip's cry, "Tu m'as cassé la jambe," he grills Craig closely. Is there any visible indication that Phillip was actually injured? Any blood? Any obvious signs of pain? Did Phillip have any difficulty crawling forward in *Midnight Slider* and cutting the bow line? No? No.

By the time Craig's story has been scrutinized twice, it's 2:30 in the afternoon. Craig's testimony is the only evidence, so the next step is for the two sides to present their legal arguments in favour or against letting the jury hear some or all of the statements Craig has attributed to others. What are the other cases where courts have considered this issue? What were their findings? What was their reasoning? What guidance do those findings provide to Chief Justice Kennedy?

But—heading into an extended recess—do the lawyers want to embark on the next act of this extended drama? Would it, Justice Kennedy asks, be counsel's preference to present these arguments when the court convenes again six days hence, on Monday? Luke Craggs thinks so, and Shane Russell doesn't object. He has already provided the court with three relevant cases on the subject, and now he tenders four more.

"This is stuff we've gotta get right," declares Justice Kennedy. "We don't want any statements going to that jury that are not admissible, or we don't want them being produced for the wrong reasons. I am going to have to talk to the jury at some point in relation to these statements. I want to hear complete arguments Monday morning at 9:30, counsel, and I hope to give a decision shortly thereafter."

He bangs his gavel, and everyone except James Landry goes home for six days.

By the time the court re-convenes, Luke Craggs has accepted the admissibility of all the fourteen contested statements reported by Craig Landry, except for "You broke my leg." Crown counsel Steve Drake seeks to have the statement admitted not as evidence of Phillip Boudreau's state of mind, but for the truth of its content: in other words, Phillip's cry that his leg was broken establishes that the leg *was* broken. This was a spontaneous utterance; Phillip had no time for "any calculated insincerity" or "conscious reflection" so his statement "fits squarely into the res gestae exception" to the hearsay rule. Furthermore, in his June 7 statement to the RCMP, James himself said he thought his third shot hit Phillip in the hip somewhere and confirmed that Phillip shouted "You broke my leg." James also noted that Phillip only crawled to the bow of the boat to cut the bow line, which is consistent with an injury to his leg.

"On the other hand, counsel, he's being shot at," says Justice Kennedy. "I don't think he'd walk to the bow of the boat."

"That's a possibility as well, My Lord," says Drake. But he considers that the weight of evidence shows that "You broke my leg" is both reliable and credible, and should be submitted to the jury.

Luke Craggs disagrees. The hearsay rule has to do with fairness, with the recognition that it's impossible to test the reliability of "something that was said out of court by someone who cannot come to court." The hearsay rule should not be set aside lightly. He argues that Phillip's behaviour after the rifle shots doesn't provide any real evidence that his leg was actually injured, and that his main concern would have been to say something—anything—to make the shooting stop.

Craggs points out the forensic evidence from the boat: four shots were fired, all four hit the boat, and all four were very low in the boat. If any shot had hit Phillip Boudreau, it would have hit him somewhere near the ankle, not the hip. Craig Landry has testified that there was no sign of bleeding or attending to an injury. Phillip crawled to the bow of the boat to cut the bow line, which is consistent with him not being injured. Phillip's boots have been recovered, and they show no evidence of any shooting. Justice Kennedy agrees.

In short, the "You broke my leg" exclamation is "highly prejudicial" within the totality of the evidence, Craggs argues, and there is fairly compelling evidence that the statement is not reliable. It should therefore be excluded.

Justice Kennedy reviews the fourteen contested statements, one at a time, and finds them all admissible, including "You broke my leg"—which he views as "not reliable to the extent that it should be" and "highly prejudicial," but nonetheless a "classic spontaneous utterance." The Crown can use it.

With that, the voir dire is over. The jury returns briefly and is dismissed until 1:00.

Earlier that morning, Luke Craggs submitted a letter to the court on the subject of media coverage. Justice Kennedy has already reminded the media that all the testimony and argument in a voir dire, because it is taking place in the absence of the jury, cannot be reported in the press "until such time as the jury is sequestered."

Now he takes up the issue raised in Craggs's letter: a front-page story from the Halifax *Chronicle Herald* of November 18 in which Joel Pink assured a reporter that his client, Craig Landry, had not made a deal to have the charges against him reduced in return for testifying against James and Dwayne. Craig, said Pink, was "very truthful. Basically his story has not changed since Day 1." But when it was pointed out that Craig had indeed changed his story, Pink swivelled smoothly to say, "Oh no, his first statement, as you will see, was not truthful. You'll hear how it came about that he gave that in his testimony."

Luke Craggs now tells Justice Kennedy he's concerned about the source of these comments, and about their prominence in the paper.

"The best comparison I can come up with is if Wayne Gretzky offered his commentary on who's going to win the Stanley Cup," he says. "Someone who's highly regarded as a lawyer is offering commentary on the credibility of what I would characterize as *a* key witness, if not *the* key witness." The Crown has other evidence— "but really, without Craig Landry, the Crown's case is missing some important pieces. My concern is that a juror will be struggling over Craig Landry's testimony—and there's Joel Pink, this first-rate, highly respected lawyer, saying he's telling the truth. Well, maybe that tips the scale in favour of the Crown's case.

"At this point, My Lord, of course that's speculation. I think we have a good jury, but in terms of publicity and the possibility to sway jurors one way or the other, this is essentially the atomic bomb."

He wants the court to poll the jurors privately and individually to see whether they've seen the Pink article, and if so, whether the article has affected their view of the case. If the court does find clear evidence that jurors may have been swayed by Pink's comments, the outcome could be a mistrial—but it's better to have a mistrial than an unfair trial.

Shane Russell thinks Craggs is giving Pink a little too much credit, and not giving enough credit to the jurors themselves. Joel Pink, he says, "may be Wayne Gretzky, but those twelve jurors are the ref. They decide the issues, they decide the facts."

Russell reminds the court that Craggs himself gave an interview to the same newspaper a week or so earlier, saying that Craig Landry's credibility and reliability would be questioned and noting that Craig appeared to have benefited a great deal from his cooperation. The prosecutors didn't think Craggs's comments deserved the court's attention, and they don't think Pink's do either. Russell points out that the jurors have been repeatedly cautioned—strongly—to disregard any information or opinion that isn't presented to them in court, and in particular to ignore anything they pick up from the media. He suggests that if Justice Kennedy firmly instructs the jury on this point again, that will suffice.

Justice Kennedy sets his jaw and declares that he'll rule on the matter after lunch. In the meantime, he says, "my life would be somewhat easier if lawyers did not talk to the media during the course of ongoing trials. The other thing is that it shouldn't come as a surprise to too many people that Mr. Pink believes his client, but Mr. Pink is not on the jury. We will recess, please, until 1:00."

On his way out of the courtroom, Joel Pink is wearing a huge grin.

"Wayne Gretzky!" he says. "Hey! How about *that*!"

After lunch, Justice Kennedy addresses Luke Craggs's concerns about Joel Pink. He discerns two factors. First, "we have a good jury here under oath or solemn affirmation that they will determine this matter based solely on the evidence that they hear in this court-room. I trust this jury."

Second, this particular jury was carefully selected. Its members were challenged in the selection process about the very fact that a good deal of publicity and information about the trial was already in circulation, and so "it was important that every member of that jury assure this court that they would be true to their oath, that they would determine the case based solely on the evidence that they would hear in this courtroom. And they assured us, each and every one, that they could. That's why they ended up on this jury."

The judge undertakes to reinstruct the jury to disregard all pub-licity and media coverage. The jury returns.

The Crown calls Craig Landry.

"State your full name," says the clerk.

"Craig Claude Landry."

Craig Landry is going to tell, yet again, his story of how Phillip Boudreau died. I'll be interested to see what happens when he is cross-examined, but I have heard Her Majesty's Story already—twice, in fact. I find myself thinking more about matters that the court doesn't really care about: not how Phillip died, but how he lived.

7

A ONE-MAN CRIME WAVE

THE MISSING PERSON IN Courtroom 3 is still Phillip Boudreau. The missing factor in James Landry's trial is motivation. Did the three crewmen on the *Twin Maggies* really kill Phillip Boudreau over the loss of some lobsters? Or were their motives deeper than that?

Even in communities entirely reliant on the fishery, poaching is not a capital offence. A persistent poacher may well get a ferocious beating—but he'll live to tell about it. However, Stephen Drake's label, "murder for lobster," is catchy and convenient, and it will stick. Years later, Edgar Samson, whose Premium Seafoods company has markets all over the world, will remark that wherever he goes, people ask where he's from. If he says "Petit de Grat, Nova Scotia," they'll look blank. If he says "Do you remember a case about murder for lobster?," they'll say "Oh, *that* place!"

But people in Isle Madame hated the label from the beginning, and still loathe it. Jake Boudrot, the Isle Madame journalist who edits the Port Hawkesbury *Reporter*, is scathing about his own profession's lazy adoption of the phrase. That label, he says, "just totally missed the entire case. It wasn't a murder over lobster. The media painted these guys as greedy murderers, and they all parroted that, *The Chronicle Herald*, all of them. I'm so disgusted with them, even *The Globe and Mail*, who I was helping out. I said, Is there any way you can talk to your editors and tell them for the love of God to stop calling it 'murder for lobster'? That's just ridiculous, I said. It's insulting to people here. It makes us sound like a bunch of hillbillies killing each other over a few lobsters. Do your work! Do some digging! Do your jobs!"

As the jury settles in to hear Craig Landry present Her Majesty's Story, I find myself thinking about all the things the jury does not know—the crucial facts that are not in evidence. The case does have something to do with lobster, but lobster is far from the heart of the story.

ISLAND VOICES

"Some fishermen would give him a few traps to set for himself, just give them. The deal was, if I give these to you, you don't bother my traps."

"Jackie said to him, 'Phillip, if I do these repairs for you, I don't want you to turn around and come back and steal stuff off of me.' And Phillip said, 'Jackie, I would never steal from you. You're a hardworking man with young kids. But some of these fishermen that make three or four hundred thousand a year— what's a few lobsters to them?'"

"Murvin and Billy Marchand, their boat went missing. They found out Phillip had stole it. They called the cops, said they were going after him, and the cop said, 'When you catch him, we'll pick him up.' 'Yes,' said the boys, 'you'll pick him up all

*right, what's left of him; you can come and scrape it off the
road.' 'Now, now,' said the cop, 'none of that'—so the cop went
with them. But they never found the boat. Oh, the boys were
wild. You should go ask Murvin."*

Murvin lives right beside the bridge leading onto Isle Madame, on
the Cape Breton side. He's in the auto towing and recovery business.
When you call the Canadian Automobile Association from Isle
Madame, Murvin is the guy who comes by with his big tilt-bed truck
to carry your disabled car to the shop. He's a dark-haired, husky, no-
nonsense kind of man who is perfectly happy to talk about his experience with Phillip Boudreau and the stolen boat.

"Well, I didn't see him take it, but I seen him with it—and he's
pretty evil. He *was*. I had my boat tied to the post down there,
and when it forecasted a windstorm I went down to tie the back
of it. I get down—there's no boat. Then a fellow told me he knows
where my boat's at, so I went in Arichat, in Petit de Grat—and
sure enough, I seen Phillip Boudreau with it, going up around the
cove by his parents', and he went up there for about twenty minutes, and then I see him coming back down. He knows my truck,
so I hid my truck by a building and I seen him going in by his
brother's wharf."

Murvin figured Phillip would tie up the boat and leave it. So he
and his brother and a friend waited fifteen minutes and then drove
to the wharf to grab the boat. But it wasn't tied to the wharf.

"He was still sitting in the boat with it idling, and when he seen
us he put it in gear and he waved to us, more or less saying, 'I'm out
in the water and you can't get me.'

"And you know that's the same stuff that he was trying with the
Twin Maggies. He figured they had a lobster boat and he had a
speedboat, so they ain't going to get him—but he tangled with the
wrong people there. You know people get fed up. He thought that

he had everybody scared in Petit de Grat, but there was a couple of people he didn't scare."

Murvin and his team went out three times to look for his stolen boat. On one occasion they were told that Phillip was on Green Island, a rocky island just seaward of Petit de Grat Island. He doesn't mention the name of the fellow who took the Marchand brothers to the island, but on the way out the wind rose to a gale and a steep sea came up, forcing them to turn back.

"Then I got a call from the police the next day saying that they had got Phillip. He said, 'We got a tip, and we were waiting and we got him.' But the day after, he was let go from court! You know, the Mounties were doing their job. They got him after three months of trying—but the following day after court, he was let free again. Then here he is out there cutting their traps and stealing their lobster.

"When I came in the second time that we went out to try to find him, one old fellow, I don't know his name, he said, 'Did you get him?' I said no, and he said 'I wish you would,' he said, 'before lobster season opens, 'cause we can't keep our traps.' I said, 'If you know where he's at, tell me'—and he said, 'If he catches me talking to you, he'd probably burn me out.'

"I said, 'He knows I'm looking for him, so why wouldn't he come burn me out?' That's a coward, that's going to go and tantalize the older people, you know. And he got away with it for so long. How many times was this fellow in jail and how many times was he let out and what kind of a record did he have? Why was he let out that time?"

I said that I'd seen Phillip's record—and that if you added up all his jail time, he'd spent something like twenty-three years behind bars, more than half his life.

"So what does that tell you?" said Murvin. "And here's James Landry—how old was he, seventy-some years old? And never had a criminal record. What brought this on him? Phillip thought everybody was scared of him, but then you get these guys that just wasn't. They were fed up. They'd had all they could take."

I had heard that when he called the police to say he was going after Phillip, the police said "If you catch him, call us, and we'll come and pick him up."

"That's exactly what they said."

"And you said . . . ?"

"If I got him, he would've got a beating. I wouldn't go as far as what they did, 'cause that ruins *my* life for a person like him. But he would've remembered stealing my boat."

Murvin never recovered his boat—but for him, the worst loss was that Phillip stole his sense of security.

"You know," he said sadly, "I never lose anything here. I'm here between thirty-five and forty years, and I never lose nothing. The boat was the only thing. Never lost nothing since."

On a nippy winter afternoon, I sat in a workshop with a successful fisherman named Guy Landry. I'd heard a Phillip Boudreau story that involved him and wanted to check it out. A member of Phillip's family lives just down the hill from Guy's home, and I'd been told that Guy had had a conversation with Phillip one day when a wedding reception was in progress down the hill.

"Lot of lobsters at that party, eh?" Phillip is supposed to have said. Guy nodded. "Know where they came from?" No. "Out of your traps."

"Yeah," said Guy. "That happened."

How did he feel about being taunted like that? How did he handle it?

Well, said Guy, his own philosophy was, don't confront Phillip, just go talk him down. It might take you a day or two to get him down, but that way nothing would happen. You have to realize that Phillip knew how to work the system perfectly. If the cops have a complaint against you, for instance, you have a right to know who complained—and once Phillip found out it was you, he could come back and "play a trick" to get back at you. He'd do $10,000 of damage to your property, they wouldn't catch him, and who would pay for the damage? You would. You'd be the one to suffer.

Since the cops weren't going to do anything anyway, what was the point of complaining? The cops claimed they didn't have the resources to take any real action—and the Fisheries guys said that their budgets had been cut so badly that they had guns but no bullets. And each of them said it was the other one's responsibility. If Phillip's stealing lobsters from a fisherman's traps, that's theft, and it's a police matter. If he's setting traps illegally, that's a Fisheries matter. So each of them would send you off to talk to the other. In the end you were going to deal with it yourself anyway, so why involve the authorities?

I had been told that the Department of Fisheries and Oceans called a pre-season meeting of all the lobster fishermen in the district every year—and that every year the fishermen asked "What are you going to do about Phillip Boudreau?" and every year they received bland assurances. Nothing was ever done—and now, amazingly, the minutes of those meetings seemed to have "disappeared." Guy nodded. He was at the meeting before the 2013 season, just a few weeks before Phillip's death.

For Guy, Phillip was simply a fact of life, and you dealt with him as best you could. In effect—though Guy didn't use these words—Phillip was running something like a protection racket. He'd reportedly driven a pickaxe into the engine block of a boat belonging to a fisherman who'd crossed him—and that served to remind people like Guy of the high cost of displeasing Phillip. Marine diesel engines aren't cheap, as Guy had reason to know. When we spoke, he had just put a new Cummins into his own boat. The engine cost him $50,000, the installation another $30,000.

Nevertheless, some of Phillip's antics were quite amusing. He would board and rummage through one boat after another at the fishermen's wharf, snacking and browsing as he went. The fishermen didn't mind that—a few bottles of pop, a bag of chips or whatever, who cares? On one occasion a group of them were having a few drinks aboard a boat and ran out of booze. Phillip offered to go get some, and soon returned with a bottle. A bit later, another skipper came along complaining that he'd been robbed of a bottle. Too bad, said the boys, that's terrible. Sit down, have a drink.

"Phillip wasn't a bad kid," Guy concluded. "He was quite likable, really." That said, he was rumoured to be bipolar, so "you'd never know which Phillip you were going to be dealing with. He shouldn't have been sent to jail all the time; that was no good for him. He should have gotten treatment. He didn't have much education; he should have been sent back to school. They said he had a mind like a four-year-old. I wonder if he really understood that what he was doing was wrong."

ISLAND VOICES

"You got better deals from Phillip than you ever got from Walmart."

"They didn't have to kill him. They could have boarded his boat, beat the shit out of him, broke his knees, and called the cops. They could have said he threatened them with a rifle. They would've got a rap on the knuckles—but with his record, Phillip would have gone to jail for ten years and come out a broken man in his fifties, no threat to anyone."

"No. Wouldn't have worked. Phillip had his own friends, you know. All it would have taken was one phone call: 'I'll give you two grand to burn that fellow out.'"

"Phillip was sort of a strange genius, because he figured out exactly where the holes were in the system, and he used them. He didn't 'fall between the cracks.' He lived in the cracks."

RCMP Staff Sergeant Daniel Parent was posted to Arichat twice, the second time as NCO in charge of the detachment. Now retired, he lives in Auld's Cove, on the mainland side of the Strait of Canso, and runs a small business doing household maintenance and repairs. He has vivid memories of Phillip Boudreau, whom he refers to as "Phillip à Bowser."

"Over the years I've investigated him several times," he said, sitting at his kitchen table one afternoon. "At one point I had twenty-six criminal charges against him, twenty-six to thirty criminal charges. Most of it was property related, but there were also some threats to this one and threats to that one, different people from the area. I was trying to find him, but he just couldn't be found. He was hiding but he kept committing these crimes, one after the other. He was quite active. A source called me and told me where he was, so I went out there and I grabbed him—I just barged into the house and went upstairs, and he didn't have the time to move or anything.

"We got him charged and he was kept in custody without bail, because he kept on doing his things. So we had to put a stop to that. At some point he was being transferred back to Sydney and he asked the driver of the sheriff's department van to stop so he could go relieve himself—but when he went down the ditch, he just started running again and disappeared.

"One time he cost us a brand-new Chev. A fisherman had his boat at the wharf, and he had a generator. It was part of his tools, I guess. So one day the generator went missing." The problem, said the fisherman, was that if he had a breakdown when he was forty or fifty miles offshore, he'd need his power tools—and without the electricity from the generator, the power tools were useless. That changed Parent's view of the offence. It wasn't just theft or property crime; it was a crime that put people in danger, so he took it seriously. It turned out that Phillip was responsible.

"He just unloaded the generator and hid it into another boat," Parent recalled, "and a few nights later he and some others came back to pick it up. We were watching. We tried to stop them, but they took off."

The thieves were in an all-terrain vehicle, designed for beaches, bogs, and dirt tracks. Parent went after them in his brand-new squad car, leaving his lights off. The narrow road to Alderney Point twists and turns, and it's lined with houses, so he didn't want to risk a high-speed chase.

"I would not turn on the lights until I had them some place where I knew that they could not escape. They were heading back toward his family's place, and there's a trail there that goes up to Cap Rouge." The trail is a narrow ATV track that snakes across the moorland near the beach and then rises steeply up the rim of a seaside cliff. "They had a 4x4, and I had the brand-new Chev. So they took off and I took off behind them, and it was like a roller-coaster kind of thing, quite a wild chase." Pounding over rocks and through ponds, the Chev took a terrible beating, and eventually its transmission failed. That ended the chase, and pretty much ended the Chev, too.

"But the next day, two guys show up at the office," Parent said. "They were sorry blah, blah, blah, they had been with Phillip only to go and pick up the generator, and that's all they were involved in. So anyway we solved that one—but it cost us a Chev."

Like Murvin Marchand, Staff Sergeant Parent found the community deeply divided about Phillip. "Half would be hiding him and the other half would be in fear of him," he said. "Once in the fall when he was on the loose and we were seeking him, older people kept asking, 'Are you going to get him?' The big concern was they could not go to pick berries because they were in fear of him.

"When he wanted to be nice he could put the smile on and just butter you. Those who liked him would fall to his charm, to his stupid joke or whatever. And if they laugh with him, they're friends. But if they don't laugh—'I'm going to get you.' That's basically how he was dealing with most people. Especially elderly people. Most of the people complaining at the time we were searching for him were elderly people. The younger crowd, the younger generation, some of them could stand up to him. Not that they would always challenge him either, because he was sneaky and could come at you from behind."

ISLAND VOICES

"The lobsters that he stole, there's lots of people around here bought them. There's lots of guilt to go around."

"You can't blame a poor man for buying food cheap when he can get it. And somebody else was going to buy it anyways."

"I blame the cowards that hired Phillip to do their own dirty work. Now he's dead, but they're the ones to blame. How do they sleep at night?"

Marcel Heudes, whose home isn't far from Phillip's, was frank about having helped to hide him. Yeah, he said, "I had him hiding in my house for a year, underneath the basement." Genial, vigorous, and earthy, Marcel is whatever he needs to be, and he gets along just fine. Sometimes he's a fisherman. Sometimes he's a construction worker. Sometimes he's a concrete contractor. Sometimes he's in Alberta, sometimes in Ontario. Sometimes he's in Alderney Point. Phillip certainly exasperated him, but he and Phillip were friends all their lives.

Marcel Heudes is also the only person I've met who made a sustained and realistic effort to help Phillip turn his life around. The only time Phillip ever held a steady job was when he worked for Marcel in Calgary for nine months. That sequence of events actually started, Marcel said, when Phillip was in prison. Whatever he needed in jail he would have to buy—like a TV, for instance.

"He would go and phone his brother or sister or mother," Marcel recalled. "He'd get nothing. So then he'd phone me. It's a collect call from Phillip in jail. The guard would say, 'Do you want to talk to Mr. Boudreau?' 'Yeah, sure,' I'd say. 'What do you want?' He said, 'I'd like to have a small thirteen-inch TV.' I took the guard back on the phone. I said, 'How much is your TV?' 'Seventy-five bucks.' So I told the wife to write a money for $80, send it to Dorchester, and get him a TV.

"A week after, collect call from Phillip Boudreau again. What the fuck now? He says, 'My TV broke down.' Then the guard come on the phone—'No,' he says, 'Phillip broke his TV. He smashed it on the floor.' 'Well,' I said, 'you're not getting another one. Bye.' But a week after he calls again, says I have to buy him another one. So I bought him another one."

Phillip was nearing the end of his sentence then, and the correctional service was looking for someone to help him adjust to life outside. At that time Marcel was living in Alberta, but he was willing to help.

"I said, 'Fuck, if he wants to move to Alberta, he can stay with me. I got a house, I own my own company, he can work for me.' They had one of the correctional centre guys come and check what kind of man I was, if I did drugs, if I drank, whatever. Everything was good—and then he asked me, 'Do you think Phillip will get after your son?' I looked at him. 'Phillip is not a murderer,' I said. So he came and stayed with me."

Every month Marcel and Phillip would visit a probation officer together—a man from Halifax, as it happened. Marcel was paying Phillip $16 an hour, a thousand dollars every two weeks. Phillip had no idea how to handle money, but he opened a bank account for the first time and got a credit card with a $1500 limit. He was also eligible, for the first time, for Employment Insurance.

"Fuck, was he ever happy!" said Marcel. "He was good, he was good, he was a good worker. But I'm going to tell you what happened to him one day in Alberta. In Alberta if there's change in your truck or something, they take your change—and your cards, they'll spread them all around. That's what happened to me. My cards were all over my lawn. Well, Phillip had left his wallet in the cubbyhole of my truck, and I don't lock my truck. He gets up and there's no wallet. We found all his cards from his wallet—and was he ever mad!

"I looked at him and I said, 'Now you're mad, but how do you think the people felt back home when you stole from them, you little prick?' I said, 'How do you think they felt when they were getting up in the morning and their three-wheeler was gone and you had it?' Was he ever mad! I couldn't believe it.

"I got all his papers, you know."

You do? Could I see them? While we talked, Marcel's mother went off hunting for Phillip's records. Eventually she found them, and Marcel handed them to me.

"Look, this is everything there, all the stuff that the correctional centre gave me, his bank statement, I kept everything he had. Here, you can read it all. This is his first payroll. This is his bank receipts or something. He had $66 left in the bank. I wanted to give all this to the family as a memorabilia, but I said, 'They don't give a fuck for this. I might as well just keep it for myself as a memorabilia,' and that's what I did."

The papers included a couple of documents from the correctional service about Phillip's transfer to Calgary, and his time there. The first, dated April 14, 2008, was written by a Sydney officer who knew Phillip well, having "supervised him, on and off, throughout the past fifteen to eighteen years." She reeled off a long list of problems: a dysfunctional family background, an incredibly impulsive nature, minimal stress management skills, functional illiteracy, and so on. The prison sentence he was just completing had been extended by six months because Phillip had threatened a female correctional officer—though the writer noted that he actually had "no history of violent and/or aggressive behaviour." She feared, however, that if he were sent back to Petit de Grat, the result would be the same as on previous occasions: unemployment, drugs, bad company, more offences, more jail time.

But she had phoned Marcel Heudes, who clearly knew Phillip well. He and his wife, Kim, had already bought Phillip an airline ticket to Calgary and were prepared to "see to it that Phillip has a flight back home if things don't work out.

"The current opportunity to relocate and to live and work with an old family friend represents a 'once in a lifetime chance' for Phillip Boudreau," wrote the parole officer. She noted that Phillip was "expressing a desire to alter his lifestyle at this juncture. He has stated that he is getting older and does not want to spend the remainder of his life incarcerated." The officer was "not optimistic that Phillip will last in Calgary in the long term," but she concluded that "if Phillip stands any chance of breaking his long standing offence cycle, this could be it."

The second document was filed less than a month later by a Calgary parole officer, who noted that Marcel and Kim Heudes were providing Phillip with "emotional, moral, residential and financial support." In addition, Phillip was receiving "positive support" from Marcel's brother Gilles (the officer misspelled the name as "Gil"), who was also working with Heudes Contracting Ltd. The pace and intensity of life in Calgary were sometimes a shock to Phillip; at one point, Marcel remembers, Phillip had a full-blown panic attack in the roaring traffic of the six-lane Deerfoot Trail.

Small wonder. He had spent almost his whole life in rural Nova Scotia, and, said the Calgary report, "file information suggests that he suffers from ADHD, Tourette's syndrome, and is borderline schizophrenic." This is the only official comment I've seen on Phillip's mental health, although his sister Maggie said he had been diagnosed as bipolar during one of his prison terms.

Nevertheless, the Calgary parole officer was generally satisfied with Phillip's progress. He had been "adjusting well," had stable housing and employment, was going to counselling, and had taken various steps to integrate himself into community life, like opening a bank account. Although he was still easily frustrated, he had a positive attitude towards the changes in his life and was generally cooperative with his supervision team.

A handful of documents: the official residue of Phillip Boudreau's life. Canada Trust. Province of New Brunswick, Correctional Service, Health and Wellness. Canada Revenue. Fading echoes of a troubled life.

ISLAND VOICES

"One time my cousin Frankie was down inside the hold of a boat at the Premium wharf, heaving up totes of fish. Phillip comes along. One of the totes is lying in the sun. 'Hey Frankie,' says Phillip, 'you should move that tote out of the sun.' 'Yeah,' says Frankie, but he doesn't do it. Phillip tells him again. Frankie ignores him. Phillip comes over and starts kicking at his head. Later on Frankie mentions it to his father, that would be my uncle Dennis. Dennis is a big man. He goes looking for Phillip, and he finds him. Phillip was just a shrimp, you know. So Dennis pins him up against a wall with one hand, and he tells Phillip exactly what's going to happen to him if he does anything like that to anyone in our family ever again. And that was the end of it. He never ever gave any of us one minute of trouble after that."

"Phillip was a bully, and a bully is a coward. Phillip was a nice guy when you spoke to him alone. When it was people around, Phillip would make comments, try to draw attention, trying to be a bully, which he was. A lot of times if he saw someone was scared of him then he would bully him."

"I'm going to tell you who he knew in jail: he knew Mom Boucher, that really bad bastard from the Hells Angels in Quebec. Mom Boucher used to call him Booboo. So Booboo was his name in jail."

Omer Boudreau is eighty now and says he's not the man he was, but he still looks trim, compact, and powerful. He started fishing when he was fourteen years old. I heard he had a memorable run-in with Phillip when he was the captain of his own swordfish boat. I wanted to know if it was true.

A swordfish is a magnificent animal—a far-ranging, fast-travelling predator found throughout the temperate oceans. Adults are commonly ten feet or more in length, weighing over a thousand pounds and swimming at up to sixty miles per hour. They can dive to nearly ten thousand feet, although they are often found basking in the sunlight at the surface. Swordfishermen often speak of them almost poetically—their beauty, their speed, their energy and agility. They like to swim along the axis of the seas, right inside the waves, and when a big sea forms a wall of water between the fisherman and the sun, the swordfish can be seen surging along as though encased in liquid green glass. When hooked they fight fiercely, and have been known to drive their swords right through the planks of wooden fishing boats.

Today they are mostly hooked on long, baited lines, but traditionally they were fished from modest-sized boats using harpoons. The man with the harpoon is called a "striker;" his station is in a steel pulpit at the tip of a long slim stainless-steel walkway called the "stand," which runs out from the bow of the boat. It is no small feat to harpoon a moving swordfish from a plunging, soaring pulpit. Omer Boudreau was particularly good at it.

Swordfish live in the open ocean, so fishermen pursue them far offshore, staying out for days at a time. On one occasion, Omer had stocked his boat with food, drink, and other supplies, like cigarettes. ("This was a long time ago," he noted. "Everybody still smoked then.") Then he sent his crew home to get some sleep before they sailed out in the evening.

That night they went to sea. Six hours later, off the northeastern tip of Cape Breton, Omer—who was at the wheel—said to a crewman, "You should get me a pack of cigarettes out of that locker."

"There's nothing in there."

"Sure there is," Omer said. "I put the grub in there myself."

"Well, there's nothing in there now."

Omer took a look. Sure enough, the locker was empty. So were the other lockers where their supplies had been stored. Without supplies, the trip was impossible. They turned around and headed home. Six hours later they were back in Petit de Grat. Phillip was selling their supplies on the wharf.

What did Omer do?

"What *could* you do?" said Omer. "He's got no money. The police won't do frig-all. We just loaded up again and went back out.

"I'll tell you another one he pulled on me. I had a nice four-wheeler parked out behind the house here. Usually I put it in the shed, but this night I didn't. And mostly I sleep with the window open, but this night it was raining and windy and the curtains were blowing all around, so I closed the window. Phillip and another one came in the night and dragged it and put it up on a trailer, and gone. It's all gravel back there, and you could see the scuffs where they turned the wheel and dragged it sideways. Right under my bedroom window!

"Anyway, a day or so later I'm at the Corner Bridge, and Phillip is outside the store, sitting on a five-gallon bucket of poached lobsters, selling them right there in the open, and he waves me over. 'Listen,' he says, 'if you want to know who stole your bike, it was me. And if you want it back, I'll tell you how you can get it. I sold it up in Troy, at the trailer park there. You can go there and buy it back.'

"I said, 'Listen, you little bastard'"—by now Omer, just telling the story, was trembling with rage and frustration—"'listen, you little bastard, I'm seventy-five years old and you know I can't put a beating on you like you deserve. If I was a little younger I'd give you a beating you wouldn't forget.'"

I had heard the story before, the bike that was sold in Troy, not far from the Canso Causeway. But I hadn't heard who the victim was.

"It was me," said Omer. "Oh, that little bastard. I got the insurance for the bike, but it was only about $4000, and the bike cost me twelve. They said it was old, so they depreciated it—but it was hardly used. I don't use a bike much, just running out to the cabin I had in Gros Nez."

Gros Nez—Big Nose—is an island that looks like the nose of a giant lying supine in the sea. The phrase also refers to the nearby eastern tip of Petit de Grat Island. There are no roads into that area. You get there by boat or ATV. A friend and I had cruised along that shore in a small motorboat a week or two before, and I'd noticed a couple of little shacks along the shore. Phillip slept in those cabins sometimes. I had heard that Omer's brother Peter had a cabin out there too, and that Phillip had trashed and burned it.

"That was my cabin," said Omer. "Mine and Peter's. I bought the materials and we built it together. And what a job they did on it, you. They picked up a small log and used it for a ram, and punched right through the walls. They wrecked everything, everything, everything. We didn't know what to do, pull it down or fix it up, but then a couple of weeks later it was burned."

By Phillip?

"Well, I don't know who burned it, but I don't think it was Phillip. I got a suspicion who it probably was. It could have been Phillip, though.

"I damn near hit him with my car one time, head-on, without wanting to. A guy from Boudreauville was planting pot plants, and Phillip didn't like him. Maybe he was short of marijuana himself, I don't know. Anyway, he went to Boudreauville, wherever they were planted, somewhere in the woods, with his four-wheeler. Stole them all. Packed them on the front of his four-wheeler, tied them up. There were seven or eight of those plants, and they were maybe four or five feet high.

"I go to see his brother once in a while, Gerard, he's a good friend of mine. So this night I was coming home, and it was turning dark, about eight o'clock at night. There's a big curve that goes right down along the water there. I had my park lights on—and all of a sudden this thing's coming at me around the curve, partway on my side of the road. I didn't know what the hell it was. You know, he had the plants in his rack there, all tied up together. He had no lights on, and he was comin' about thirty, forty miles an hour, and I was comin' the same speed the other way, fifty, sixty kilometres, and first thing, this is in front of me! I never had a clue what it was. I couldn't see him or nothing; you could barely see the bike. He got by me all right, but I damn near hit him head-on."

Later in the evening, as Omer was sharing some reflections on how people should treat one another, he told me about an episode with his father. He was very young, possibly ten or twelve, so it must have been around 1950, a time of wrenching poverty in rural Cape Breton. Omer and his father were out on their woodlot one winter day cutting firewood. They'd loaded the wood on their sled and were heading home when they met a desperately poor neighbour who had no woodlot and had been gathering dry sticks and dead branches. The man had several children, and Omer knew that they didn't even have blankets; the children huddled together in their coats to keep warm.

"Along comes another fellow, he owned the next woodlot. He was pretty well off, but he was an asshole. 'Where'd you get those sticks?' he said. 'Over there.' 'That's *my* woodlot,' said the asshole. 'Those are *my* sticks. You put them back.' My father said, 'Aw, come on, it's just a few sticks'—but this arsehole insisted. It got quite heated. Finally my father said, 'All right, my friend, put the sticks back and then you come with me.' We got him up on the sled and we drove to his house and we dumped our whole load of firewood. 'There,' said my father, 'that'll keep you going for a while.'

"I don't think I ever saw my father so mad," said Omer, his eyes brimming. "But why would you do that? Just to hurt another man? He had lots. He was never going to use those sticks. They meant nothing to him. I can't understand a thing like that. I still can't understand it."

ISLAND VOICES

"I had given him some gas for his four-wheeler, and he looked around my shop and he said, 'What do you need here? What do you want? I'd like to give you a gift.' I said, 'Phillip, there's nothing I need that I don't have.' If I'd of told him there was something I wanted, he'd of went and stole it, and I didn't want that."

"One time there was a ship in here and half a dozen survival suits got stolen off of it. Them things are expensive, maybe $3000 each. The ship couldn't sail without them, and it was going to take a while to get new ones. Phillip sent somebody to tell the skipper he could get them back for $300 each or something. Well, what would you do? Pay $18,000 and wait ten days—or pay $1800 and sail tonight? Didn't take him too long to do the math."

"When James gets out he'll be seventy-some years old, the fucker. I can probably kick his fucking cane and walk on him."

"If Phillip was my brother, I would have been up on a roof somewheres with a rifle, outside the courthouse, and I would have picked them off, every one of the ones that killed him."

Some people claim that Phillip couldn't have been poaching the morning he was killed, because he only poached at night. Not true, said Omer. He poached in the daytime, too, when it served his purposes.

"There was a fellow he didn't like. I won't name the guy. Now, Phillip's got a little speedboat that does twenty-five miles an hour, and the other guy's in a fishing boat that does maybe eight knots. So Phillip would go out in the morning, and he'd stay one trap ahead of the guy, and he'd haul the guy's second trap while the guy was hauling his first. And then whatever lobsters were into it, he'd hold them up and say, 'Look! Look what nice lobsters I got from your trap!' And then he'd put them in his boat and leave the trap open and go on to the next trap. And then of course the fisherman, when he was finished with his first trap, he'd have to come over and haul that trap again. It was empty, of course, but he'd have to bait it again and close it.

"Phillip would do that all along the string of traps until his mind was satisfied. And then he was taking the lobsters in and selling them.

"The guy hollered, 'I should shoot you'—he's allowed a gun to shoot seals if they're on his nets, something like that, so he had a 12-gauge shotgun, and he held it up to his shoulder, and he said, 'You little prick, I should fucking shoot you!' Phillip laughs and he holds up his .22 rifle that he had in his boat all the time, and he says, 'My gun can shoot farther than yours.' So that's pretty brazen, eh? He done that to three or four fellers."

"Are you serious?" I said. "He'd go down the string of traps cleaning out each one in turn, right in front of the fisherman that owned them?"

"That's just what he'd do."

"Jesus Christ," I said, "was he *trying* to get himself killed?"

8

COURTROOM 3:
THE COCKAMAMIE STORY

BACK IN COURTROOM 3, Luke Craggs is beginning what one reporter will describe as a "blistering" cross-examination of Craig Landry, who has just told Her Majesty's Story again.

"How was jail, Mr. Landry?" Craggs demands.

Shane Russell immediately objects. What's the relevance of the question to the matter before the court?

"Well, I have some sense of where the defence is going," says Justice Kennedy. "I'll allow the question."

"Did you like it?" Craggs asks. "Did you want to get out of jail?"

"Yes."

"And why did you want to get out of jail?"

"I don't know how to answer that."

"Well," Craggs continues, "if you didn't like it, what specifically did you dislike? Was the food good? Were the clothes comfortable? Were there scary people there? Did you meet any of them? Did you sleep at night? How did you feel about not being with your three-year-old daughter? You were charged with murder: did you know

what the potential sentence might be for murder? Were you concerned you might be in jail a long time? During the three or four
weeks you were in jail, were you thinking of ways you might be able
to get out of jail?"

Under Craggs's questioning, Craig says he hasn't seen any of the
Crown's evidence that was provided to his defence lawyer—no video
statements of the other accused, no photographs, nothing. Yes, he
was taken in for questioning on June 2, shortly after midnight. He
went voluntarily, and he voluntarily gave the police a statement that
was not true. Craggs wants to know if the purpose of giving the
statement was to mislead the police.

"No," says Craig. He gave the statement because "we were told to."

Craggs gives Craig a copy of the transcript of that interrogation,
in which the police make it clear that Craig is not under arrest and
is free not to speak or to leave at any time. Craggs starts to lead the
witness through the tissue of falsehoods that make up his statement.
For instance, Craig told the police that he didn't see other boats, and
that he didn't see Phillip Boudreau—but both of those statements
are false. Then Craggs puts up a flip sheet on an easel and asks the
witness to start making a list of his own lies as they emerge from
the transcript.

Shane Russell objects. It's possible for the defence to establish
that Craig lied repeatedly on June 2 "without embarrassing the witness or engaging in theatrics." Justice Kennedy excuses the jury and
asks Craggs his intent. Craggs says he wants the witness to record his
own lies. The Crown doesn't think the witness should be asked to do
that. Justice Kennedy agrees, but notes that it's perfectly acceptable
for Craggs himself to keep a running tally of the witness's lies. As
presiding judge, it's his job to ensure that Craggs's record is accurate,
but the defence is certainly entitled to keep a visible record. Craggs
moves the easel closer to himself. The jury files back in.

Craggs painstakingly leads the witness through lie after lie, tick-
ing them off on the flip chart. The lies occur on page after page of

the transcript—pages 2, 12, 13, 15, 18, 19. On page 21 of the transcript, Constable Rob Daley, the interrogating officer, says, "All right, and you want me to believe that?" Craig responds, "What do you want me to tell you?" The officer replies, "The truth." Craig responds, "I did." Towards the end of the interrogation the officer tells Craig that the body will be found and that the remains will show the cause of death.

"Are you sure he's dead?" Craig replies. "Don't misunderstand, I'm not—I'm not—I'm just saying that he's done this before."

And why had he said that? Craggs asks the witness.

"It's just what I was told to say."

Luke Craggs summarizes: he's noted down fourteen lies, and he wants to know if these were all lies that Craig was instructed to tell: Did Craig himself really have no role in fabricating this detailed cover story? His meeting with Dwayne, James, and Carla late on June 1 had lasted only ten or fifteen minutes—and in that length of time he had heard and absorbed this whole story so that he was able to repeat all the details to the police?

"Yes," Craig responds. That's what he's saying.

"You weren't in fear yourself of possibly being charged?"

"No."

"The motivation behind your telling all of these lies was not to save your own skin?"

"No."

"It was just doing as you're told? Why? I mean, you're not a trained seal or something—I need to understand why you went to the extent you did, just because you were told." But Craig just keeps repeating that he did it because "that's what we were told."

It's 4:30 in the afternoon, and Craggs gives up. He's done with this line of questioning. Justice Kennedy adjourns the session.

———

The next morning, Craggs grills Craig Landry again. After Phillip Boudreau's death, and after the crew of the *Twin Maggies* landed their lobsters and he helped Dwayne clean the rifle, what did he do? He got home about 1:30, after which he smoked and watched TV until Carla Samson called him late that afternoon. No, he didn't reflect on the morning's events, didn't think about what he should do next, didn't think of calling a friend, or the police, or the priest. Yes, he did think about the morning's events, but he didn't really think about what might come next.

The events in Mackerel Cove happened fast, maybe ten or fifteen minutes from start to finish. Did he make any objection to what was happening other than to cry, just once, "Stop, no more shooting"? He did not. He says he just stood passively by and silently watched things happen—the attempt to tow Phillip's boat, the three rammings, the whole process of gaffing and towing and sinking Phillip. He was arrested on June 6 and charged with murder on June 7, and he gave no detailed statement then because "I was told to keep quiet." Then, on June 26, in the presence of his new lawyer, Joel Pink, he told—for the first time—the story he had just told the court again the previous day, the account that became Her Majesty's Story. The next day he re-enacted the whole episode with the police because the police "wanted to see where things had happened."

Craggs establishes that Craig has lived in Petit de Grat, specifically in Alderney Point, almost all his life; he can actually see Mackerel Cove from his yard. Soon after the re-enactment, he was released from custody. How did he feel?

"It was good to be home."

Craig had subsequently testified at the preliminary inquiries for both Dwayne Samson and James Landry. Craggs shows him the transcript of Dwayne's preliminary on November 26, 2013, followed by the transcript from James's preliminary on December 17, and then takes Craig back to the transcript of his interview with the RCMP on June 26, some months earlier. And then, finally, he gets back to the meeting of the four accused at Dwayne and Carla's house the day of Phillip's death. How long was the meeting? On June 26 Craig said it lasted "two or three minutes," maybe "three or four minutes"—but today he said it lasted ten or fifteen minutes. So which of these assertions is accurate?

"Without being sarcastic, I never had a chance to look at my watch," Craig responds. "It was however long it took, I'm sorry." But it was brief, because "I had a two-year-old to take care of."

Craggs asks about Craig's relationship with James.

"I've known him all my life," says Craig. He and James went hunting for ducks and deer a number of times, but he no longer hunts. He's not allowed to have firearms, but in any case, "I'm not interested in guns now." James, he says, isn't an especially good shot, but he "shoots as well as the rest of us. It depends on the day he's having, like everyone else." Craggs reviews the sequence of shooting, including Craig's observation that after James's second shot smoke came out of Phillip's engine and it stopped. Craig says he assumes the slug hit the engine, but in earlier testimony he'd stated positively that the shot hit the engine.

After the third shot, Craig says, he turned away because he was scared—and after the fourth he cried, "No more shooting!"

Did anything else happen to you at that point? Craggs asks.

"Yes," says Craig. "I messed my pants." What does that mean? Did he defecate in his pants? "I don't know what the word means." Poo in his pants? "Yes."

And then did he clean himself up?

Shane Russell objects. The witness is clearly feeling awkward, and what's the purpose of pursuing this line of questioning? Is Craggs pursuing some material point, or is he elaborating on this matter to embarrass or agitate the witness?

"This kind of question is embarrassing, I'm sure," says Justice Kennedy. "But this is not a tea party. It's a murder trial. Sometimes those kinds of questions get asked in trials of this nature. What took place on board the *Twin Maggies* at times pertinent from beginning to end is relevant to this trial, and you may continue, Mr. Craggs."

Craig admits he finds this question uncomfortable. But on two previous occasions, while testifying under oath, he had volunteered this information, had he not?

"It was asked," Craig responds icily.

"It was asked of you. So someone actually asked you, Did you defecate in your pants, or poop in your pants?"

"They asked me the story, and I told them."

Craggs goes back to the two transcripts and has him read the testimony aloud. In both cases, Craig says he was so frightened that "I pooped myself." He wasn't asked questions specifically about that point. So isn't it fair to say that he offered up the information voluntarily?

"Yes," Craig concedes.

All right, says Craggs, "and did you offer it up because you were trying to make your story sound more believable?"

"No."

Craggs returns to the question of when he cleaned himself up. Craig says he did that at 1:30 in the afternoon, after he got home. Probing further, Craggs determines that Craig had fished the rest of the morning, taken a lunch break, returned to the wharf, unloaded the boat, gone to D'Escousse and helped Dwayne clean the rifle, driven James home—and only then, hours later, did he clean himself up.

"And after the shooting stops," Craggs says, "are you looking around you as the *Twin Maggies* circles around and comes toward Phillip's boat? Are you saying anything like 'What are you guys doing?' Were you concerned about Phillip, the guy you're friendly with?"

"I was just surprised. And scared."

"And as the *Twin Maggies* went over Phillip, do I understand your evidence to be that as far as you knew Phillip was in his boat until it actually got hit the third time?"

"I can't say for certain."

"But you can say for certain that it was run over three times."

"Yes. I heard a thud three times."

"So where were you?"

"At my post."

"And where were your eyes?"

"In the back."

"In the back? Looking over the stern of the *Twin Maggies*? And you don't see Phillip's boat at all?"

"I don't remember seeing it."

Craggs hammers away at three major points that undercut the witness's credibility. First, Craig Landry resolutely maintains that he was little more than a passive bystander. He didn't really participate in the killing, but—aside from exclaiming "No more shooting!"—he did nothing much to stop it, either. He didn't implore the others to leave Phillip alone, he didn't try to prevent the ramming, he didn't even go over to the rail to take a closer look at what was happening. He just stood silently at his post, as though he were still fishing, while the other two aboard carried out a sustained and deadly attack. Really?

Second, Craggs repeatedly implies that Craig has made a deal with the Crown, giving testimony that damns his shipmates in return for leniency towards himself. Craggs notes that on June 2 Craig told the police the Cockamamie Story—that Phillip charged out of the fog and collided with the *Twin Maggies* on Friday—and stuck to it rigidly because "I was told to." Then he engaged Joel Pink, the Gretzky of Nova Scotia criminal lawyers. Next, for no apparent reason, and certainly not in hope of any benefit for himself—perish the thought!—he was swept by an urge to come clean. So, accompanied by Gretzky, he told the police what became Her Majesty's Story. And the Crown, in a sudden spontaneous upwelling of generosity, decided he should be released on bail and that his charge should be reduced from second degree murder to accessory

Phillip Boudreau and his dog Brudy.

A view of Petit de Grat, Nova Scotia, looking westward from the bridge and the fishermen's wharf.

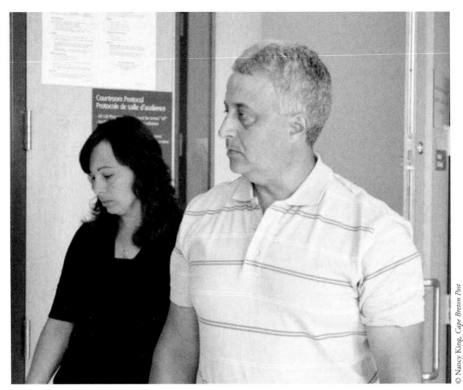

Dwayne and Carla Samson leave the courtroom after he wins day parole, June 19, 2018.

James Landry, convicted of manslaughter November 28, 2014, released on parole December 19, 2018, died November 3, 2019.

Craig Landry leaves the courtroom September 11, 2015, after sentencing.

Twin Maggies, the fishing boat that became a weapon in the Phillip Boudreau killing.

Police guard the fishing boat *Twin Maggies*, June 1, 2013.

The battered hull of *Midnight Slider*, Phillip Boudreau's boat, displayed for the jury in the courthouse basement.

The Port Hawkesbury Justice Centre.

Nash Brogan (left) and TJ McKeough, Dwayne and Carla Samson's defence lawyers.

Crown Prosecutors Shane Russell (left) and Steve Drake.

Luke Craggs, James Landry's defence lawyer.

Joel Pink, Craig Landry's defence lawyer.

James Landry's boat *T-Buddy*, fished by his daughter Carla Samson during his incarceration.

Marcel Heudes, Phillip Boudreau's friend and sometimes employer.

Thilmond Landry, Phillip Boudreau's neighbour.

after the fact. Luke Craggs clearly does not believe all these events were completely unrelated.

The lawyer doesn't spell it out, but the truth is that if Craig did admit that he cut a deal to speak out in return for leniency, that admission itself might wreck the deal. The courts have often viewed such pacts as hopelessly coercive, and therefore have dismissed the resulting evidence as being fundamentally unreliable. If Craggs can convince the jury and the court that Craig's testimony is tainted, he will neutralize a major part of the prosecution's case.

Third, having established that Craig is very good at memorizing a story, at following instructions, and at sticking to the script, Craggs focuses on discrepancies between Craig's earlier and later testimony. As he continues the cross-examination, he asks about the top speed of the *Twin Maggies*, and Craig says he doesn't know. But he *did* know on June 26, 2013, as Craggs proves by having the witness read aloud from his earlier testimony, in which he said that Dwayne ran the engine at 1900 rpm, which gave the boat a speed of 8.2 knots.

Yesterday, Craggs continues, Craig testified that Phillip was wearing a black T-shirt, a black sweater, and rubber boots, although he didn't remember the colour of the boots. But a year and a half earlier, in his June 26 statement, he was asked if he could describe what Phillip was wearing—and he couldn't. And he says he hasn't looked at any of the police information disclosed to his counsel. So how is it that he recalls things now that he couldn't recall then?

"You remember little things," said Craig.

All right, says Craggs, let's move on to the gaffing of Phillip. "You described a total of three times when you saw James Landry trying to drown, and then successfully drowning, Phillip Boudreau, correct? With a gaff? Now, as all this is happening, you're still standing at your table. Are you able to see what's actually happening in the water, with the gaff?"

"No."

"Do you actually see the gaff touch Phillip's body?"

"No."

"And as you're watching this, are you thinking, 'James is trying to drown Phillip'?"

"Yes."

"But you didn't speak up and say, 'James, don't drown Phillip'?"

"No."

"And you don't know how Phillip got physically hooked with the gaff, right? You don't know if it hooked his arm, or his neck, or his clothing? Because you didn't see it."

"Correct."

Craggs directs the witness to the transcript of the November 26 preliminary hearing for Dwayne Samson. On page 22, Craig says unequivocally that James hooked Phillip with the gaff and caught him by the shirt. Why had he said that?

"I must have assumed, 'cause I could not see it."

"You saw Phillip Boudreau between the gaffings? Are you sure he wasn't dead at that point? Are you sure he didn't die from the thirty-five-foot lobster boat running over his boat?"

"Yes. He did not."

After a few further questions, Craggs moves into the final phase of his cross-examination, almost a summation, still hammering away at the possibility of a deal. When the murder charge was reduced to accessory after the fact, how did Craig feel? Better? Relieved? And he still hadn't entered a plea? Did he recognize that he might be found guilty, and might be sentenced? Uh-huh. Is it fair to say that if you're found guilty, you'd prefer not to go to jail?

"It's fair to say, yes."

"And is your cooperation with the Crown and your testimony, is that geared towards getting a lighter sentence if you're found guilty?"

"No."

And Craig had told the police the Cockamamie Story on June 2 because someone told him to tell that story? And on June 6, when the police tried to interview him, someone had told him not to talk to them, so he did as he was told that time? But suddenly, on June 26, his motivation changed. He wanted to tell the truth.

"Yes."

"Did anyone tell you to change your story? Are you just doing as you're told to try to get a lighter sentence? Have you switched people around in your story and told this court that other people did things that you in fact did?"

"No."

"Has your concern for caring for your family factored into anything that you have done since this incident happened?"

"I must say yes. Taking care of my three-year-old girl."

"You mean being a father to her, right? You can't be a father if you're locked up, right?"

"No."

"You've been out on bail for almost a year and a half now, correct? And are you still living in Petit de Grat? Okay, in the course of living there and going about your day-to-day life, have you been approached by people to talk about this?"

"Yes."

"Did this happen once, twice, a few times?"

"Few times."

"Have you felt pressured by anyone to tell your story? Have you felt any pressure from anyone in Phillip Boudreau's family?"

"Most of them won't talk to me. I'm not allowed to talk to them. I have no contact."

"Is that a yes or a no?"

"I can't talk to them, so I don't know."

Craggs pauses. When he resumes, his tone is harsh and aggressive.

"Sir, what if I told you that the most James Landry did was to shoot at Phillip Boudreau and miss? Would you agree with that?"

"No."

"Okay, what if I told you that James didn't say anything to Dwayne, and Dwayne drove the boat around and drove over Phillip? Would you agree with that or disagree?"

"I disagree."

"Did *you* say anything to Dwayne? Did you say 'Run him over' yourself?"

"No."

"What if I told you that your story about James tying Phillip's bow line to the spar and helping the *Twin Maggies* tow him out was a fabrication on your part, would you agree with that or disagree, sir?"

"Disagree."

"What if I told you that the gaffing incident that you described was a fabrication on your part? You just made it up. What if I told you that the anchor, dropping Phillip in the water with the anchor, was fabrication on your part?"

"No, sir."

"You didn't say anything to make your story sound more believable? You didn't try to make things sound more punchy?"

"No, sir."

"Your understanding, when they fired the rifle at Phillip's boat, was that the purpose was to give him a scare, correct?"

"Correct."

Craggs asks for a five-minute pause to review his notes before he concludes the cross-examination. When the court resumes, he reminds Craig of his testimony the previous day to the effect that when the *Twin Maggies* eventually stopped towing Phillip, the victim was wearing only a black T-shirt. Craig could observe that because when Phillip rolled over face down, Craig could see his bare buttocks.

"Would you agree that the first time you mentioned that to either the police or the court was when you testified yesterday? Okay, is there a reason why you didn't mention it before? Is it because you made it up?"

"No."

Craggs reminds the witness that he was originally charged with murder but is now charged only as accessory after the fact. Did he know anything about how he came to be charged with the lesser offence?

"No," says Craig. "I don't know. I just talked to Mr. Pink, that's all."

Craggs has no further questions.

On redirect examination for the prosecution, Steve Drake takes Craig back to the question of James's marksmanship and Craig's experience hunting with him. When James hunts deer, Craig confirms, he uses a .30-30 rifle, like the one in evidence. It fires a single projectile, a bullet. When he hunts ducks, he uses a shotgun, which fires fifty or sixty pellets. The pellets expand, which "gives you a better chance to hit your game."

"The times you went to hunt ducks with James Landry, with a shotgun, have you seen him miss ducks with a shotgun, with forty or fifty projectiles coming out of the barrel?"

"Yes."

Drake clears his throat.

"When you go hunting ducks, do you go to *scare* the ducks?"

"No."

"What do you go to do?"

"Kill the ducks."

"Kill the ducks. And you saw James Landry miss."

"Everyone misses."

Drake has no further questions. The witness is excused. The court breaks for lunch.

After lunch, the Crown prepares to show Exhibit 25, the video of James's interrogation at the RCMP station in Arichat on June 2, 2013, positioning the screen so that everyone—judge, jury, gallery—can see it. Justice Kennedy, as always, is very thoughtful about the ability of the public and the press to see the video. This is, he reminds us, a public courtroom, and the public is entitled to attend, to have a good view, to hear the testimony, to see whatever the lawyers and the jury can see. When the video begins, though, nobody can hear very much. The sound is terrible—thin, scratchy, faint.

"This is what happens when lawyers get near technology," says Justice Kennedy. The hearing pauses while the staff scurry around looking for better speakers.

Eventually, just before 3:00, the video begins to play. The images are black and white and fuzzy, recorded by a single camera mounted on a wall. The camera is focused mainly on James, who sits on a utilitarian chair in a corner of the room. The plainclothes Mountie conducting the interview, Brian Richardson, has his back to the camera. It's 3:32 p.m. on June 2, 2013—the day after Phillip Boudreau's disappearance.

Richardson begins by identifying himself as an officer with thirty-four years' service. He makes sure that James acknowledges that he's not under arrest, he's free to go, he's aware that the conversation is being recorded, nobody has offered him any threats or rewards, and he's speaking voluntarily.

Richardson wants to know about the collision on June 1 between *Twin Maggies* and Phillip Boudreau in *Midnight Slider*. James is ready with the Cockamamie Story: the collision occurred the previous day, when *Midnight Slider* rammed *Twin Maggies*. But on Saturday?

"Never seen him," says James. "The only boat we seen, we seen a big blue boat coming out of Petit de Grat when we were finished hauling."

Richardson ignores James's denial and goes back to the ramming. There are two possible scenarios, he explains. First, *Twin Maggies* rammed Boudreau's boat "with the intention of causing his death. Well, if that were the case, we would be talking about a murder investigation here. The other scenario would be that you intention-ally ran into that vessel, but there was no intention to kill, so in that situation the charge would be criminal negligence causing death. Do you understand those two different scenarios?"

James does not understand, and so Richardson carefully goes over it again, noting that he wants to be sure he's making things clear, particularly because he realizes that James's first language is French. Eventually James says, "You explained it good to me, so I get it. You got to explain it good, I'm not that smart. We can't all be cops, lawyers, and priests. There's got to be fishermen." And he isn't yielding on the question at hand: "I'm telling you we didn't see him, the only boat we seen was that blue boat, that's all."

"Give me one good reason why I should believe you when you tell me that," says Richardson.

"Well, it's true. I'm telling you the truth. Why would I lie? I got nothing to hide."

Richardson explains that this is a criminal investigation, and that "whatever you talk about here today, I may be required to go to court and testify to it." He tells James that the other two crewmen have already been interviewed, and have given their stories. The police are out on the scene talking to other people. A forensics team is out looking for Phillip's body, and "I feel confident that that body will be located." Phillip's boat has been found; a forensics team is examining it, too. The *Twin Maggies* has also been seized and is being examined. In short, the evidence that's being gathered will allow the police to determine what really happened, and they need James to tell them his story so that they can get a complete picture. One way or another, Richardson implies, the police are going to get the true story, so James might as well tell them the truth now. Lying is a hopeless strategy. The police even have eyes in the sky.

"Since 9/11 the Americans have put a lot of satellites in the sky," says the Mountie. "For example, have you ever heard of Google Earth? On the internet you can type in a civic address and a satellite in the sky will zoom right in to that address, and it'll give you an image like you're walking down the street. That's how far technology has come.

"I'm told there's satellites passing over us each and every day, day in and day out, okay? I've heard of a company that provides a service to the police and the military that if you give them a location, a date and time, they'll go back and they'll check their satellite images and there's a very good likelihood that the satellites that they have passing over would have taken an image of that location at that particular point in time, okay?

"They can blow those images up and it will give a clear picture of what was taking place. Now I don't know if the investigators have considered doing that, but if they were to go back and contract one of these satellite companies, and get an image of that collision taking place between those two vessels, what would that image show the investigator?"

"The collision," says James—and that's all he ever says about the idea. If you got a photo of the collision, it would show the collision. Period. What more is there to say?

At Richardson's request, James reviews his day. On June 1 he rose at 3:00, was picked up by Dwayne at 4:25. The crew loaded bait on the boat and left the Premium Seafoods wharf in Arichat at about ten minutes to 5:00. The *Twin Maggies* steamed to Cape Auget and started hauling traps. They had several strings of traps, including a string of 125 traps running in towards Petit de Grat, and they finished hauling them between 7:00 and 7:30. They were back at the wharf in Arichat at 12:05, as usual.

Richardson needs him to slow down, because he's getting only little bits of what James is saying. He asks James to review the day again, starting from the time they left the wharf at 4:50. James does so, in great detail. Richardson doesn't know the area, and apparently doesn't have the benefit of a map. He also doesn't have much of an ear for French, so his attempts to follow James's lobstering itinerary provide some inadvertent comedy. James talks about setting fifteen traps in an area known as "Hautfonds," the Shallows; Richardson can't decipher that name.

"Old—?" he says.

"Hautfonds, they call that the name," says James.

To Richardson, it sounds Chinese.

"Au Fung?" he says. "F-U-N-G?"

"Yeah, that's it," says James. "We got fifteen there at Hautfonds." He continues, but Richardson is completely lost, so they start again.

"Tell me everything about that, leave nothing out, from the time you left the wharf . . ."

The conversation goes on. No, he didn't see Phillip Boudreau, he saw the blue boat that he believes was a shrimper going into Arichat for ice. Tell me about your afternoon, says Richardson. So James does, twice. He denies that the *Twin Maggies* saw *Midnight Slider* at all on Saturday; he insists that the two boats collided the previous day, in heavy fog. He says Phillip rammed the *Twin Maggies* twice, waving a baitchopper, a long heavy knife comparable to a machete.

"He rammed the bow of the boat because he was either on dope or drunk or what, but he ran into the bow of the boat with his boat, and then he turned around and he hit it again. He showed me the chopper. He said, 'I'm going to cut all your traps.' He had the chopper in his hand. He wasn't an easy fellow, I'll tell you."

"He wasn't *what?*" says Richardson, flummoxed again. On Isle Madame, "not easy" means not easily pushed around, stubborn, forceful in pursuing what one wants.

"He was a bad fellow," says James. "Maybe he's hiding in the woods, you don't know."

As the interview draws to a close, Richardson asks whether James would be willing to take a polygraph examination, a lie detector test. A polygraph, says Richardson, is "very accurate."

"Yeah," says James, "but they don't work all the time."

Richardson persists: A person who is being truthful will have no problem with a polygraph examination. Would James be willing to take such a test?

"If I have to, I will. I have no choice."

No, says Richardson. It's voluntary. Would he be willing to do it?

"I'm telling you, if I'm forced to, I'll have to." And that's all James will say. Soon afterwards, Richardson takes him home. The interview has taken just under two hours. The screen goes blank.

Back in the courtroom, Justice Kennedy dismisses the jury for the day, and then expresses his concern about the Mountie's suggestion that James should take a polygraph exam. It is, he says, "manifest that the officer overstated the reliability of the polygraph. Now he was doing it for a purpose, but I worry about the jury having some sense that if Mr. Landry had only taken a polygraph he could have cleaned this whole thing up. In fact, results of polygraph examinations are not admissible in court in this country, and they're not admissible for good reason. They're not nearly as reliable as the officer would have suggested, but the problem is that triers of the facts might very well think they're definitive when they're nothing of the sort. So I may say something to the jury in the morning about the polygraph."

Both the prosecution and the defence agree. Luke Craggs also wonders about a more general issue.

"This goes back to the concern I had at the outset," Craggs says, "that police will say things that are either hearsay that they gathered as a result of the investigation, or things which flat-out aren't true, such as the polygraph—or you may recall the earlier example the officer gave about satellite imagery being available, and overstating the availability of that imagery. These are interrogation techniques, and I think it's important that the jury understand that they *are* interrogation techniques."

Justice Kennedy agrees.

"I could tie that into a repeat of what I said at the very beginning: that it's what Mr. Landry says, not what the officer says, that they are to consider." He could also remind them that this interrogation took place very early in the investigation, so the officer asks James to consider how his story will look when Phillip's body is recovered and examined—which didn't happen. When the jury returns in the morning Justice Kennedy will address these matters, reminding the jury that the only actual evidence in the video is what James Landry says; what the police say is not evidence.

There is something surreal about this. As a spectator in courtrooms, I sometimes feel I am watching actions taking place in an alternative reality. For example, anyone who watches courtroom dramas on television has heard judges say things like "The jury will disregard that remark." The trial then continues as though the jurors have obediently wiped those words from their cranial hard drives. But in fact the jurors can't un-hear the remark; it has lodged in their memory, and it will have an effect, try as they may to disregard it. Similarly, when Nash Brogan introduced that extraordinary petition of Isle Madame citizens calling for Dwayne Samson's release on bail, he didn't really expect the judge to send Dwayne home. But by demonstrating that the people who knew Dwayne best considered him a trustworthy man in a bad situation, he was ensuring that everyone in the courtroom understood how spectacularly out of character it was for Dwayne to be accused of any misdeed at all, let alone murder.

All of which creates some serious questions when a jury watches a video replay of an interrogation such as James Landry's. Confessions are by far the most persuasive form of evidence, and the police will go to a lot of trouble to obtain them. Constable Richardson's approach has been based on the Reid technique, developed in the 1950s by a former Chicago policeman turned security consultant named John Reid, who was also involved in the development of the polygraph. Reid developed his interrogation technique in part as a more civilized alternative to the traditional third degree, which obtained confessions by using serious physical threats and actual torture—beatings with rubber hoses, sleep deprivation, and the like. Not surprisingly, many third degree confessions were false.

The Reid technique is more subtle, but it too relies heavily on coercion, as Nash Brogan's original description of the police procedures makes clear. Reid interrogations start by holding the accused in a bare room on a hard chair, waiting for hours for something to happen. The room is often unheated or overheated; throughout the June 2 interrogation, James is constantly complaining that the room is stiflingly hot. Holding a suspect over a weekend allows the police to prolong the isolation and discomfort.

When the interrogator finally arrives, he stands, looking down on the suspect, and declares that the police now have evidence that clearly shows the suspect is guilty. It's obvious to everyone. So tell me about it, and don't lie. If the suspect wants to remain silent, the officer disregards that and continues pressing the suspect to talk. If the suspect tries to claim innocence, the interrogator overrides, interrupts, and ignores the comments. Next, the officer produces an account of the case—what happened, how it happened, the obvious guilt of the accused. The officer may lie, dissemble, mislead, and threaten in order to get a confession.

Finally, the interrogator turns to "moral minimization," sitting down and talking sympathetically with the suspect. I understand why you did what you did. Your wife nagged you, kept wasting money, wouldn't discipline the kids. You lost your patience. Could have happened to anyone. I've felt that way myself. You're not a bad person. Just tell me about it. I promise you'll feel better. In an astonishingly high proportion of cases, the Reid technique results in a confession, which the officer goes on to flesh out, record, and have the suspect sign under oath. But a shocking number of those confessions are false.

In the United States, the Supreme Court confronted the shortcomings of the Reid technique as far back as 1966, in the celebrated Miranda decision. In that ruling the court held that, to guard against bullying interrogations in a hostile setting, people arrested must be informed of their right not only to remain silent but also to have a lawyer present during questioning. "If you do not have a lawyer, one will be provided to you." How often have you heard that sentence in American police shows? You never hear it in Canadian shows, because Canadian law doesn't provide such safeguards. James Landry, for instance, repeatedly said that his lawyer had advised him to say nothing, and that's what he wanted to do. Sergeant Richardson simply ignored those wishes and went on with the interrogation.

One disturbing result of a Reid interrogation is that a jury watching the video will hear a great deal of false information from the interrogator, and no matter what the judge says, the jurors will probably remember it. They may or may not realize that it's false, and in their deliberations they may or may not, with the best will in the world, distinguish between what they're allowed to remember and what they've been ordered to forget.

The truly appalling feature of the Reid technique is its tendency to generate false confessions and wrongful convictions. The Innocence Project is a non-profit legal organization based in New York that works to reverse wrongful convictions through DNA testing. In a study of three hundred wrongful convictions reversed by DNA evidence, the project found that 25 percent of the original convictions involved false confessions, self-incriminating statements, or guilty pleas.

As a result, the Reid technique lay under a heavy shadow even in 2013, when James Landry was being interrogated. The previous year, Alberta Provincial Court Judge Mike Dinkel was faced with a confession obtained by Calgary police after an eight-hour Reid interrogation during which the accused fruitlessly asserted at least twenty-four times that she wanted to remain silent. The interrogation, Dinkel found, "had all the appearances of a desperate investigative team that was bent on extracting a confession at any cost." He threw out the confession, finding that the Reid technique "has the ability to extinguish the individual's sacred legal rights to be presumed innocent until proven guilty and to remain silent in the face of police questioning. I denounce the use of this technique in the strongest terms possible." He ruled that the confession obtained from the interrogation was involuntary and therefore inadmissible.

In 2015, the RCMP officially discarded the Reid technique in favour of a new Phased Interview Model for Suspects, an approach that interviewing specialist Sergeant Darren Carr described as "less Kojak and more Dr. Phil." The new phased interviews, which were adopted "forcewide," said Carr, are "all about getting the person talking, letting them say what they have to say and focusing more on things like provable lies and slowly dismantling the story rather than accusing them." Perhaps the most important difference is that the new approach is focused on gathering information rather than getting a confession. As Carr put it, with the new technique, "we aren't blindly chasing after the confession."

But that development would take place in 2015. On June 7 and 8, 2013, Dr. Phil was nowhere in sight. Kojak and the Reid technique were alive and well and living in Antigonish, Nova Scotia, where James Landry sat in a bare interrogation chamber, waiting to record another conversation with Brian Richardson for a jury of his peers to review.

9

COURTROOM 3:
JAMES LANDRY'S STORY

NOVEMBER 26, 2014

ON WEDNESDAY, NOVEMBER 26, Justice Kennedy begins by telling the jury that the presentation of evidence is coming to an end, and that he will soon deliver his charge to them. By the afternoon he'll be able to give them "some idea of what your future holds." He also instructs them to disregard Sergeant Richardson's suggestion in the interrogation video that James should take a polygraph examination. In Kennedy's view, the officer shows "exaggerated confidence" in the accuracy of lie detector tests.

"Polygraph evidence is not admissible in Canadian courts," Justice Kennedy says. "We don't allow it to come into the courtroom. And there's a reason why we don't allow it, because it's not nearly as accurate as the officer suggested." In Canada, he says, "when we're determining credibility, we do that with juries, not polygraphs. So my suggestion to you is that you ignore any reference to that polygraph."

Shane Russell introduces the next video, Exhibit 26, which is Sergeant Richardson's interrogation when James was arrested on

June 7, a week after Phillip's death, and charged with second degree murder.

Richardson begins by confirming that James knows what he's been arrested for and that he had a chance to speak to a lawyer. Did he understand the lawyer's instructions to him?

"Yeah, he told me not to spoke a word, not to tell you nothing. So that's what I'm gonna do."

Richardson acknowledges that advice, and repeatedly assures James that he doesn't have to say anything. He also reminds James that anything he does say might wind up in court. James repeats several times that he's not going to say anything. Richardson acknowledges the comments, but continues the interrogation. Things have changed since the earlier conversation, he says. On that occasion, James was free to leave at any time. Now he's not free to leave. All three of the *Twin Maggies'* crew have been arrested and charged with second degree murder; the investigation has continued and has turned up a range of evidence; and the evidence shows that James was lying in his earlier interrogation. The police know that there was an altercation Saturday morning; that shots were fired; that the *Twin Maggies* rammed *Midnight Slider* and ran over it.

"That's totally contrary to what you told me," Richardson says. "There is now no doubt whatsoever that you and the other two crew members are responsible for Phillip's death. Craig was arrested yesterday. Dwayne is under arrest. He's being charged with second degree murder as well, okay?"

Richardson keeps on talking, trying to get James to say something, anything. He talks about Phillip, calls him a tyrant who was poaching lobsters, cutting traps, "causing a lot of grief for a lot of people in that area. It was only a matter of time before something happened. He in some regards was the author of his own misfortune." James is a hardworking fisherman trying to provide for his family, and Phillip is "taking away from you and your family. We know what he's been doing."

"He's been doing that for ten years," James grunts.

In Courtroom 3, Justice Kennedy stops the video playback. He wants the jury to remember that Richardson's extensive comments and questions are not evidence. The only evidence here is what James says. The interrogator is trying to get a statement from James, and he says various things "that the other evidence doesn't reflect. He's saying things to James Landry, some of which will coincide with the evidence in this case, and some of which almost certainly won't." In other words—in keeping with the Reid technique—the officer will tell James the truth if the truth is useful. If a lie is useful, he may well tell a lie. But Justice Kennedy is not so rude as to explain the point that baldly.

The video resumes. Richardson slowly gets a few grudging responses from James. James has been fishing for forty-eight years, says Richardson. No, fifty-two years, James corrects him. He started with his father when he was thirteen. Five years ago, when he turned sixty, he signed his licence over to his daughter.

"You worked hard," says Richardson.

"Worked hard," James agrees. "I had three jobs, me, to pay my licence from my uncle."

And then a guy like Phillip goes out and cuts your traps.

"Twenty in one day he cut, and ten the next day. Listen, I'm not the only one that hated him either."

Richardson goes on and on, explaining how he understands James's frustration, how he can see that James would be enraged to come upon Phillip cutting his traps, how it's natural that James's rage would lead him to do something he wouldn't have done if he hadn't been pushed to his limit. But, says the officer, other people are affected by the consequences. Craig is forty, with a young family. Dwayne has twin eight-year-old girls. They've got their entire lives ahead of them; they've got children depending on them. If James had been thinking of that, he wouldn't have done what he did.

"I didn't do nothing," says James.

"We know that's not true," says Richardson. "We're way beyond that." And he goes through his litany again: you're a good family man, not a criminal. A criminal would have prepared the situation, planned how to get rid of the evidence. But in this case there was no planning, and "you've left all kinds of physical evidence behind."

And James, he says, "you were really the skipper out there, the guy with the experience, the guy who's really calling the shots out there." James denies this, but admits he "showed them the ropes." Exactly, says Richardson, "so in my mind you're probably the skipper out there." And it's the skipper's duty to accept responsibility so that other people don't suffer for his mistakes. The police know there was an ongoing conflict between James and Phillip. They know there was a conversation with Phillip's brother Gerard the previous night. They know that while James at sixty-five is working hard, Phillip at forty-three is drawing welfare and stealing.

"He's been doing that for fifteen years," says James. "Stealing bikes, doing everything."

"But what I'm trying to understand is what was going through your mind," says Richardson. He describes some of the physical evidence, like pieces of fiberglass from *Midnight Slider* embedded in the keel of the *Twin Maggies*, proving that the fishing boat went right over the speedboat. James reverts to the Cockamamie Story: yes, we had a collision the previous day; Phillip ran into us. No, says Richardson, we can establish without a doubt that your vessel drove right over top of his vessel. The fragments of the speedboat are embedded *in your keel*, at the very bottom of the boat.

He wants to know whether James has been truthful with Carla, because Carla has said she's between a rock and a hard place. She doesn't want to be involved, and she wants to believe her husband and her father, but what they're telling her is not the same as what the police are saying, and the police seem to have evidence. She wasn't out there that morning, but, says Richardson, James and Dwayne have brought her into the mess because she's the owner of the vessel.

James says nothing.

Richardson circles back to Phillip, who really is "the author of his own misfortune. He put himself there. He generated the situation that caused his death because he's out there fucking around with fishermen's livelihoods." James still says nothing, and Richardson goes on.

The story that Richardson is developing has James as its central figure—the authentic skipper, the real leader, bearing a long-standing grudge against Phillip. On June 1, the conflict boils over. Seeing James's fury, the younger men "found themselves in a situation that they had to do something to help you out, they had to support you in what you were doing. For God's sake, man, you gotta dig inside yourself, into your heart, and find the courage to tell the truth, because your actions brought them into the situation and now they're paying the consequences for it."

James still doesn't bite. Richardson goes on. And on. He is as relentless as a dripping tap, and he's sniffing his way through James's conscience and emotions like a tracking dog with a scent. The chink in James's armour is the well-being of Carla and the two younger men. Richardson closes in on those feelings, backs off, circles through other issues—Phillip's activities, physical evidence—and comes back to the younger people.

Finally he starts to play a clip from Carla's police interview—but in the courtroom it's 12:10 and Justice Kennedy doesn't want the jury to hear that clip. He excuses the jury and instructs the prosecution not to play the clip; when the trial resumes in the afternoon they are to restart the video just after the clip. Carla's comments are, he says, "manifest hearsay," and despite the fact that neither the prosecution nor the defence sees a problem, he wants to avoid any complications that might later arise.

And with that, he halts the proceedings for lunch.

———

Before the jury enters after the lunch break, Justice Kennedy tells the defence and the Crown that he expects evidence to be finished today, Wednesday, and that he will discuss with counsel the elements of his charge to the jury at the end of the afternoon. He'll hear closing arguments tomorrow. Then, on Friday, he'll charge the jury in the morning. After lunch on Friday, the jury will be deliberating.

The jury returns, and Justice Kennedy tells them the schedule he's proposing. When they come to hear the charge on Friday, he says, they should bring an overnight bag and leave their electronic devices at home. If they don't reach a verdict by around 6:00 p.m., they'll be sequestered in a hotel for the night and will continue deliberating on Saturday morning.

The video continues, picking up after the excerpt from Carla's interrogation. Richardson's comments, however, do give us a notion of what she said. She started to say that her father was a—but she doesn't finish the sentence because, Richardson says, "she respects her father. And she expects her father to do the right thing in this difficult situation. She doesn't want to be involved in this; you hear her say that herself. Have they done something out there that's wrong? Well, they're going to have to bear the consequences. Well, right now she's bearing the consequences too, because her livelihood has been taken away, the ship's been seized. She doesn't want to be part of this. Don't make her part of something she doesn't want to be involved in. You guys have done that. She needs an explanation as to why this happened."

Richardson goes on about how James must love Carla, and how regrettable it is that even though she wasn't directly involved, "when you folks come in after this very unfortunate set of circumstances that took place off Petit de Grat—and the ship that's registered to her, that she runs that company, is involved in the death of another person—you brought her into the fold. You made her involved. Regardless if she wants to be here or not, she's there."

"Oh, I know she's there, right," James says thoughtfully.

Richardson continues implacably. Is it fair that Craig, who was only an employee, should bear the consequences of James's emotions and actions? Because "the beef wasn't with him and Phillip, the beef was with you and Phillip." But the person who really caused the confrontation was Phillip. "It's not your fault. He's the one that generated that animosity by doing what he did. He's not a nice person. He's a leech." James is a good person. Richardson is "sure this event has gone through your mind time and time again."

"You think," says James.

Yes, says Richardson, because that's the way it would affect a good person. You're not a cold, calculating person. A cold, calculating person "wouldn't give this a second thought, and next lobster season, if somebody else is fucking around with your traps they would do it to them too, 'cause they wouldn't care about the consequences. I hope that's not you."

James slowly shakes his head. Richardson keeps on about the difference between James—a good person who made a mistake—and a real criminal. He thinks James has regrets. Finally he asks him outright.

"Do you regret what happened?"

And finally James breaks.

"Yeah, I regret it."

"It wasn't something you set out to do, was it?"

James shakes his head.

"This is something that spiralled out of control that morning."

James nods.

"Was he out there fucking up your traps again when you guys approached him that morning?"

"Yes."

And slowly, short questions followed by short answers, Richardson elicits the story. Yes, James fired four shots at Phillip. He thinks he may have clipped Phillip with the second shot. He used a .30-30 rifle, and he "put it in the water. Where I throw it, you'll never get it. In thirty, forty fathoms of water. Can I call my daughter and tell her that I told you the truth?"

Sure, says Richardson, but not just yet. Where is Phillip?

"Don't mention him," says James. "They should have done that ten years ago."

"Well, perhaps that's the case. But we need to know what happened to his body."

"Ah, gee, I can't tell you that."

Was the body tied to the boat when it was going out?

"Oh, no, we didn't have the body. We passed over the boat, we never see him after."

And about the ramming—?

"We ran over it, and that's it. The boat tipped, and that's it."

"How many times did you run over it?"

"A couple of times, maybe."

And who was operating the boat at that time?

"I was. I jumped at the wheel. I told Dwayne to get out. I was mad after him and that was it. I regret to do it, but somebody had to do it. You asked me for the truth, so I told you the truth. I was trying to help my son-in-law and the other fella."

And when he fired at Phillip, what were his intentions?

"Killing him. He's no good. If I could go back, back in time, maybe I wouldn't a done it. But I was so mad, madness into me, that I didn't care. I had bad emotions. I was pushed to the limit. There had been ten or fifteen years he'd been doing that—stealing bikes, I'm telling you, doing everything. 'I'm gonna burn your house, I'm gonna burn your shed.' You know, half of the night you weren't sleeping."

Had he had any conversation with Phillip that day?

"No. I was looking to destroy him, not looking to talk to him, mad like I was."

Richardson goes back to the original sighting. How far away was James when he fired at Phillip?

"He was way in front of us, he was hauling our pots, and he was waving the knife and making fun, 'cause he had a boat that was faster than ours," James says. "He never thought I had the gun aboard. I thought I might have hit the motor, 'cause the boat stalled right away. That's the only way we could get him, 'cause he was faster than us. Making fun. I said, 'Your fun is getting short.' I regret it now, but it's gone. I'll have to take my punishment."

Richardson wants to know more about the ramming. James reiterates that he "pushed Dwayne, the skipper, aside. I said, 'Give me the wheel.'"

"And tell me what you did then."

"I ran her right over him."

"What were your intentions in doing that?"

"Because I wanted to destroy him. You know, the only thing I could see was black. I was seeing black, I was so mad."

Richardson still wants to know what they were towing.

"His body wasn't around the boat at all," James says. "If we were towing something, it must have been something caught in the basket [around the propeller]. I never looked behind. Then we turned back and we went to the rest of our pots. He had cut ten more—that was thirty in two days."

"How were you feeling once you started to settle down?"

"I told the boys, I said, 'We made a mistake. I made a mistake.'"

Richardson takes James back to the telephone conversation when Phillip's brother Gerard told James, "There's only one thing you can do. Get rid of him." What had James been thinking?

"Well, not too much. I figured maybe he had cut some traps, and what can you do?" But then he passed the Corner Bridge store, where Phillip was waving his knife at James, and "making fun of me." And that enraged James so that he wanted to "jump out of the truck and cripple him."

Richardson returns to the question of the gun. When had they taken the rifle aboard? Oh, a long time, says James. What make was it? A Winchester, he thinks. Now, says Richardson, the investigators have discovered that nobody on the boat had a seal licence, a permit to have a gun aboard.

"Well, I didn't know that," says James.

How long had James owned the gun? Maybe twenty years. And how long had it been aboard the *Twin Maggies*?

"Oh, geez, only a couple of weeks."

Richardson, in a tone more of sorrow than of anger, tells James that he himself has been honest with James, but James hasn't been entirely honest with him—because a witness has reported that he saw a firearm wrapped in a blanket being taken off the boat, and so Richardson believes "that when you come off the boat that day, that gun came with you."

"Yeah," says James, without further argument. His original lie about dropping the gun overboard has obviously failed, but he instantly creates a new one.

"Yeah," he says, "I got it hid."

Where?

"You'll have to let me go and I'll get it for you. You won't find it. But I'll be honest with you, I'll get it for you."

Richardson keeps pushing, pointing out that James is under arrest and can't go get the gun, so James suggests that he tell Carla where it is, and she can get it. But he absolutely won't tell Richardson where to look for it. Richardson clearly finds this puzzling and frustrating, and he evidently doesn't want James talking to the co-accused, who happens to be his daughter. He calls time out, in effect. They're both hungry and thirsty—"my tongue is some thick," James notes—so Richardson will arrange for some food. James wants a McDonald's cheeseburger, onion rings, and a Pepsi.

The two of them vacate the interview room for forty minutes. When they come back, waiting for the food to arrive, Richardson tells James that he's talked to the other investigators, who have obtained warrants to search both James's house and Carla's. They were about to do the searches when Richardson told the others where he was with James's interrogation.

"I don't want to see them go and start tearing homes apart needlessly," he says. And he doesn't want James to tell Carla where to find the gun. So he proposes an alternative plan.

"How do you feel about it if we were to take you for a drive, for you to take us to the firearm? That way we're keeping Carla out of this altogether. She's involved enough now. There's no point in getting her involved any more in this."

"Okay," says James. "I'll get you the firearm."

"And you can show me where it's at."

"Right, so you don't have to break no home or nothing." But he'd like to talk to his daughter.

Not just yet, says Richardson. "I'm not suggesting for one moment that you're the type of person that would say something to Carla that would interfere with the investigation," says Richardson, thereby suggesting exactly that.

"No, no, no," says James earnestly.

"But some people have done that to us, right?"

"Yeah, yeah, yeah, but I wouldn't do that," says James. The conversation rambles on, and a few minutes later James says, "If I tell you the truth, it might help the other two boys, you know? I'd like to keep the other boys out of it."

Yes, says Richardson, but everyone has to take responsibility for their own actions. And then he circles back to James's Friday night conversation with Phillip's brother Gerard. That night, James says, he came home from fishing, cleaned up, and went to the Island Nest restaurant. He came back, fed his dog, and saw that he had a message on the phone. Gerard had called, and James called back.

"He said, 'My brother Phillip is gone with his speedboat again at the end of Cape Auget, messing in your traps.' I said, 'What are we gonna do with him?' And Gerard said, 'There's only one thing to do, get rid of him.' That's what the man told me." And, said

James, "it made me feel, if I was gonna get a chance, I was gonna cream him."

Cream him?

"Well, get rid of him."

Richardson tries repeatedly to get James to say that "get rid of him" meant "kill him." But James won't quite say that.

Their hamburgers and onion rings arrive. While they eat, Richardson leads James through the events of the morning. When he gets to the point where the *Twin Maggies* meets Phillip, James says that Phillip was "making fun, going with his boat. He was ahead of us. You may depend, you're not gonna get a speedboat with a big boat." Later he explains that Phillip was "skipping three or four, so we couldn't get close to him. And he never thought I'd surprise him."

Surprise him?

"When I fired at him. I didn't wanna hit him, the first time—and then I got really mad, because the pot that we hauled, it was cut."

Piecing James's comments together here and elsewhere, it appears that Phillip was not merely "fooling with their traps," as Her Majesty's Story seemed to say. It sounds as though he was doing exactly what Omer Boudreau described—poaching and vandalizing right in front of the *Twin Maggies*, robbing each trap in turn and cutting the buoys, waving his knife and taunting them, keeping out of reach by staying three or four traps ahead. Secure in the knowledge that his speedboat could easily outrun a bulky, plodding fishing boat, he was simply toying with their helpless fury. The immediate result, James indicates, was that he aimed the second, third, and fourth shots directly at Phillip, and one of them—James thinks—hit him. Then, filled with boiling rage, James pushed Dwayne aside and rammed Phillip's boat.

"The first time I only nicked the boat," he says. "The second time I passed right over the boat, and then we never seen him."

Richardson clearly doesn't believe that Phillip simply disappeared. He turns the conversation to the body. He has witness accounts, he says, that the *Twin Maggies* came up right beside *Midnight Slider* and there was some activity before the ramming began. Richardson thinks the activity had to do with disposing of Phillip's body. James denies it. Richardson persists: divers have done a careful search of the area, and they've found Phillip's outboard, his boots, and his cap—but not his body.

"If he went out of the boat there," Richardson concludes, "he should have been there."

James doesn't budge. After the ramming, they didn't tow him, they didn't see him. There was a strong tide running out of the harbour. Maybe the tide took the body.

Richardson isn't satisfied, but he moves on to the question of who was at the wheel. If James pushed Dwayne aside and took over the controls, presumably Dwayne's account will confirm that, because Dwayne is also being interrogated at this same time.

"Okay. I'm telling you what I done."

"What was Dwayne saying while all this was going on?"

"Nothing. He never talked. He turned pretty white. I guess he felt he had done wrong too."

"I don't want you being straight up with me today about firing those shots and then trying to take the blame for something someone else did."

"No, no," says James. And then, a bit later, "If I had to do it now, I wouldn't do it. But it's too late."

Richardson returns to the question of the gun and the shots that were fired, but nothing much else is revealed. At 5:31 he leaves the room, returning a minute later to say that Staff Sergeant Gerry Landry, a colleague from New Brunswick, is going to join them. The three will drive down to James's home in Little Anse so that James can retrieve the rifle. They leave the interview room at 5:53.

———

Back in Courtroom 3, Shane Russell stops the playback, and Justice Kennedy calls a fifteen-minute break. When the trial resumes, Luke Craggs points out that the police took a small voice recorder and recorded all the conversation in the car. The audio quality is very poor, and much of the conversation is inconsequential. Nevertheless, he will be referring to some passages from that audio material in his closing statement. He suggests that, rather than making everyone suffer through three hours of terrible audio, the Crown might agree to simply give the jury a transcript. Or the two sides might consent to providing a transcript of only the relevant passages. Or the jury could receive a whole or partial transcript along with a copy of the audio.

"This is not a controversial issue," declares Justice Kennedy. "Work it out. If there are issues, I'll deal with them in the morning. Bring in the jury, please."

The video of James's interview resumes, picking up the conversation at 10:43 p.m. on June 7. Staff Sergeant Gerry Landry, who's now joined Brian Richardson in the interview room, notes that James and his RCMP escort have just arrived back from Little Anse, where James has retrieved a rifle from under his mattress. But although the Mounties don't know it yet, this will turn out to be the wrong rifle. The actual weapon—the rifle belonging to Dwayne— has just been seized from Dwayne's home, so James's hoax will almost instantly be exposed. James has tried once again to help Dwayne and Craig by assuming more blame than he deserves.

James still wants to talk to his daughter—he has been asking frequently ever since he admitted his involvement in Phillip's death— but Richardson keeps putting him off, assuring him that it will happen, but not just yet. James is clearly getting tired.

Richardson still believes that the *Twin Maggies* towed Phillip's body out to sea, and he tells James that there were witnesses who saw the whole episode from the shore. James scoffs at the idea. Who was up walking the shore at 6:00 a.m.—and what could they possibly have seen, given the distances involved?

The two Mounties, Richardson and Landry, begin to show James a video interview between Constable Rob Daley and Phillip's brother Gerard, whom James calls "Bowser." In the video, Gerard says that "James Landry called me up the night before, and he asked me if Phillip was around. I said, 'Yes, Phillip is sailing around in the harbour' and he said, 'This is his last night on the water. He won't be on the water tomorrow.' So that was all right—he hung up—"

James interrupts the playback, saying "Aha. I never said that. I never said anything. I never said that at all. That's a lie."

The Mounties continue the playback. What happened on the water that morning, says Gerard, was that Phillip "was standing up, then I don't know if they had a few words among them. I can't say that; I didn't hear them. The only thing I heard was two gunshots, and then the motor stopped. Then Phillip was sitting down, so he shot the motor. I don't know if he hit him in the legs or not, I can't see it. Anyway, he was sitting down and then I looked at the *Twin Maggies* again. He shot three more shots and then they went around the boat and the speedboat was on that side of the boat. I seen him on the stern and farther out, and then that was it. Then the motor was gone, Phillip was gone, and they were smacking the boat with the big boat. But I know they towed something from there, going that way.

"They towed him, that's what I see. It could have been his body, but they didn't tow the motor. They found the motor, they found the boat, they found everything else but him. So I figure it's him."

Daley asks, "How certain are you that they were towing something?"

Gerard responds, "Because I seen it, it was flapping on the water like that."

The Mounties stop the Daley video, and James says, "I'd like for him to see that from his place when we were—I'd like to see it. You go at his place and you look and see how far we are from there."

Staff Sergeant Landry notes that Gerard had binoculars—and also notes that Gerard's account of what happened is in agreement with other evidence—Phillip did stand up and then sit down, the *Twin Maggies* clearly did run over *Midnight Slider*. In all, Richardson concludes, "he had a pretty clear account."

"Yeah," says James, "he had a pretty clear account. Maybe he had drank twenty-four beer before he said that."

For the record, James is correct about the distances. From a boat in Mackerel Cove, Gerard's house is little more than a small white blotch on the Alderney Point shore. Even with binoculars it would be hard to distinguish a person at that distance, let alone see what the person was doing.

Another parenthetical note: Gerard says that James told him that this was Phillip's last night on the water, and adds, "So that was all right." Clearly, that was not all right—but the phrase is an interesting feature of Isle Madame storytelling; it means "That's the end of that part of my story." Often it fits well with the story—"The road was all plugged up with snow, so I got my four-wheeler with the plow blade and cleared it. So that was all right." On other occasions, the phrase sounds very odd indeed. "When we find him, his leg is broke and he got a concussion. So that was all right." Then comes a transitional phrase—"Next thing I know, he's screamin' at me"— and before the final act of the story, often the raconteur will use the phrase "last goin'-off," as in, "Last goin'-off, he's arse over teakettle in a snowbank, and that's where he stayed."

So that was all right. Next thing, in the video, James is telling the two Mounties that Gerard must have stolen his very detailed story from Pigou—Venard Samson, the fisherman who towed Phillip's boat to the wharf. Pigou was fishing not far away, and he could have been close enough to see what Gerard describes. In James's view, Pigou told the story to Gerard, who then adopted it as his own. That would account for the very odd fact that Gerard claims to have seen the whole thing—the murder of his brother—but didn't call the police for several hours because, he says, he didn't have the number. ("The number is 9-1-1," scoffs a neighbour. "How hard is that?")

In addition, Fisheries officer Norman Fougère says he called Gerard at 9:00 that morning—he has the phone record—and that Gerard told him he had sent Phillip to Mackerel Cove to pick up a couple of traps that the sea had tossed up on the shore, where Gerard couldn't go in his big boat. Phillip, Gerard said, had already brought one trap out and had gone back for another. But Gerard said nothing about watching the death of his brother two hours earlier.

So that was all right. Back on the video, because James had asked about who saw the rifle being passed up from the *Twin Maggies* to the wharf, the two Mounties show him photos of *Midnight Slider* and the bullet holes in the hull. A metal rod is running through one of the holes "to show the direction of the bullet," says Staff Sergeant Landry.

"And when they followed it through," Richardson says, "they actually found one of your bullets still in the boat, okay?"

"Okay."

"Is that bullet going to match the gun that you gave us tonight?" asks Staff Sergeant Landry.

"Yeah, .30-30 I guess," says James. "I didn't lie. Why would I lie to take you home to give you the gun?"

So that was all right. The discussion goes on, reviewing the scuff marks, paint scrapes, and marks on the two boats, going over and over the elements of James's story. And then Gerry Landry, wondering whether James is misleading them about the location of the body, says, "If the body tomorrow was to show up, the question is, Could there be a bullet hole in his head?"

"No, no, no."

"Est-il possible?"

"Impossible."

"Impossible."

"Impossible," says James. "There's not a bullet in his head."

The conversation continues, rambling and discursive, reviewing some of the evidence. Finally Gerry Landry says, "James, did you tell the complete truth today?" James says he did.

"Are you ready to swear a statement to tell the complete truth?"

"Do I have to do that tonight?"

James seems flustered, and asks once more to speak with his daughter or his wife. He wants to tell them where his wallet is and to make sure they feed his dog. He wants to tell them that he told the truth, that he gave the gun to the police, that he's all right.

"That's it," he says to the Mounties. "I told you the truth, the whole truth, and I can't tell you no more. If you find him, good luck—but you know from my prayer that I'm going to say tonight that I hope you don't find him."

Gerry Landry wants to know why he doesn't want the body found. Is he afraid that the evidence from the body will contradict James's story?

"No, no, I'm not afraid. I hope you do find him, but leave the crabs to eat him. They don't have to put him in the cemetery. He don't deserve a Mass."

Another Mountie, outside the room, talks to Carla and to James's wife, Ann. Meanwhile Richardson leaves the room and Landry speaks to James for thirteen minutes in French, which is translated in the transcript provided to the jury. Somehow the police have confirmed that during the altercation, Dwayne was actually at the wheel. Landry wants to know why James lied about that, saying that he rather than Dwayne was driving the boat—why he didn't tell the truth about that in the first place.

"Well, to save him a little bit."

But the truth is that Dwayne was driving the boat, right? Yes, he was.

"Was he as angry as you?"

"Ah, I think so, yes."

Landry returns to the question of the gun: Dwayne asked Craig to get it, then Craig loaded it and handed it to James with four bullets in it. After a few more questions and answers, the reason for this line of questioning becomes clear.

"This is the important part," says the Mountie. "Because we were talking about seal hunting. When you go seal hunting you have a lot of bullets. But there were just four bullets. It's pretty obvious that there was a problem with Phillip." So he believes that James and Dwayne were thinking, "We'll have the gun, and if we find him we'll get even with him."

"What?" says James, taken aback. Landry keeps pressing the suggestion that they had only four bullets because they weren't hunting seals, they were hunting Phillip. But James rejects the idea completely. There were only four bullets in the gun because they only had four bullets, and that's all there is to that.

Landry leaves the room and returns fifteen minutes later with Brian Richardson. By now it's midnight, and James finally gets to speak with Carla—on a speakerphone, with audio and video recording, and two policemen in the room. It isn't much of a conversation. James tells Carla that he's told the truth, and Carla responds that "whatever you said, we just take that and move on, okay?" James explains where his wallet is, and Carla confirms that she's fed the dog. James tells his wife and daughter that he loves them, and they tell him that they love him. And that's really what the call is all about.

James is tired, but this long interrogation is not over. The policemen want him to give a sworn statement attesting to everything he's told them today.

Back in Courtroom 3, Shane Russell stops the video playback. The only remaining video evidence, he says, is James giving his sworn statement, and we'll see that tomorrow morning. After that, Justice Kennedy tells the jury, the defence will have an opportunity to present evidence, and then the two sides will make their closing arguments. He reckons that will take all of Thursday. Friday morning he will give his charge to the jury, who will retire to determine their verdict.

The jury is excused, and Justice Kennedy describes to the lawyers the charge—the instructions—he'll provide to the jury. He will review the verdicts available to the jury, lead them through some tricky issues about evaluating the evidence, and talk about the cause of death and when Phillip's death actually occurred. He'll remind them that the absence of a body doesn't mean an accused can't be convicted of murder. He frequently refers to "Watt," which turns out to be *Watt's Manual of Criminal Jury Instructions*, written by Mr. Justice David Watt of the Court of Appeal for Ontario. If you're seeking a little light reading, you should pick it up: it's only 1350 pages and it costs just $366.

Both Shane Russell and Luke Craggs have some concerns they'd like the Court to address in the charge. Justice Kennedy agrees to address these issues, and adjourns the trial overnight. In the morning we will hear James Landry's formal, sworn, recorded statement: his KGB statement.

To me, "KGB" is the Soviet secret police, Vladimir Putin's finishing school, but to a Canadian lawyer it's a statement made in accordance with the rules set down in *R. v. B. (K.G.)*, a 1993 Supreme Court of Canada case. In that case, three of four youths involved in a murder had given statements claiming that the fourth youth (known by the initials K.G.B.) had actually stabbed the victim. At trial, they withdrew those statements. One way or another that made them liars; either K.G.B. had stabbed the victim or he had not, and the three had now sworn to both. The prosecutors argued that they had told the truth the first time, and that their original statements were reasonable evidence that K.G.B. had indeed done the stabbing, despite the later denial.

The court agreed, ruling that such evidence could be considered on three conditions. First, the person must have spoken under oath, with appropriate warnings about the legal penalties for lying. Second, the whole interview must have been videotaped. Third, it must be possible for the person to be cross-examined by opposing lawyers at trial.

When the police obtain a KGB statement, they try to meet these three conditions—and after that, whatever the accused says is considered to be evidence that speaks to the facts, not just to the credibility or the state of mind of the accused. If James says he was driving the boat, that's eyewitness evidence that he was indeed driving the boat, no matter how he may change his story later.

On Thursday morning, Shane Russell tells the court that the two sides intend to submit an additional agreed statement of fact noting that there were no bullet holes found in Phillip Boudreau's engine. They've also agreed that the jury should be provided with the audio recording and a transcript of the mostly trivial conversation that took place during the long drive to Little Anse for James to retrieve the rifle.

The jury returns, and Justice Kennedy reminds them that in the video they're about to see, what the police say is not evidence and certainly not truth.

"Truth comes from witnesses who testify before you under oath, subject to direct and cross-examination," he says, "and truth only becomes truth because you decide it is. You decide what the facts are in this case. You decide who to believe, you decide whether you can believe people beyond a reasonable doubt. We'll talk about that in my charge tomorrow, but by this time I sense that this jury has a pretty good sense about how these things work."

Shane Russell restarts the video playback. On the video, it's just after midnight, which makes it June 8, 2013. The Mounties have sent for a commissioner of oaths. James is really sleepy—he's been up for twenty hours—and he threatens to fall asleep in his chair.

If he does, he says, "you'll have to throw me a water in the face." A little later, when they ask if there's anything he needs, he says "a bunk."

The commissioner's name is Corinne Sears, and she arrives at 12:33 a.m. She has James swear—as usual—to tell the truth, the whole truth, and nothing but the truth. In this case, though, the commissioner wants him to understand that lying under oath is perjury, and it's a criminal offence. Richardson further informs him that if he tells any falsehood he could be charged for fabricating evidence, for obstructing justice, or for public mischief, all of them offences under the Criminal Code. James confirms that he's making the statement voluntarily and that he hasn't received any threats, promises, or favours.

Then he goes over the story again. They came upon Phillip cutting traps right in front of them, taunting them as he did so. But then his motor caught on a trap line and stalled. Then, says James, "we got him." He fired the four shots, and he thought he hit the motor, but since he now knows there are four holes in the boat, he's "pretty sure I hit him, but I couldn't guarantee with that."

Which is an interesting thing: when he first told the story he said categorically that he'd hit Phillip; now, having heard that all four bullets hit the boat, he's not so sure. So was Phillip wounded or not? There's evidence on both sides. The truth will be what the jury decides is true.

James admits that he gave a false statement on June 2, and confirms that his intention was to "get rid of Phillip, kill him or whatever." When they rammed Phillip's boat, they sank it—but "we never seen Phillip after." When the police ask him why he said that he, not Dwayne, was at the wheel when they ran over Phillip, he says he did that "because I wanted to cover my son-in-law and Craig. I wanted to take the blame myself."

He repeats his story that he took the rifle home and hid it under his mattress. And he says again—as he has said many times during his long day of questioning—that he regrets what they did, that he recognizes that he will have to take the consequences, and that if he had it to do over, he wouldn't.

But when he's asked to sign the statement, Richardson mistakenly calls him "Phillip" and James flares right up.

"You call me Phillip again, I won't sign."

"It's been a long day," says Richardson. "I'm getting tired."

"Well, I won't touch you for that, but don't call me Phillip. Any other name."

He signs. And James's long day is finally over. So is the video evidence, at last.

With the video turned off, Shane Russell reads out the new agreed statement of fact: "RCMP members inspected the fifteen-horsepower Evinrude outboard motor at the bottom of Petit de Grat Harbour. There were no markings on the motor to suggest that it had been hit by any bullet."

After a break, Russell provides the jurors with a poor audio recording and transcript of the conversation between James and the policemen during the drive to pick up the rifle. Luke Craggs has said he wants to refer to that conversation in his final argument.

With that, the Crown closes its case. Justice Kennedy asks Luke Craggs whether the defence wishes to call evidence in the matter.

"No, My Lord, the defence will not be calling any evidence."

It's noon, so the court calls a lunch break. When we resume, Justice Kennedy tells the jury that what they are about to hear are the two counsels' views of the evidence, their opinion about what the evidence shows, and their attempt to guide the jurors in drawing conclusions from the evidence. But their comments are not in themselves evidence. Whenever the lawyers' understanding differs from that of the jurors, "it is your understanding of the evidence that prevails."

Shane Russell thanks the jurors for their time and their commitment, then reminds them that they are the finders of fact while His

Lordship is the authority on the law. The Crown's purpose is to highlight certain parts of the evidence and try to connect the dots to show just what happened to Phillip Boudreau and how James Landry played a key role in it. He will give them five reasons which, taken together, will justify finding that James is guilty of second degree murder beyond a reasonable doubt.

His first reason has to do with Phillip's body. Its absence doesn't mean that James can't be found guilty; if that were so, then any murderer could escape criminal liability by effectively hiding the body. Phillip was observed alive early on June 1, 2013, by his sister Margaret Rose and his brother Kenny, who described what he was wearing—items that have been recovered and placed in evidence. Neither one has heard from Phillip during the intervening seventeen months, nor have other friends.

At 6:55 that morning, Venard Samson—Pigou—found Phillip's boat capsized and mostly submerged, but he didn't find a body, which led to an elaborate and fruitless search. But Craig Landry's testimony explains why the body was never found. And James himself—though he has denied towing and dragging and sinking Phillip's body—has testified that he hopes the police don't find the body. All this evidence satisfies the Crown's need to prove two things: first, that Phillip is indeed dead, and second, what led to his death.

The second reason to convict is that James knew Phillip and had a motive and opportunity to kill him. In his statements, James talks at length about his frustration with Phillip; it's "a long frustration," says Russell, "and it runs very deep." James believes Phillip has been cutting his traps and robbing him and his family for years. The issue was directly on his mind the previous evening, when he talked about it with Phillip's brother Gerard. James has said that if he got a chance, he was "gonna cream him." He also met Phillip at the Corner Bridge store, when Phillip said he was going to cut more traps. James wanted to jump out of the truck and cripple him. And on the fatal Saturday, James says, he was looking to destroy Phillip, not to talk with him. This long history gave James the motive to "cripple him, cream him, destroy him, get rid of him and, most significantly, kill him."

The third reason to convict, Russell continues, is the physical evidence: the gun, the battered boat, the bullet holes, the paint scrapes on the *Twin Maggies*, the bow line, the gaff, the boots, the hat, the motor, the gas tank. All of these items, Russell says, "play a significant role in explaining what occurred." Four bullets were fired, and only four—not because James decided to stop shooting, but because four bullets were all he had. All four hit the boat, suggesting they weren't intended as warning shots. Russell particularly emphasizes the orange bow line, which was cut off short, supporting Craig's description of Phillip crawling forward to cut his boat free when it was under tow. The cut line thus supports Craig's larger story about the *Twin Maggies* towing Phillip out to sea, where James and Dwayne tied him to the anchor. James has plenty of opportunity to call off the attack, but he doesn't; instead he directs it, and tells Phillip, "You won't cut any more traps." It's these actions after the shooting, the directions he gives Dwayne as well as his physical actions, that tie James to the events that led to Phillip's death. And when James talks about the events, he always says "we"—as in "we ran him over, we got him, we just missed him, we hit him."

James was involved "all the way," Russell concludes. "James was not driving the boat, but he was driving the agenda." At this point, Russell notes, James's story and Craig's diverge. James says Phillip went into the water and "we never seen him after." There's no mention of the towing, no mention of the gaffing, no mention of the anchor. Which brings Russell to his fourth reason to convict James: the testimony of Craig Landry.

Craig has a three-year-old daughter and was employed as a deckhand on the *Twin Maggies* for a mere eight weeks before his employment ended on June 1. He was paid a weekly wage, and had no share of the profits. Unlike James he grew up with Phillip, saw him every day, and never had any problems with him. Russell says there are certain "hallmarks of credibility," notably whether what a witness says is corroborated by other evidence, and he specifies a number of points on which Craig's evidence is indeed corroborated. Craig says that four shots were fired, that James used a .30-30, that one of the shots was fired while Phillip was heading away, that he believed one of the shots hit Phillip, that after the fourth shot James had no more shells, and so on—all of which matches up with other evidence. One important point: Craig says that after the ramming Phillip was wrapped around a red gas can, whereas James says he simply disappeared. If Craig is right, Phillip was still alive after his boat had been swamped.

Was Phillip gaffed and towed? Russell actually says "we know" that happened, and in support of Craig's credibility he cites the divers' testimony that if Phillip had drowned in Mackerel Cove his body should have been there, along with his boots, his cap, his boat, and so forth. He also notes testimony saying that the body should have surfaced in a few days—but not if it were tied to an anchor. None of these things in itself would be enough to show that Phillip was indeed dragged and drowned—but all of them taken together make an extremely convincing case that Craig has been telling the truth.

The fifth and final reason to convict James Landry "is James Landry." Russell uses a baseball analogy: Reggie Jackson of the New York Yankees, the team's sparkplug and leader, described his role as being "the straw that stirred the drink." James Landry was the straw that stirred the drink during the attack on Phillip Boudreau. James Landry, "through his words, actions, and direct conduct, murdered Phillip Boudreau." Russell reviews yet again the alleged sequence of events and James's leading role in them: the shots, the instructions to Dwayne, the ramming, the gaffing, the towing, the drowning. James is the catalyst, the inspiration, the one who gives the orders and directs the attack. And in his interrogation, James says "I hope you don't find him. Let the crabs eat him. They don't have to put him in the cemetery. He don't deserve a Mass."

Based on the totality of the evidence, Russell concludes that James Landry's intention was to murder Phillip—and he did.

After a ten-minute pause, Luke Craggs takes the floor, thanks the jurors for their service, and sets out to dismantle the Crown's arguments.

"Looking back at the trial," Craggs says, "up until the time that Craig Landry testified, most of what you heard set up the circumstances." But in order to understand what really happened, jurors have to look primarily at the testimony of the three men who were on the boat. The jurors have heard direct testimony from Craig Landry and watched three video interviews with James Landry, both of whom were on the boat, but they haven't heard from Dwayne Samson at all. So they have to put together the story as best they can from the two men who were on the boat and have spoken.

The first sixteen or seventeen witnesses provide the context. Phillip went to his boat around 6:00; an hour later the boat was found badly damaged in Mackerel Cove. He'd been wearing the baseball cap and rubber boots that are in the courtroom and that were found near the damaged boat, along with the gas tank and the outboard motor.

"So something happened there," Craggs says. "The question really is, What happened?" Again, we know a number of things. The *Twin Maggies* docked a little late, something looking like a rifle was removed from the boat, and so on. "There's really no reason to doubt the authenticity of all this evidence"—and the same is true for the expert testimony: the trajectories of the bullets, the ballistics that match the bullet to the rifle, the evidence about paint and fiberglass, the evidence from the eight days of fruitless underwater searches.

This is pertinent information, Craggs concedes, but it doesn't directly speak to James Landry's guilt or innocence. What really counts is the evidence provided from those who were on board the *Twin Maggies*—and that evidence, "in my respectful submission, is lacking. It does not establish proof beyond a reasonable doubt." This brings him to Craig Landry—the person who came to court and was able to answer questions in front of the jury. His testimony should be scrutinized very carefully. It's a crucial element of the Crown's case.

Some of Craig's testimony was not controversial. Both he and James, for example, said that four shots were fired. It's his account of "the actual things that caused Phillip's death" that needs to be examined. Craig wants his testimony to be believed not only by the jury but also by the police, the prosecution, and the community. He doesn't want to be known as a killer, and he doesn't want to be convicted of murder. He has told his story with a great deal of care. He wants everyone to believe that he was in the classic situation of being in the wrong place at the wrong time. He had no share in the fishing business, and no reason to hurt or kill Phillip.

But, says Craggs, "the reality is that he has charges pending, he wants to get the best outcome from the charges, and he has to go back to living in his community." So the jury should keep an open mind about what his motivations might be. When someone is arrested and charged, says Craggs, they really have only three choices: they can remain silent, they can tell the complete truth, or they can lie. Then he goes through his reasons for suggesting that the jurors should, at the very least, be very skeptical about what Craig Landry has said.

The essential problem with Craig's testimony, Craggs declares, is that it was illogical. It seemed "scripted. It seemed as if it was carefully tailored to distance himself from anything bad that may have happened." What he means by "illogical" is behaviour that's inconsistent with normal human behaviour. When enough illogical things pile up, you have to question whether the overall story is true. With Craig's story, the oddities accumulate in a snowball effect. You don't think much about the first ones, but they keep accumulating, and "the more you see, the stranger it gets."

Craig started by describing a fairly ordinary day—until he caught sight of what turned out to be Phillip, in among their traps. At that point his language changed; his choice of words became very cautious. He reported a consensus that they should keep an eye on Phillip, and maybe the gun should be loaded. Dwayne told Craig to put three shells in the rifle. Craig did—but he didn't put any shells into the chamber, he didn't check whether the safety was on (though he's an experienced hunter), and he didn't bring the rifle on deck. He did the bare minimum that was asked of him, and his language distances him from responsibility. And when James starts shooting at Phillip, a man Craig knows, Craig doesn't protest or interfere.

Craggs is particularly skeptical that Craig actually "pooped himself" and then went for six or seven hours before cleaning up. There was a toilet on the boat. Why would he not have cleaned himself? Instead he resumed fishing, took a lunch break, drove to Dwayne's house and cleaned Dwayne's rifle, and so on—and only then did he clean himself. In addition, Craig reported that after the shooting Phillip was just sitting in the stern of his boat—not bleeding, not apparently in pain, but not taking any action at all while the *Twin Maggies* circled and picked up his bow line not once but twice. According to Craig, throughout the story Phillip takes no action to escape or to defend himself. How likely is that?

Craggs finds similar problems with various other parts of Craig's story, including the gaffing and towing, which sounds like "a horrifying and barbaric death." But the actual homemade gaff seems too flimsy for the purpose, "a poor choice of murder weapon. This weapon just couldn't do the job." He wants the jury to find that the evidence about the gaffing "is fabricated"—and so is the evidence about tying Phillip to the anchor and dropping him; the railing of the *Twin Maggies* is too far above the water for a small man like James to reach, lift, and manipulate the weight of another man's limp body.

Again, the exchange between James and Dwayne about the precise depth of the water—12.2 fathoms—should have enabled the divers to find the body. But it didn't. And the business of going to Dwayne's home to help him clean the gun is strange. Dwayne owns a couple of guns: how can he possibly not know how to clean one?

"I'm going to say—and I'm going to ask you to believe—that Craig Landry was following a script," Craggs concludes. "He knew what he had to say. He chose his words carefully to make it look like he didn't want anything to do with it out on the water, and all he did was help get the gun off the boat and help clean the gun after the fact. Because as soon as he went off script, he didn't know what to say." He did and said things "because I was told to," as though he had no choice. There's almost no physical evidence to support the grisly events he describes as having happened after the ramming. Craggs reminds the jury that Craig is "motivated to mislead" because he's been charged with murder himself, and he wants to be a father to his young child. So "maybe there are noble intentions behind his dishonesty." In any case, soon after he tells his sensational story to the police, his murder charge is dropped and he's charged with the much lesser offence of accessory after the fact.

The only other eyewitness testimony from the *Twin Maggies'* crew is James Landry's video testimony, which Craggs considers to be "not fully satisfying." Craggs sees problems not only with James's truthfulness but also with its motivation, "which may lead you to wonder whether the things that he said, incriminating himself, are actually accurate." In general, he says, "people don't voluntarily confess to crimes unless they actually did them." In these videos, nothing happens for some time—and then, well into the interrogation, James opens up. He says he regrets what happened, and then he tells his story.

But look very carefully at what the officer has been saying to him, says Craggs, because the officer's questions provide motivation for what James then says. Over and over again, Sergeant Richardson

says that James is the real skipper; he's sixty-five years old, he's operated the boat and the licence for decades, his kids are grown up, and
the two younger men respect him and look to him for guidance.
They have young families, and long lives ahead of them. Since James
is mainly responsible for what happened, he should tell the truth,
bear the consequences, and take some of the pressure off Dwayne,
Carla, and Craig.

So now "a very interesting thing happens," says Craggs. "James
Landry now says that he did everything. He says he shot the gun,
and he pushed Dwayne Samson aside and took control of the boat.
He says the other men stood by, didn't say anything, didn't do anything—and really he sticks with this story that he did everything
until he speaks with Staff Sergeant Gerry Landry in French towards
the end of the June 7 statement.

"Why did he do this?" Craggs asks. "He was trying to take the
fall." But after the "I did everything" story falls apart, he says—many
times—that he was trying to "help my son-in-law and the other
fellow," and "I don't want to put my daughter in trouble." He says he
"told the boys, we made a mistake" and then corrects himself to say
that "I made a mistake." He says it again in the car when the Mounties
take him to Little Anse to recover the rifle, a .30-30 Winchester, and
he leads them to a .30-30 under the mattress of his bed.

Craggs pauses slightly. "What he did is, he led them to the wrong
gun." The lawyer walks over to the evidence table and points at the
.30-30 rifle that has been entered in evidence. "This is Dwayne
Samson's rifle. And James keeps this charade up. He never told the
police that he had led them to the wrong gun. He told them that
that was the gun he had used to shoot at Phillip Boudreau's boat.

"Now, most of us would like to think that if someone we cared
about were in peril, we would make a sacrifice for them. We'd jump
in front of a car to save our kid. Fortunately, most of us never get
tested. James Landry actually did it. James Landry tried to take the
fall for a murder, and the police believed him for a while. And now

the Crown is playing his statement, and asking you to pick out the portions of it which are convenient for their case—and believe those.

"You have to remember that this is a criminal trial. You have to have proof beyond a reasonable doubt. Essentially what you have is testimony from two people on the *Twin Maggies*. It would appear that James Landry overstated what he did, and Craig Landry understated what he did. So where does that leave you?"

The evidence confirms that James shot at Phillip; it does not confirm that he hit him. It confirms that James had reason to wish Phillip would "go away," but it does not prove that James sent him away.

"We're talking about criminal acts," says Craggs. "We're not talking about morality, or about the right thing to do; we're talking about whether James Landry's actions tied him in to a criminal offence. My respectful submission is that he shot the rifle to scare him, and that's where his criminal liability stops. There is no credible evidence before you that he encouraged or helped Dwayne Samson drive the *Twin Maggies* over Phillip Boudreau's boat"—and it's Craggs's contention that Phillip died then, when the boat went over him. That, he says, makes sense; the whole gaffing and sinking story does not make sense. And, although Craggs does not spell it out, if Phillip died in the ramming, that also makes Dwayne the killer, not James.

"James Landry did not behave well that day," Craggs concludes. "James Landry did things wrong. James Landry lost his temper. What James Landry did not do, however, was commit a crime. I would ask you to find James Landry not guilty."

Thank you, says Justice Kennedy. He tells the jury that he will charge them in the morning, and that they should leave their phones and other devices behind but bring a change of clothing in case their deliberations keep them sequestered overnight.

Justice Kennedy does want to say that he has reviewed his notes and "can see no evidence that Reggie Jackson was ever on that boat." That brings a good laugh to end the day. And I go home to Brigadoon.

IO

VISITING BRIGADOON

"WE WERE STANDING IN front of the co-op store and it was closed," said the woman from Southern California. "There were three or four teenagers across the street, and they came over towards us. I was scared. Teenagers terrify me. Where I come from, when a group of teenagers comes at you, you jump in the car and lock the doors. You get out of there, unless you want to be beaten and robbed.

"But these kids came over and said, 'Hi, that's store's closed, but if you want to buy some food or something, there's a convenience store up the hill and another little store not very far down the other way.' I thought I was dreaming. They came over to help us, can you imagine?"

In May 2000, Charles and Peg Bosdet were visiting Isle Madame because his family came from the island. The Bosdet family home was the spectacular old mansion still standing at the very end of Bosdet's Point Road in West Arichat. Charles, a journalist by trade, worked in the aerospace industry writing manuals for jet engines and the like; Peg was an artist and also a writer, the author of a couple of authoritative books about buttons as markers of social history. Somehow or other my wife, Marjorie, and I met them, along with another professional couple that had moved to Isle Madame from Halifax.

We told Peg and Charles that the four of us had developed our own whimsical terminology to describe the deep security that stems from mutual reliance and trust between you and your neighbours. For instance, people don't lock their doors because, as a neighbour once said to me, "If you lock your doors, how can we get in?" They're not coming in to make off with your valuables or stifle you in your bed. They're coming in to return a tool or a book, drop off some rhubarb or a loaf of fresh bread, borrow a cup of sugar. Neighbours spontaneously solve one another's problems. If someone neglects to beach a rowboat properly and it's beating on the shore, any passerby will haul it up. If a car's interior light is on, someone closes the door properly so that the light goes off and the battery doesn't run down.

This is what we'd come to call "reverse vandalism." You return from a trip, and your property has been improved. Your newspapers are stacked neatly at the back door, your plants are watered, and your boat cover is tied down snugly. One day I was writing about this very phenomenon when I looked out the window to see my own red flat-bottomed skiff chugging across the harbour. At the helm was Bill Martin, the retired mechanic next door. A few days earlier he had tuned up my ancient outboard, but later, when I took it out for a run, it stalled repeatedly. I didn't tell Bill about this, but a friend happened to notice it and mentioned it to him. Now Bill was out there in the harbour trying to find the problem and fix it. Reverse vandalism.

"Rustic engineering" is the combination of imaginative problem-solving and traditional techniques that neighbours come up with when they get together to accomplish some difficult task. We need to move a building. Okay, we'll use rollers, levers, tackles, jacks, and wedges, and maybe a backhoe. We need to raise a pole? Put the top of the pole between the horns of an extension ladder and then extend the ladder. Somebody needs a wharf. Wait till the harbour freezes, bore some holes in the ice, and bang some pilings down through the holes with the bucket of a backhoe. Look what we can accomplish when we tackle things together.

"Just in mind delivery" is when you're vainly looking for something and a neighbour overhears. Hey, he says, I got three of those, I'll bring you one. It happened all the time when I was building my boat. One time a neighbour named Eric Samson—"Eric the Puss"—dropped into my workshop to see how the boat was coming along. How are you going to move that one-ton block of lead ballast? he asked. I didn't know. I got a couple of little industrial dollies, said Eric. Perfect for that. I'll bring 'em over. Keep 'em till you're done.

The Bosdets hung out in Isle Madame for several days. Later, Peg wrote from Los Angeles to say she felt as though she'd been on a visit to Brigadoon, the enchanted Scottish village that rises out of the mists for a single day once every hundred years. She could hardly believe such a place existed.

Isle Madame is not Brigadoon, of course; it's present every day, all year round, a very real community with all the normal human conflicts. It was a bitter labour–management conflict in the fishery, after all, that brought me to the island in the first place. I had no real intention of staying, but I liked the place, I was writing a book, and I had no particular reason to go anywhere else. When the book was finished, six years later, I discovered that I had settled in to stay.

One thing that held me was my curiosity about how people handled conflict in a community so small and long settled, where people knew one another so well. I had spent all my life in cities—Vancouver, Berkeley, London, Halifax—and in a city, if you don't want to see anyone ever again, you can often dodge them indefinitely. Not so in Isle Madame. It didn't take long to see that privacy was not much valued here, and was not easy to obtain.

"Privacy?" cried a friend. "*Privacy?* I'm an Acadian, me—I don't know what that is."

I came to realize that although I didn't have much privacy, I didn't greatly care. I wasn't doing anything I was ashamed of, and my neighbours' attitude towards one another's foibles—and mine—was one of amusement. Over time, I came to feel that the two great Acadian values are truth and tolerance. Acadians want to know what's going on, want to understand who you are and what you do. There had never been a freelance writer here before, and people were intensely curious. What kind of exotic bird was this, perching in their local tree? Eventually my neighbours decided I was a trades-man, like a pipefitter or an electrician working construction. My home was a base, I had no one employer, I was highly skilled, and I travelled a lot. It's an excellent analogy—far better than the mystical nonsense about the tortured role of the artist so common in literary and cultural circles—and it satisfied my neighbours' passionate need to understand.

But they never used their knowledge to wound me. I was alone and I welcomed company, so people dropped in, invited me to par-ties and barbecues. One time, early on, the man filling my order in a lumberyard asked if I was married. No, I said, divorced.

"But you got a woman wit' you?"

"No," I said. He fell silent and looked out to sea for several long moments. I wondered what he was thinking. Then he turned back to me, looking apologetic.

"I don't know any women," he said sadly.

Acadians, I concluded, want to know you and understand you, not in order to judge you but to determine how they should conduct their relationship with you. They want to draw you into the web of mutual assistance that has been their greatest resource for four hundred years. Around here we look out for each other, they'll say. You never know when you're going to need a hand yourself. We're like a family here. We all pitch in. Everyone benefits.

So I joined the fire department, served on the board of the little local credit union, spoke at the high school graduation. When the cod fishery collapsed, I joined the effort to build a replacement economy, serving on the board of Development Isle Madame and, for its first seven years, chairing the board of Telile, the island's unique non-profit community television station. The work was sometimes a strain, but it was mostly a pleasure.

So what about conflict?

Acadians on Isle Madame can flare right up, sounding terrifyingly violent. "If I catch you, you little bastard, I'll tear off your arm and beat you with the wet end," as I once heard a loving mother say to her defiant child. Fistfights? Yup. Beatings, sometimes fierce ones? Now and then. Brawls? Occasionally. A friend of mine once went to the Petit de Grat branch of the Royal Canadian Legion and found the door locked. He could hear a proper donnybrook going on inside. He went to the back door, tapped in code, and the bartender opened the door a crack.

"What's going on?"

"Ah," said the bartender, "the comrades are restless tonight."

But although Acadians tend to flare right up, they flare right down again too. When a squabble is over, it's over, and there's no point holding grudges. I've tried to learn that skill, with some success, but it's not the way I grew up; my wise Aunt Ethel once remarked that in our Scottish family we have a habit of "nursing our wrath to keep it warm."

I rarely see any such brooding in an Acadian, but that doesn't mean the contretemps is entirely forgotten. If someone rats you out you don't forget it, and you don't trust him with sensitive information again—but otherwise you treat him the same as you always did. The memory of the fight becomes encysted, so to speak; it's not gone, but a membrane grows over it, and if nothing happens to rupture the membrane, the memory ceases to trouble you. You go on living together as you always did.

You see this in people's acceptance of Phillip's depredations. Your four-wheeler is gone. Your rifle is gone. The groceries are stolen. The traps are empty. But Phillip is Phillip; he has no money, so there's nothing to be done about it; you just get on with your life. You see the same thing in local politics. Isle Madame once had a stormy revolt of citizens against a planning bylaw proposed by the county council, a bylaw that was clearly designed for urban settings and made no sense in a rural community. At a loud and raucous community meeting, our local councillor—who could be quite pugnacious herself—stood up and said, "Hey, hey, everybody. Let's all settle down. We're all going to be here tomorrow. We all have to live together. Let's take it easy."

What would rupture the membrane over the encysted memory of a quarrel? Repetition, I think. You took my chainsaw and brought it back damaged. We had a scrap: fine, we've put it behind us. But if you do it again, then it was a mistake to forget it the first time. Now we have a pattern, and that sore spot is open and raw again. It won't skin over so easily the second time. And if you do it a fifth time, or a tenth, the sore won't heal at all.

Like other human societies, then, Isle Madame has an intimate knowledge of bitter conflict, violence, despair, and abuses of power— but those conflicts rarely result in homicides. How rarely? I doubt if there's any official statistic about that.

So I went to see Raymond LeBlanc.

Ray LeBlanc is among my oldest and dearest friends. My first home in D'Escousse was right across the road from his, and I soon got to know not only him and his wife, Pearl, but also his parents and all five of his children. At the time he was the municipal clerk and sheriff of Richmond County, a job he soon gave up to become a paralegal assistant at the Port Hawkesbury law firm where he spent the rest of his working life. Liberal Party leaders, he says, implored him not to retire as sheriff until after the 1974 election, "because they'd promised the job to ten or eleven other people"—so for some months he held both jobs, despite the fact that he is what's known in Nova Scotia politics as "a rank Tory." On September 9, 2018, Pearl made a note that, after nearly fifty years of discussion, Ray and I had agreed on a political subject for the first time. We'd been discussing Donald Trump.

Nevertheless, I knocked on doors for him when he ran successfully for the municipal council, and when I was once approached to run for the NDP, which he thinks is a silly party, I told him I wouldn't even consider it unless he would manage my campaign.

"Yah, I'll do it," he said, grinning, "and I'll use every goddamn dirty trick in the book to get you elected, too."

For decades, Ray was the returning officer for Richmond in provincial elections, as his son Ronnie mentioned in his testimony about organizing the petition urging Dwayne Samson's release on bail; Ray and Pearl also offered to post bail. The two have also been leaders in the North Isle Madame Recreation Association and the D'Escousse Civic Improvement Association, which operates the community hall. In its heyday, the hall made tidy profits from its Saturday dances; it used them to create a scholarship fund that supported any child from the village who went on to higher education.

Raymond does the income tax returns for half the people of the community. He and Pearl operate the village's only remaining general store, which is built onto the side of their home. Over the years they've carried many of their neighbours—including me—through difficult financial times by giving us food on credit, sometimes for months on end.

In the early 1980s, when I wanted to explain in a national magazine why I love village life, I used my relationship with Ray as an example. I do business with Ray, I said, but I also dance with his wife, employ his son and his father as carpenters, buy firewood jointly with him, ask his help with my projects, and chase his goat out of my yard. I have seen his kids grow up. I know how hard he is to beat at chess. I know him drunk and sober, at night and in the morning, at work and at play. I've seen him angry enough to fetch his rifle and sad enough to cry. And he knows me the same way. I find some of his attitudes and opinions primitive, and he considers some of my ideas dreamily sentimental—but those differences do not dampen our pleasure in each other.

After my article had been accepted, the magazine's fact-checker called Ray, who confirmed all these things. Then the fact-checker said, "Just out of curiosity, Mr. LeBlanc, how do you feel about having someone write so frankly about you in a national publication?"

At the time, Lech Wałęsa and Solidarity were struggling for liberty in Poland. Without missing a beat, Ray replied, "If that's what he sees, that's what he says. We're not in Poland here."

Could there be a better defence of free speech? It's Milton's *Areopagitica*, in fourteen words.

"So Raymond," I said, "I think the last time someone from the island was tried for murder it was Eugene Landry, right?"

"Yeah, probably so." We both remembered the shock of that killing. Enraged by a fierce family argument, Eugene went and got his gun, stuck the barrel through the kitchen window, and shot his father-in-law dead.

"Now when was that, exactly?"

"In the 70s," said Raymond. "Come on in here. I think I got it in my genealogy."

We went into the cluttered room that doubles as an office and a living room. Settling himself behind a big desk, Raymond consulted his computer. After a moment he announced, "I got Eugene. He died on February 17, 1990. That doesn't give me the date of the murder, though—wait now, the date of his father-in-law's death would be the date of the murder. Henry Landry. Let me see— September 30, 1977."

Thirty-six years from Henry Landry to Phillip Boudreau. What about even earlier killings?

"That would be in the 1950s, probably," said Ray. "I remember one back then that people thought was murder, but I don't think it went to court. They called it a hunting accident." I wondered how many "hunting accidents" or "traffic fatalities" or "accidental drownings," here and elsewhere, are actually murders. People do get away with murder all the time; the Halifax police website, for instance, lists seventy-two unsolved homicide or missing person cases.

Ray also remembers a case where two men got into a scuffle in the tavern in Louisdale, on the Cape Breton side of the bridge to Isle Madame. One man knocked the other out and thought he'd killed him, so he threw the body off the bridge. The victim wasn't actually dead, however, but he was unconscious, and he drowned. Legally that wasn't murder, though, since there was no intention involved.

So Eugene Landry remains the last person tried for murder in Isle Madame. He was a scary man, very different from the *Twin Maggies'* crew. When he returned to the island after a decade or so in prison, he came around to see me. I was president of the local NDP at the time, and he was, he told me, suffering from a terrible injustice: the government wouldn't grant him a firearms permit. Good for the government, I thought, as I explained that the president of an opposition party's local constituency association really had no influence whatever over such matters.

Permit or no, Eugene did get guns, Raymond remembers. The police knew he had them, too, but none were willing to go to his house and confront him. Then, late one night, probably after a dance at the hall, Raymond heard a ruckus outside. He looked out the window and then opened it for a better view. Eugene and his sidekick, Bucky Short, were in a shouting match with a third man, who was bellowing "Murderer! Murderer! Who you going to kill next?" To which Eugene replied, "Follow me home! I'll show you who's going to be next!" A Mountie came up the road from the hall and broke it up, with Eugene still threatening to murder the other fellow.

Eugene and Bucky died together not too long afterwards. One bitter winter night they rode a three-wheel all-terrain vehicle to the Louisdale tavern. On the way home they took a shortcut over the ice of Lennox Passage. The ice gave way, and the two of them drowned. Bucky's body was found the next day, but Eugene's wasn't found for three months. The community reaction was summarized by one of the boys who socialized each evening in Poirier's Garage.

"No, sir," he said, "they ain't gonna be too many tears shed over that one."

Eugene was actually a distant cousin of James Landry's—and, Raymond thought, also of his. He'd been peppering our conversation with asides that one person after another "is my cousin."

"Ray," I said, "is *everyone* your cousin?"

"Well, I got ten uncles and aunts on my mother's side, and ten more on my father's. And one of my uncles had twenty-eight kids. I got a lot of cousins."

Alas, any history of crime on Isle Madame would have to include a chapter on the Roman Catholic Church. Originally, Isle Madame was the seat of the Diocese of Arichat; the soaring wooden church in Arichat, constructed in 1837, was the cathedral, and the imposing building across the road, now a law office, was the bishop's palace. The palace was also the first campus of what became St. Francis Xavier University. In 1886 the diocese was moved to Antigonish, on the mainland, whereupon all of eastern Nova Scotia, including Cape Breton Island, became the Diocese of Antigonish.

The diocese has had a noble history. In the 1920s and 1930s, two Cape Breton–born priests spearheaded a powerful self-help movement that gave people throughout the region the tools to get through the Depression. Father Moses Coady was the director of the university's extension department. His cousin, Father Jimmy Tompkins, also taught at the university before being exiled to parish work. The two of them criss-crossed the Maritimes preaching a gospel of cooperation, showing people how to set up credit unions, co-op stores, co-op industries, consumers' co-ops, and more. Go into almost any co-op organization in Nova Scotia and you will see a portrait of the revered Father Coady proudly displayed. The Antigonish Movement spread abroad, particularly into the Third World, and to this day students come to Antigonish to study community development and co-op economics at the world-renowned Coady International Institute at St. Francis Xavier.

In June 1991, however, two years after the child abuse scandal at the Mount Cashel Orphanage in Newfoundland, four Cape Breton priests were charged with the sexual abuse of children: Father James Mombourquette, Father Dan Doucet, and the twin brothers Fathers Clair and Claude Richard. All but Clair Richard had served in D'Escousse and elsewhere in Isle Madame. Mombourquette and the Richards were convicted. Dan Doucet was acquitted. He was much loved on the island, and several of us testified to his character. Christian theology teaches that we are all sinners, but I am quite sure that whatever Father Dan's sins may be, they do not include pedophilia or any other abuses of power.

I was equally sure that the others were guilty—and that the Diocese of Antigonish had a lot to answer for. I'd been told that when parishioners had complained that one of the priests was a child molester, Bishop William Power simply moved the man to a distant parish. When that priest was later assigned to Petit de Grat, where he had served earlier, a delegation from the village told the bishop in no uncertain terms that if he wanted a quiet life he should reconsider that decision. The bishop took the hint—but he didn't take the matter to the police, and he didn't take the priest out of parish work. Indeed, Power's successor, Bishop Colin Campbell, reacted to the Newfoundland scandal by suggesting that the sexual relations were consensual, or that the boys had seduced the Christian Brothers involved. A torrent of outrage, largely from Catholics, soon ended that line of argument.

These were, of course, only the early tremors of an earthquake that continues to shake the Catholic Church worldwide, not least the Diocese of Antigonish. Over the next two decades, dozens of victims came forward with stories of abuse by numerous priests stretching back more than sixty years. In August 2009 a new bishop, Raymond Lahey, negotiated a $16 million settlement with 125 victims. A month later, when Bishop Lahey was returning from an overseas trip, his laptop was inspected by Canada Border Services and found to contain "disturbing images." He was charged with possession and importation of child pornography, and was ultimately convicted and defrocked.

Meanwhile, the diocese had to raise $16 million. How would it do that? By borrowing $6 million and by pillaging its own parishes—the very communities whose children had been violated by the disgraced priests. Parish bank accounts were vacuumed, parish properties were sold, parishes were merged. Isle Madame had four parishes, each with a church and a glebe house. The diocese sold the properties in D'Escousse and West Arichat, adding their parishioners to the congregation in Arichat. Today the gracious old glebe house in D'Escousse belongs to someone in Ontario, and St. Hyacinth's Church stands deconsecrated and empty.

I believe I was only the second non-Catholic householder in D'Escousse, but I miss that church very much. Its regular masses were like the heartbeat of village life. The church was the place where we celebrated the great transitions in our lives—marriages, deaths, births, and baptisms. Without it there is something missing at the core of our lives together.

I also miss the priest who served there for years and years, and who lies in the cemetery up on the hill behind the church. Father John J. Macdonald was a big lumbering Scot from Antigonish

County who had a bumper sticker that read "It's Hard to Be Humble When You're Scottish." But he was fluent in French, and he loved Acadians in general and Isle Madame in particular. In canon law, the priest is responsible for all the souls of the parish, whether Catholic or not. I told John J. that it pleased me to think he was therefore my priest too, even though I was an infidel.

"Oh, hardly an infidel!" he exclaimed. "But I'm glad you feel that way."

"Father JJ" could be uncompromising and acerbic, but he was deeply devoted to his people and also to the ideals of the Antigonish Movement. That dedication took him to the highest levels of the credit union movement both nationally and internationally.

"I loved your article on Lee Cremo and his fiddle music," he said to me once. "Guess where I read it? On the plane between Geneva and Bologna."

I counted on his counsel—and perhaps because I was outside the Church, Father JJ occasionally used me as a sounding board. When the four priests were charged with child abuse, he came to my door looking devastated.

"I can hardly hold my head up," he said. "I'm supposed to be the moral leader of this community, but I feel like everyone's looking at me and asking themselves, *What about him?*

"And you know what's even worse? I went to see one of our oldest parishioners, and he was trying to comfort me. You know what he said? 'Don't worry about it, Father, 's nothin' new.' *Nothing new?* What's he telling me? *Nothing new?*

"Who'll trust me now?"

I would, always. And perhaps the finest moment in our friendship came five years later, when my wife, Lulu, was dying. Father JJ drew me aside to say that people understood that Lulu was not a practising Catholic, and were wondering what arrangements would be made for her funeral. She and I had discussed that, I told him, and we wanted an event where friends from a range of spiritual traditions would talk briefly about the meaning of death within their faiths and would share with us an observance that was part of their own ceremonies of farewell—a prayer, some food, the burning of sweetgrass. We would like the pulpit to be shared with friends who were not only Catholic and Protestant but also Jewish, Muslim, Sikh, Buddhist, and Mi'kmaw. I told Father JJ about Lulu's delight in the idea.

"It sounds wonderful," she'd said, grinning. "It seems a shame to miss it."

If we possibly could, we'd like to hold the event in the church. And we'd like him to act as host.

"Of course," said Father JJ. "It's the community temple."

"Do you have to ask—you know, anyone?"

"My philosophy," he said, with a wicked glint in his eye, "is ask *not*, and thou shalt receive."

So that is what we did, and John J. preached about it later. If organized religions had tried to pull off an ecumenical event like Lulu's funeral, he said, they probably wouldn't even agree about the shape of the table for their discussions. But look what open hearts can do. Look how easily ordinary people can bridge those same religious divisions when they come together in sorrow and generosity to honour someone they loved.

I miss that man, and I miss that church. But maybe we see in people like John J. the animating spirit that sustains people's faith despite scandals, lawsuits, and financial catastrophe. All of which is captured in one parishioner's reaction when I asked him how he felt about the institutional Church after all the sordid goings-on.

"Well, we're not too impressed with the Church," he said. "But we didn't give up on God."

And God did not give up on any of His children, including Phillip Boudreau, noted Marie-Louise Sampson, an ex-nun who had enjoyed a playful, teasing friendship with Phillip. Writing on Parker Donham's public affairs site, Contrarian.ca, she reminded readers of the overflow crowd at another unorthodox ceremony, the "Service of Farewell" for Phillip, held on August 9, 2013, just a couple of months after his disappearance. She wanted readers to remember that Phillip had people who loved him, and particularly that "Phillip was a human being, who was created and loved by God as much as you are."

The service was indeed remarkable. The church was packed, and the crowd included some surprising people, like Phillip's parole officer and some of his former cellmates, not to mention a large cross-section of Petit de Grat. Clearly many of those people were not big fans of Phillip, though some were. Many went because attending a village funeral is simply a thing that one does when a member of the community dies. But the event also embodied a need to come together in a moment of shock and regret. In a way, perhaps the huge turnout was the counterpart of the petition presented at Dwayne Samson's bail hearing. If the petition said "Dwayne is a good man in a bad spot," then the funeral said "Phillip should not have died."

That's close to Marie-Louise Sampson's view.

"Phillip was not always what he had become," she wrote. "People responsible for this know who they are, many of them who ARE LOSING SLEEP AT NIGHT THROUGH GUILT TRIPS. Society has failed him, at school, he was bullied, he was a child starving for love, expecting that maybe, just maybe, someday someone would have chosen to let him know that in his 'own little way', he too was SPECIAL!"

A human life is an endless process of becoming, a constant dance between character and circumstance. Every funeral is an occasion for reflection. How well did this person play the hand he or she was dealt? And how well did the rest of us manage our evolving relationship with the person we've lost? Our communities shape us, and then we shape our communities. Perhaps Brigadoon is less a place than an ambition, a value, a condition we create together.

———

Peg and Charles Bosdet did return from California. In 2002 they moved to Isle Madame permanently, bringing Peg's mother with them. Mary Louise Van de Berg, then eighty-two, was a concert pianist by training, a woman of great dignity and refinement. She fit right in, playing at local events and benefit concerts. One of her favourite people was a particularly foul-mouthed workman.

"That's all right," she said, when asked if she was shocked. "That's his language. That's how he expresses himself."

In trying to explain the move to people in California, Peg said, they would describe the island as "a charming place that's like fifty years behind the current time. That's not a negative. What we meant was, they still cherish family, and their extended family as well. Everybody knows everybody. They're still friendly to strangers, and not afraid of them. The young people are friendly, even to adults. People still don't lock their doors. They don't lock their cars. They find it odd that we do."

Charles laughed, remembering an island man driving him somewhere on an errand. When they stopped, Charles said, "'Aren't you going to lock the truck?' He said no. I said, 'Aren't you even going to take the keys out of it?' He looked at me as if I had an extra head. He said, 'What if somebody needs to move it?'"

"People here still cooked," Peg said. "They made their own bread. The last place we lived in California, the lady next door to us—who I only met when she was moving out—she had a beautiful kitchen, and she informed me that she and her husband had never cooked in it once. They ate out twice a day. The kitchen was for the caterers, when they held big parties. That's not unusual. When Charles and I got together, I was the first woman he'd ever been with who cooked."

Not only did Peg cook, she was also an entrepreneur. She had established and operated an import business, bringing products to the United States from India, and she was an award-winning baker, having baked birthday cakes for the likes of Bob Hope, Barbara Eden, and President Gerald Ford (who had the presidential seal in icing on his cake). Isle Madame needed jobs and tourist magnets. While Charles continued to commute to his work in California, Peg astonished the island by opening a chocolaterie. What, in Arichat? A *chocolaterie*?

The Candy Shop was an instant hit—bright and airy, decorated in white and crimson, bursting with superb chocolates and whimsical confections. Almost before it opened, Peg had to double its size. It turned out that people would happily drive two hours to buy first-rate chocolates in Isle Madame. Before long the shop and the factory had thirty-two employees. Economic development agencies sat up and took notice. Maybe the business could grow again. National distribution. Export markets. Why not?

It all crashed on February 5, 2008—Super Tuesday in American politics. The Bosdets had driven three hundred kilometres to the U.S. Consulate in Halifax to cast their primary ballots for an inspiring, improbable presidential candidate named Barack Obama. On the way home, their car skidded off a snowy highway. Peg broke her back. For the next three months she lay flat in a hospital bed, forbidden to move a muscle lest her spine be further damaged. She was bedridden at home for a further six months. She made a good recovery, but she tires easily, and she still uses a cane. And the Candy Shop was gone.

But what a contribution she had made, and what an important example she had provided.

A decade earlier, when the island was reinventing itself in the wake of the fisheries collapse, the redevelopment group devised an initiative that we called "Grey Tigers." Isle Madame is a sailor's heaven—an archipelago, a stunning network of beaches, islets, and inlets—and so we decided to lure early retirees with cruising sailboats and other young seniors who might bring or start businesses. People like the Bosdets, in fact. We had some successes, most notably with a short-lived bilingual call centre, but we never made a sustained effort to market the idea.

Today, it's apparent that we didn't need to; it happened spontaneously. The island is now home to, among others, a book cover designer, potters, consultants, artisanal food producers, a constitutional lawyer (and apiarist) whose legal practice is mainly in Ontario, a solar energy entrepreneur, a graphic designer, and a pair of cruising sailors—one of whom is a nuclear power millwright by trade—who reached the island from British Columbia via Cape Horn and now manufacture wooden bowls. Brigadoon doesn't need much marketing.

Peg Bosdet remembers that, in her early years here, she and her mother were sometimes spooked by a superstitious feeling that the island might indeed vanish, that it couldn't possibly be real.

"It's like a magical sort of feeling," she explains. "You're afraid that it can't be what you think, or that you won't see it again. For the first two years, at least, we'd be away and we'd feel like, 'What if it's disappeared? What if it wasn't real?' And you know, you come along the highway from Port Hawkesbury, and you come up over this little rise, and all of a sudden you can see the island's lights. And my mother, because she felt the same way about it, would always say, 'Oh, it's still here! Brigadoon is still here!'"

11

COURTROOM 3:
DELIBERATIONS

NOVEMBER 28, 2014

THE EVIDENCE HAS ALL been submitted, the witnesses have all been heard, the lawyers for both sides have made their final arguments. Today the case goes to the jury.

But not right away. First, Chief Justice Kennedy will confer with the lawyers, and then he will deliver his instructions to the jury. Only then will the jury retire to deliberate. Before the jury enters, Justice Kennedy tells the lawyers that he's received their two separate written theories of the case, and that in his instructions he will put both theories before the jury. He'll also give the jury a version of what are known as "WD" instructions because they arose from a case, *R. v. W.D.*, in which the testimony of the accused contradicted the testimony of other witnesses. WD instructions direct the jury to assess and weigh the testimony of an accused exactly the same way they would assess the testimony of any other witness. Craig Landry's live testimony and James Landry's videotaped statement are both legitimate pieces of evidence.

On another point, Canadian Press has asked for access to James Landry's video interview. Kennedy agrees that the tape, once played, is a public record and should be made available. The problem is that once the jury has begun its deliberations, the evidence—including the interview—belongs to them, and they may well want access to it. After the verdict has been rendered, though, there's no reason why the tape shouldn't be available.

When the jury enters, Justice Kennedy starts by thanking them for coming in on a stormy day. His next task is to "charge" them. He is an old hand at this. He has been on the bench for thirty-five years, the last fifteen as chief justice of the Nova Scotia Supreme Court. He's well aware that he is instructing twelve people whose experience of the courtroom ranges from limited to nonexistent, and he intends to ensure that they understand exactly what they are to do and how they are to do it. His charge will be detailed, meticulous, and repetitive. It will take about three and a half hours to deliver. He will, he says, "explain to you your function as a jury, and make reference to the charge against the defendant, Joseph James Landry."

And so he begins.

"The Crown prosecutors called witnesses whose evidence in their opinion proves that James Landry is guilty of second degree murder. The defence, on the other hand, would say no, that the evidence is not of sufficient weight or sufficient credibility to convict the accused. You have heard the addresses of both counsel, and it's your duty now to weigh all of that evidence and do that with fairness after listening to what I have to say with respect to the law.

"You the jury are the judges of the guilt or the innocence of the accused. You base your decision on the sworn evidence of the witnesses and the exhibits that were tendered as a result of that evidence, and also the two agreed statements of fact. I talk about the law. You turn evidence into fact."

He instructs the foreperson to oversee the deliberations and keep the conversation on track. Any verdict the jury returns has to be unanimous, and so Justice Kennedy suggests that the foreperson call for a vote from time to time, because "sometimes you've got unanimity and you don't know it." He cautions jurors against expressing any definitive opinion too early in the process; they need to make every effort to reach unanimity. That said, they're also obliged to obey their own consciences, which means that sometimes a jury can't reach a unanimous decision.

The two basic principles to remember are the presumption of innocence and the need for proof beyond a reasonable doubt. The defence does not need to prove anything. It is the job of the Crown to prove guilt. Reasonable doubt is based on reason and common sense, and on what the evidence tells you. If you concluded that he's "probably guilty or likely guilty," you would have to find him innocent. The key word is "sure," and jurors should concentrate on that word.

The charge is second degree murder, Murder 2, which is a form of "culpable homicide." Homicide simply means to cause the death of a human being by any means. Culpable homicide means to cause death by means of an unlawful act; it can be murder, manslaughter, or infanticide. Murder occurs when a person means to cause either death or bodily harm likely to cause death. First degree murder is planned and deliberate murder, including assassination or contract killing. Killing a police officer or a prison guard is also Murder 1. Murder 2 is any murder that is not Murder 1.

To prove Murder 2, the Crown must establish five things, beginning with the identity of the accused and the time and place of the event, neither of which is at issue here. It must further establish that the accused committed an unlawful act, that the unlawful act caused the death in question, and that the accused meant to cause death or bodily harm likely to result in death. In this case, the Crown alleges a series of unlawful acts: that Phillip Boudreau was shot in the hip or leg; that he was gaffed and towed, which constitutes assault; and that he was tied to an anchor and dropped to the sea bottom. These would all be unlawful acts.

The next element is causation, proving that the unlawful act caused or contributed to Phillip's death. The act doesn't have to be the sole cause of death, says Kennedy, or even the principal cause; it just has to be a significant contributing cause of death. He notes that this is a murder trial without a body, and yet there's strong evidence supporting the claim that Phillip is dead. He was a fixture in Petit de Grat, but he hasn't been seen since that fateful day. His boots, hat, and boat have been found, however, and Craig Landry "told you what happened to Phillip Boudreau."

Justice Kennedy reviews Craig's testimony in detail: Craig saw a puff of smoke from Phillip's outboard; Phillip said he wasn't cutting any traps and also that his leg had been broken. One issue is the question of when Phillip actually died. Did he die in the ramming, as James suggests? Or—following Craig's story—when he was being towed? Or when he was dropped into the sea? In the end, though, it hardly matters. Clearly the actions of both James and Dwayne were—certainly in Craig's account—significant contributing causes of death.

James's statement and Craig's testimony coincide up to the point of the third ramming. The rest of Her Majesty's Story rests entirely on Craig's testimony. So Justice Kennedy notes that the credibility of Craig Landry is "central to your finding on this sentence." He says he is obliged to give the "Titus warning" to the jury about the reliability of witnesses who are facing criminal charges themselves. This warning derives from a 1983 Ontario case, *R. v. Titus*, where a lower court refused to allow a defendant, Joseph Titus, to grill a prosecution witness named Miehm about an outstanding murder charge against Miehm himself. Wrong, said the Supreme Court of Canada; if the Titus jury had known about the "disreputable" witness Miehm's "background and the motive which it afforded him to favour the prosecution's case," they might have weighed his testimony differently. Similarly, in James Landry's trial, Craig might well be motivated to testify against James to save his own neck, as Luke

Craggs has strongly implied. The jury, says Kennedy, should approach such testimony with care and caution. This is "one factor for you to consider. How much it influences you is up to you." Is Craig's account of Phillip's gaffing and sinking "a fabrication, or does he give the kind of detailed evidence that a truth-teller might give? You'll decide."

At this point, based on the overall weight he's given Craig's dragging-and-drowning story in particular, I sense that Chief Justice Kennedy has personally concluded that the Crown has proven its case, that Craig is a credible witness, and that James is guilty of Murder 2. He does note, at the beginning and end of his discussion of Craig's testimony, that this is one witness's account of events— but between those brackets he talks about Craig's story without such qualifications. He doesn't say, for instance, that "Craig Landry has provided you with his account of what happened." Instead he says, "Craig Landry has told you what happened to Phillip Boudreau."

After a break, Justice Kennedy turns to intention, the fifth and final ingredient in Murder 2. The question here is whether the accused "meant to cause death." Kennedy has already noted James's statement that he wanted "to get rid of him, kill him or whatever." Now he asks, How do we figure out intention? It is fair to infer "that a sane and sober person intends the natural and probable consequences of his voluntary actions. If Phillip Boudreau's death was a natural consequence of James Landry's actions, you are entitled to conclude that James Landry intended to kill Phillip Boudreau by those actions. You are not *required* to draw that conclusion, but you are *able* to draw that inference." A bit later he says, "I repeat: he told the police that his intention was to get rid of Phillip Boudreau. Intention."

After a further quick review of the elements of Murder 2, he turns his attention to the "included offence" of manslaughter. If the jury finds James not guilty of Murder 2, they may still find him guilty of the "included offence" of manslaughter.

What is an included offence? Chief Justice Kennedy provides a careful analysis. The nub of the matter is that if the jury finds the Crown has failed to prove murder beyond a reasonable doubt, the jury must then consider whether the Crown's evidence *would* suffice to convict James of manslaughter. If so, they would acquit him of murder but convict him of manslaughter. Justice Kennedy cautions the jury that, in instructing them about manslaughter, he's not making any comment at all about the strength or weakness of the Crown's argument for a murder conviction. Manslaughter is simply a possibility that they need to understand.

So what are the elements of manslaughter?

Essentially, the difference between murder and manslaughter is intent. A murder is the consequence of an unlawful act that is intended to cause death. Manslaughter is such an act without the intention of causing death. It is conduct that is "objectively dangerous," an unlawful act that would subject another person to the risk of bodily harm which is neither trivial nor transitory. In that connection, says the judge, "remember what James Landry told the police. This is a case where the defendant in a statement says what he was intending to do on that day." The Crown would say that the relevant evidence would be about the shooting, about the gaffing, about pulling Phillip out to the mouth of the harbour while he's gaffed, about tying him to an anchor and throwing it overboard. But once again, the only evidence that those things happened, aside from the shooting, is the testimony of Craig Landry.

In summary, says Justice Kennedy, "you don't go to manslaughter unless you have found him not guilty of Murder 2."

Next, Kennedy explains that there are several different ways of participating in an offence and being guilty of it. First, one can simply commit the offence, alone or with others. Or one can help someone else commit it, which would be "aiding." One could encourage them through words or conduct, which would be "abetting." Both of these require that you know that the other person intends to commit an offence, and that you intend to help them or encourage them to do it. For example, if you consider Craig Landry's testimony credible, then the whole discussion about whether the water was deep enough to drop the body would constitute abetting.

Then Justice Kennedy delivers the WD warning about James Landry's video statement. An accused's testimony should be treated just the same as any other testimony—and "if it leaves you with a reasonable doubt, even if you don't believe it, you must find him not guilty. And even if what James Landry said does not leave you with a reasonable doubt, you may convict him only if the rest of the evidence proves his guilt beyond a reasonable doubt."

Finally, both the Crown and the defence have submitted their quite concise theories of the case, and the judge reviews them. The Crown's theory is that James Landry said he wanted to kill Phillip Boudreau, and he did. Phillip's body has not been found because James towed the body into 12.2 fathoms of water, where he helped tie Phillip to an anchor and dropped him in the water. He spirited the gun away from the boat and told police a false story to hide his tracks. The combination of witness testimony and physical evidence proves beyond a reasonable doubt that James killed Phillip. He simply did not hide his tracks well enough.

The defence's theory begins by noting that the only evidence that can speak to how Phillip Boudreau may have died comes from Craig Landry's testimony and from James Landry in his statement to police. Craig's testimony isn't credible because he clearly wanted to avoid criminal liability for his role in the killing. James's confession must be treated with great care because he wanted to take the blame for the murder in order to protect other men on the boat and their families. In short, Craig understated his involvement and James overstated his involvement. The evidence needed to convict is unclear, and it would be unsafe to rely on that evidence as proof beyond a reasonable doubt. So James must be found not guilty.

"Those are the theories of the Crown and the defence," says Justice Kennedy. "Your verdict will be based on the facts as you find them, and the law as I have endeavoured to explain it. On the back of the original indictment, handwritten, are the three possible verdicts: guilty of second degree murder, guilty of manslaughter, not guilty. There will never be any situation where you will explain your verdict, and you do not speak about your deliberations to anybody else. What takes place in that jury room is amongst the twelve jurors and nobody else. As soon as you're not twelve, you don't deliberate. For example, if two or three jurors went out for a smoke. If you're missing somebody, you stop.

"Don't wonder about consequences, please; consequences are for me or for the courts. It would be improper to involve consequences in any respect in your function of determining the matter. You've taken an oath to well and truly try the charges and render a true verdict according to the evidence; if you honour that oath you will have done what is expected of you. If you're still deliberating at 6:00 you'll have had a long day. If you'd like a little more time, that will happen, but by 6:00 it's time to get a good meal and a comfortable night's sleep."

And with that the jury retires to the jury room, where they'll have lunch before starting their task. The judge confers with the lawyers, and brings the jury back for a moment to clarify the difference between direct and circumstantial evidence. If you come in from outside and report that it's raining, that's direct evidence; if I see you come in dripping wet and folding an umbrella, I may infer that it's raining, and that's circumstantial evidence.

"Both are valid types of evidence, and the law treats both equally," he says. "Now please finish your lunch uninterrupted. Counsel will remain within fifteen minutes of the courthouse in case their presence is needed."

———

So now we wait. It's 1:00 in the afternoon; people go for a quick bite—there's no telling when the jury may return—and then hang around the courthouse lobby, talking in small groups, tapping on their cell phones, reading, listening on headsets.

It's an odd crowd—the families of both the accused and the victim, reporters and broadcasters, sheriffs, lawyers, witnesses, spectators. At one point during the afternoon I drift over to Phillip's family and fall into conversation with his sister Margaret Rose, also known as Maggie. The others in the family group include Phillip's brother Kenneth, a husky, scowling man, and his brother Gerard's wife, Linda, petite and intense, who's now fishing the family lobster licence in the vicinity of Mackerel Cove and is said to be very capable and very competitive. Maggie and her daughter have just had tattoos inscribed across their shoulders, at the base of their necks, displaying the words "Midnight Slider."

So what was he like, this brother of hers, this midnight slider? Maggie says he was a happy guy who loved to dance, and who did so quite furiously, often alone, at Saturday dances at the Social Action Centre in Little Anse, where James Landry lives, and at the Royal Canadian Legion in Grande Anse, on the Cape Breton side of Lennox Passage. He loved music but didn't play an instrument. He and his dog Brudy were devoted to each other; he was also devoted to Maggie's children and grandchildren. I use the words "thief" and "poacher" to see if they bother her. They don't—and in fact she comments that, on June 1, Phillip "wasn't poaching. He wouldn't be poaching or cutting traps in broad daylight, where everyone could see him. He'd do that at night. That morning he was out picking up two traps, one for Huntley David and one for Gerard, that had been driven into water that was too shallow for their big boats to go in there."

She says that Phillip had been diagnosed as bipolar one time when he was in prison in Renous, New Brunswick, and she mentions something to the effect that he had been tested at ten and found to have the mind of a five-year-old. The family was told he would never grow up entirely, which may help explain his apparent inability to understand and foresee the fury that his taunts sometimes engendered in others. On the other hand, several people told me of an occasion when Phillip had apparently been taken into custody and sent for a psychiatric assessment. The psychiatrist reportedly phoned the parents to say that there was "nothing wrong with your son."

"If you think there's nothing wrong with my son," snapped Gerard Boudreau, "then there's something wrong with *you*." And he clapped down the phone.

Although Maggie accepts that Phillip was a thief, she insists that he wasn't violent; he would never have done to anyone what the *Twin Maggies* crew did to him. His relationship with James Landry had apparently been cordial enough; James used to come over and have tea with their parents from time to time, and he once gave them some money to send to Phillip in prison. I find this hard to believe, but later I learn from a reliable source that James also took food and clothing to Phillip when he was hiding out in the woods, and that James sometimes bought poached lobsters from Phillip himself. Petit de Grat is a small place, and its relationships are complex.

I drift back to the assembled reporters, photographers, and cameramen. There's still no sign of the jury, which rather surprises people. Broadly speaking, the murmured consensus among the journalists and other observers seems to be that the Crown has proven its case, and that the verdict will be guilty of second degree murder. So what's taking so long? What's going on in that jury room?

At 6:00 everyone is called back into the courtroom. The jury is back, but not to deliver a verdict. They need more time. Joking that the lawyers are tired, Chief Justice Kennedy declares that the working day is over. He will bring the jury back in tomorrow at 9:30. However, he says, if all twelve jurors arrive early and find themselves in the jury room together, they can continue deliberating. But all twelve must be present. And with a little joke about the lawyers billing for triple overtime, he adjourns the trial overnight. We all file out into the early winter darkness. It's Friday evening, and the jurors aren't going home tonight.

Emerging from the Justice Centre parking lot, I turn down Kennedy Street for a steep little half-block to Granville Street, Port Hawkesbury's one-time main drag, which runs along the edge of the harbour. I've been immersed in law almost to the point of claustrophobia, and I'm enjoying the dark, chilly outdoors. Looking across the street at the cold ocean water, with the lights of the mainland town of Mulgrave visible on the opposite shore, I find myself reflecting on the nature of islands and of boundaries. Most jurisdictional boundaries are arbitrary lines on a map. But some boundaries have a deeper authenticity. Nova Scotia, for instance, is almost surrounded by the ocean, tethered to North America by only the narrow Isthmus of Chignecto. And Cape Breton is separated from the rest of Nova Scotia not by a cartographer's pen but by the Strait of Canso, the water I'm looking at right now. Until 1955 the only way to reach Cape Breton was to cross the strait by ferry.

Port Hawkesbury today presents itself as an undistinguished mill town of 3200 souls, but it boasts a harbour capable of handling the largest ships in the world—an unexpected side effect of having replaced the ferry with a causeway. Starting in 1952, contractors dumped ten million tonnes of rock from nearby Cape Porcupine into the water, creating the Canso Causeway and completely blocking the strait but for a short ship canal.

The project was propelled by the passion of a Cape Breton politician named Angus L. Macdonald, a towering figure in Nova Scotia history who served as premier from 1933 until his death in 1954, with an interlude in Ottawa from 1940 to 1945 as Canada's wartime minister of the navy. As one source puts it, he "converted his longing for the island into a fervid Scottish trope, which he used shamelessly throughout his public career in order to wrap himself in a Celtic mystique." In truth, he wrapped the whole province in Celtic mist and moonglow.

Before his untimely death—he was only sixty-three—Angus L. had opined that the causeway's opening ceremonies should feature one hundred pipers playing "The Road to the Isles." And so, when it opened a year later, on August 13, 1955, a massive crowd marched across the Canso Causeway led by ninety-nine pipers playing "The Road to the Isles." (One cross-grained piper refused to play.) They came to a halt in front of a makeshift stage on which was seated a party of politicians and bureaucrats from the capital cities of Halifax and Ottawa. Cape Breton contains some of the last strongholds of the Gaelic language in America—it even has a Gaelic College—and so when Reverend Stanley Macdonald, Angus L.'s older brother, began to address the crowd, he spoke in Gaelic, a splendid language for denunciation, sarcasm, and excoriation. Father Macdonald, a Catholic priest, reamed out the platform party as a pack of fools and knaves and ignoramuses who had made the program too short for a proper Gaelic ceremony. The crowd roared with laughter. The dignitaries laughed heartily too, unaware that they were the butt of the joke.

Gaelic can be a great convenience. Within the last thirty years, a Gaelic-speaking cabinet minister in Halifax received a delegation from his Cape Breton constituency. "I don't know what to do about the issue that concerns you," said the minister in Gaelic as his aides and officials stood by smiling. "Let us help you," the visitors responded, speaking in Gaelic as well and going on to tell him what they thought he should do. "Good," said the minister, when they finished. "That's what we'll do." They shook hands. The bureaucrats, assuming this had been a quaint exchange of pleasantries, moved to the nearby table.

"Oh, that won't be necessary," said the minister in English. "It's all decided. The meeting's over."

And—to use the Cape Breton phrase—that's as true as I'm standing here. I heard the story from someone who was there.

Cape Breton's 132,000 people speak four languages: English, French, Gaelic, and Mi'kmaw. The European settlements occupy the coasts of the island, while the Mi'kmaw communities stand on the shores of the glorious inland sea called the Bras d'Or Lake, which occupies the whole centre of Cape Breton Island. (Wikipedia notes that "Canadian author and yachtsman Silver Donald Cameron describes Bras d'Or Lake as 'A basin ringed by indigo hills laced with marble. Islands within a sea inside an island.'")

And everywhere there is music, always the preferred art of a multilingual community. The bedrock of the Cape Breton musical tradition is Scottish fiddling—strathspeys, reels, hornpipes, and slow airs—flavoured and shaped by Irish and French influences and often performed by brilliant Mi'kmaw players. One great Mi'kmaw fiddler, Lee Cremo, once told me of winning a fiddle competition somewhere in the southern U.S., where the prize was a banjo. He had never played a banjo in his life, but that evening he won the banjo competition. What?

"Nothing says a banjo got to be tuned like a banjo," he said, shrugging. "So I tuned it like a fiddle, and then I knew where everything was. Played a lotta fiddle tunes, and they never heard nothing like it."

The causeway completely transformed Port Hawkesbury, a process recorded in Linden MacIntyre's fine memoir, *Causeway.* The town had been a sleepy little place, but when the tides no longer poured through the narrow gut, the strait was transformed into a superport. And so, in the 1960s and 70s, Port Hawkesbury boomed. Heavy industries sprang up: a pulp mill, a power plant, an oil refinery, a heavy-water plant to serve the nuclear industry, a gypsum-shipping facility, and a wallboard plant, for starters. The town acted as a magnet for the hungry, the adventurous, and the avaricious, and soon became the economic backbone of the whole region; half of Isle Madame, it seemed, had jobs in the new industries. The town's boosters—who were numerous, and buoyant with self-confidence—predicted that Port Hawkesbury would rival Halifax in size by the end of the century. But by that time big industry was in decline and most of the industries had either shrunk drastically or closed entirely.

Port Hawkesbury gave me my name. I arrived in the area in 1971, having left a university teaching job in order to set up shop as a self-employed freelance writer. A dumb career move, agreed, but it gave me a life I wouldn't have wanted to miss. I bought a little house and settled in to earn a living writing feature articles for national magazines and doing commentaries and reports for CBC radio and TV.

One day in 1975 I got a call from the CBC asking me to look into an amusing local story. The Town of Port Hawkesbury had recently created a light industrial park, put in roads, and sold property to various businesses, including a Ford dealership. Only after the dealership was built did the town discover a rather important oversight: it didn't own the land. It had built the park on property belonging to the United Church and intended for a future expansion of its cemetery.

I called the mayor of Port Hawkesbury, a tavern-keeper named Billy Joe MacLean. I had never met him.

"Mayor MacLean, it's Donald Cameron calling—" I began.

"How the hell are you, you old fart?" cried the mayor.

"Well, um, fine," I said, somewhat taken aback. "I'm calling about the light industrial park . . ." After a few more sentences, the mayor interrupted me.

"Wait a minute, wait a minute, what Donald Cameron is this?"

"I'm a writer, I live in D'Escousse—"

"Oh Christ, I thought you were my buddy Don Cameron that owns the A&W drive-in here in Port Hawkesbury. I'm sorry. Now listen, how in hell did you get hold of this story . . . ?"

That's enough, I thought. That's it. I'd been mistaken for a variety of other Donald Camerons—a CBC vice-president, a senator from Alberta, a Nova Scotia politician who ultimately became premier. Shared names are a particularly common problem in Cape Breton, where a limited range of surnames and a strong sense of family continuity ensures that the little MacDonald boy will probably be named John, joining a horde of other John MacDonalds across the island. And the little Cameron boy will be Donald.

But Cape Breton also has solutions. One solution is patronymics, incorporating the name of a father or mother. If John's father was Hughie, the boy becomes John Hughie, whose son might be Danny John Hughie. This can produce some odd results. One of Cape Breton's most famous fiddlers was Bessie Archie Dan, and the last resident of the vanished community of Creignish Rear was Angus Little Rory. One day I was driving near Port Hawkesbury with the great Celtic musician John Allan Cameron—not to be mistaken for John *Donald* Cameron, then the proprietor of the music store in Port Hawkesbury, also a fine Celtic musician, who was John Allan's brother. John Allan and I weren't related, but we called each other "soul brothers." Suddenly John Allan stopped and pointed up the hill.

"Know the name of the man who lives in that house?" he demanded. I did not.

"John Angus John Archie Jim Sandy MacDonald," he said. Five ancestors in a row, lined up to identify this unique John MacDonald.

The other solution is a nickname. If one John has a farm on the shore and another lives on the hilltop, they become Johnny Up and Johnny Down. Or a name can spring from a particular characteristic or skill: Duncan the Nose, Dan the Dancer. A man born with one arm shorter than the other becomes John the Clock. A man with hemorrhoids is Archie Itchy Arse. The Acadians do the same: Pierre la Moustache, Cigarette, Soupbone, Ronnie Lobster, Raymond à Margaret à Fred Zephire.

When I spoke to Billy Joe MacLean, I was thirty-five. I had black eyebrows, a thick black moustache, and prematurely white hair. Over a snort of rum, I told the musician Tom Gallant about my conversation with Billy Joe and my continuing frustrations with my name. Tom considered my problem, narrowed his eyes, struck a chord on his guitar, and said, "The white hair. The eyebrows. The moustache. Silver Donald Cameron."

Yes, by God! And so it has been ever since.

Billy Joe's subsequent career landed him in the history books. He served as mayor from 1974 to 1981, at which point he announced that he'd be seeking the Progressive Conservative nomination for the provincial riding of Inverness South. I was at a local garage soon afterwards when the boys were discussing "Billy Joe comin' out for politics." After half an hour of careful political analysis, the proprietor summed up the findings.

"Billy Joe'll do a good job," he said. "He's that crooked, when he dies we're going to have to *screw* him into the ground, but he'll do a good job."

Billy Joe was duly elected, and Premier John Buchanan promptly named him minister of tourism (which Billy Joe understood), culture (which he did not), and fitness. He did a good job. He turned up at gallery openings and recitals full of questions and observations, making a concerted effort to understand this mysterious sector for which he was now responsible. I was then executive director of Centre Bras d'Or, a fledgling Cape Breton arts centre that approached his office looking for $10,000 to help us mount an international performing arts festival on rather short notice. In an ensuing meeting, I later heard, the cabinet decided to turn down the request; the timing was too short, the money wasn't in the budget, and so on.

But Billy Joe was a dedicated Cape Bretoner, and minister of culture, and he would have none of it. He shouted and roared and hammered on the table with his fist. This was a fine proposal, put forward by a group of eminently responsible citizens, including major businessmen, tourism operators, artists, and the president of the university. What they were proposing was a great idea that would do wonders for both tourism and culture in Cape Breton. The cabinet caved, and we got the grant—and the festival was a huge success, repeated every summer for many years. Ultimately it became the ancestor of today's Celtic Colours International Festival, which annually hosts dozens of concerts, dances, and other events all across Cape Breton for a week in mid-October. That's the time to visit the island, when the hillsides are ablaze with autumn colour and the air is full of music.

So Billy Joe did a good job. In April 1986, however, he abruptly resigned his cabinet post, and later that same day was charged with fraud and forgery in connection with $21,000 of irregularities in his expense account. In October he pleaded guilty to four counts of "uttering forged documents"—not forging the documents himself, but using documents forged by others.

What followed was worthy of Gilbert and Sullivan. Despite heavy pressure from the government and the media, Billy Joe refused to resign his seat in the legislature. The province was transfixed by what one commentator described as "the insouciance of MacLean." Jokes proliferated. The comedian known as General John Cabot Trail (of the Cape Breton Liberation Army) remarked that the weather had been so cold in Port Hawkesbury "that Billy Joe was going around with his hands in his own pockets."

Billy Joe's intransigence ultimately forced Buchanan to recall the legislature for a one-day session specifically to pass legislation created to unseat him. With Buchanan weeping openly in his seat, the House authorized the expulsion of an MLA convicted of an offence punishable by more than five years in jail, and also barred such a member from being nominated or elected for a five-year period after conviction.

Naturally, Billy Joe appealed. The Supreme Court upheld his expulsion, but ruled that barring him from running again infringed his constitutional rights. The Conservatives dumped him, so he ran as an independent in the by-election held to replace him—and won his seat back. I still have a souvenir of that campaign: a black corduroy baseball cap with the golden embossed motto "Billy Joe Country."

Billy Joe lost the seat in the 1988 general election, but in 1994 he ran again for mayor of Port Hawkesbury, and won. On Saturday, November 29, 2014, while I was driving back to the courthouse after a good night's sleep, just as Chief Justice Kennedy had suggested, Billy Joe MacLean was still in office. By the time he retired, in 2016, he had spent fifty years in public life.

So now I'm back in Courtroom 3, attending to another day of deliberations. The jury has returned, not with a verdict but with a written question to the court—the public hasn't heard what it is—and Justice Kennedy tells them he'll discuss the matter with counsel in their absence and then bring them back to deliver his answer. The jury dutifully files out again.

Justice Kennedy reads their question. "The jury as a whole requests a re-explanation/review of the charge of second degree murder. Please also explain direct and indirect cause once again, as well as party to an offence." He tells the lawyers that he will restate what he said yesterday and try to be as clear as he can, but that he is not going to deviate from the charge. Shane Russell has no difficulty with this. Luke Craggs thinks it may be helpful to remind the jury that the common thread through each of these is the Crown's burden of proof.

The jury returns. It takes Justice Kennedy most of an hour to review the matters that concerned them. But the heart of the issue is by now familiar. To convict James Landry, the Crown must prove, beyond a reasonable doubt, each of the five elements of second degree murder, starting with the identity of the accused, the time and place of the events, and the commission of an unlawful act by the accused. The prosecution must also prove that the unlawful act caused the death of the victim or significantly contributed to his death, and that the accused intended to cause that death.

What were the unlawful acts here? Shooting at Phillip and wounding him, and then gaffing him, dragging him through the water, tying him to an anchor, and dropping him in the sea.

"There's no question, I would suggest to you, about the fact that there were unlawful acts here," Justice Kennedy says. "The question becomes the cause of death and the intent."

At 10:25 the jury returns to its deliberations and the crowd to its vigil in the lobby.

Noon: let's grab a sandwich.

One o'clock.

Two o'clock.

Three o'clock.

John Langley pops into the lobby. After a distinguished career as a lawyer—he's a Queen's Counsel—John now spends much of his time cruising the world on Cunard ships, lecturing about the line and its founder, Sir Samuel Cunard (1787–1865). But he's still a lawyer, and he's intensely interested in this case.

"No verdict yet?" he asks.

"Nothing yet, no."

"The verdict will be manslaughter," says John. "I've seen a dozen of these things and I know exactly what's going on in that jury room. They're saying 'Yeah, it's murder—but the son of a bitch deserved it. Call it manslaughter.'"

The jury returns at 4:00.

The verdict is manslaughter.

12

MIDNIGHT SLIDER

"*Midnight Slider was the name of his boat, but it's a pretty fair name for Phillip, too. He was always out there somewhere, sliding around in the middle of the night—in the woods, on the water, you never knew where. He kept threatening people that he'd burn them out, he'd kill them—and how could you know that he wouldn't? Maybe one night he would.*"

"*I'm not saying Phillip was an angel which I knew he wasn't, but he was the type of guy that wouldn't hurt anyone. His threats were just that, threats. He never physically touched anyone, and in the local area everyone threat[en]s people . . .*" (anonymous letter)

"*It's not about stealing lobster. It's about a problem that continues and doesn't stop. People said 'murder for lobster.' I said,*

Look, if that guy had of come in my shed and took a screwdriver, okay, would you have said 'murder for screwdrivers'? Because it's not about the value of what he stole, it's about having someone that constantly is disrupting people's lives."

He's Ulysse, his wife is Yvonne, their daughter is Sara. Those are not their true names, but this is a true story. It started with a call from the guidance counsellor at the high school, who needed to talk with Ulysse and Yvonne about Sara.

"I thought my daughter probably told a teacher to go to hell or something like that," said Ulysse. "I never thought it was about anything like this." But it turned out that Sara had been walking near a convenience store with three or four other girls when Phillip—high on some drug or other, Ulysse thought—emerged from the shadows, grabbed Sara, put a knife to her throat, and tried to drag her off behind the store. Sara twisted out of his grasp and Phillip scampered away. Sara wanted to forget the whole thing, but the other girls insisted on telling the guidance counsellor. The counsellor in turn had a duty to call the police and the parents when anything serious—like attempted rape—came to his attention. It's unclear what the police did, if anything—but the police were the least of Phillip's worries.

"I had bought a new Civic," Ulysse told me. "Only three days old. Dark green. When I come back from the school that night, I said to Yvonne, 'I want to tell you one thing: if we meet Phillip you either buckle up or go for a walk because,' I said, 'when I get him, he's fucked.' And I went looking for him for four or five days, four or five nights, whatever. I'd travel at night just looking around for him. But he had kind of disappeared from the picture.

"So this one night I said, 'I'm going to look for Phillip. Come on for a drive.' She said, 'Let's go to Cape Auget.' We went to Cape Auget, and when we got back, I saw Phillip and some others. Anyway

I went by, and I stopped. Yvonne said, 'Don't bother with him, leave him alone.'"

But Ulysse was in no mood to listen. He turned the car around and drove back, taking his time, to where Phillip was standing with a bicycle.

"I said to Yvonne, 'Buckle up,'" Ulysse continued. "She said, 'Just go around him, don't get into it with him.' I said, 'I'm telling you one more time, you buckle up.' The car was just crawling along, right slow. When I got probably twenty feet from him, I tramped 'er. I hit the bike, demolished my grille, my windshield. He went over my car."

Ulysse stopped and got out of the car, and Phillip came running at him with a big rock in his hand. Ulysse punched him.

"I knocked him out first shot. He still had the rock in his hand, fumbling with the rock there when I hit him. And I grabbed him—they were pouring an abutment there—I walked with him in my arms. Walked with him in my arms. He was out. And I lifted him as far as I could and I tried to break his back on the abutment, on the cement wall that was there. And I walked away."

But Phillip came to, ran after Ulysse, and hit him from behind with a rock.

"I put my hand like this where you can feel the hot blood—like the blood was running down my back," Ulysse said. "Phillip went running across the road, and I opened the trunk of my car. I had a 12-gauge shotgun there. I put three shells in the pump and I just waited for Phillip to come across the road. He was probably disoriented too but he came running back. I thought he had a gun, but it wasn't a gun he come with, it was an axe.

"Anyway he was running, hollering like a fool across the road. He hadn't seen me sitting on the trunk. I got up and I was about from here to you. I said, 'Ahh, you're just a fuckin' coward. Go ahead and lift the axe.' And if he'd have lifted the axe, I would have blew 'is fuckin' head off. He'd of died right there."

ISLAND VOICES

"Phillip wouldn't have died if the RCMP and the Fisheries offi-cers had been doing their job. I heard there were fifty-two com-plaints called in about Phillip."

"We were on the beach with our golden Lab puppy and an out-board skiff came roaring in and slid up on the shore. The fellow driving it said he wanted to see who we were—he thought we were game wardens. He said, 'Holy fuck, that's a nice little dog. I could steal that dog. I bet I could get a hundred dollars for that dog.' He really spooked my wife. She didn't let that puppy out of her sight for about a month."

"It's something that had to be done. It's just a pity that it was those guys that had to do it."

"Whatever James and Dwayne get, the last three RCMPs and the last three Fisheries officers should get the same, because it's just as much their fault."

In 1995, to mark the fiftieth anniversary of the end of World War II, my colleague Charlie Doucet and I produced a film for Vision TV called *The Crimson Flower of Battle: A Small Island at War.* The film explores the wartime experiences of Isle Madame, which, like many small communities, sent an astonishing number of its people into battle. Many of them were just teenagers. They landed on the beaches of Sicily and Normandy, drove tanks, dodged torpedoes while sail-ing merchant ships in convoys during the Battle of the Atlantic, delivered lend-lease battleships to India and fighter planes to China, enjoyed torrid romances in London and Amsterdam, were captured behind German lines, built with their bare hands the airfield of

Hong Kong as prisoners of the Japanese. An epic story from a tiny island, *The Crimson Flower* is still played every November on Telile, the island's community TV station.

One of those veterans was Ralph Britten, an ace pilot who had shot down six German aircraft. After the liberation of Paris, just for a lark, Ralph flew his Mosquito fighter-bomber *under* the Eiffel Tower; a photo of that moment hung on his living room wall. Another vet was Arthur Terrio, who'd been an Irish Guard and then a military policeman. He met Mimi Connor, a fluently bilingual English nurse raised in Brussels and Paris, when the two were working as translators in a British military hospital full of wounded French soldiers after the evacuation of Dunkirk. They married, had two sons, and moved back to Isle Madame when the war ended. Ultimately they had ten children. In 1980 I married their oldest daughter, Lulu, who died in 1996.

After the war, veterans were given preference in competitions for federal jobs. When I arrived in Isle Madame, Arthur and Ralph were the Fisheries officers. Fearless, incorruptible, and devoted to public service, they were towering figures in the community. After facing the Wehrmacht and the Luftwaffe, they were not easily daunted by slippery poachers and surly fishermen. And the next generation was just about as tough. Peter Boudreau—Pierre la Moustache, Omer's brother, so named for training his luxuriant beard to cover his balding head—once demonstrated his strength by tying a rope to the front bumper of a delivery truck, taking the other end in his teeth and towing the truck down the wharf.

"Oh, yeah," says a respectful fisherman, "Pierre would take a flying leap off the wharf and land on the deck of a fishing boat eight feet out, and just take charge. You didn't fuck around with Pierre."

Compare that with the Fisheries officer who watched Phillip Boudreau approach a wharf in Petit de Grat with a boat full of poached lobsters.

"Aren't you going to do anything?" asked a fisherman, who later told Nash Brogan he was prepared to tell this story at Dwayne Samson's trial if need be.

"Do anything?" said the officer. "*Do anything?* I don't want my house burned down."

Early in James Landry's trial I met Fisheries Field Supervisor Norman Fougère in a restaurant parking lot in Port Hawkesbury. He knew everyone in the case very well; he'd played baseball against James and had been Phillip's coach. He felt sorry for Phillip when the boy was growing up, and had given him work doing things like cutting lawns, even when the lawns didn't need cutting.

He was well aware that he and his colleagues were widely blamed for failing to stop Phillip, but he wanted me to understand that there was a limit to what the local Fisheries officers could do. Their big patrol boat had been burned at the wharf—possibly by Phillip, nobody ever really knew—and it had never been replaced. Even filling up the gas tanks for their current Zodiac inflatable cost $500. If they burned that much fuel and got no results, they'd have to answer to upper management. They had no budget for overtime either. So you could take action only if you were pretty well certain of making an arrest within business hours. One time they staked out a boat, knowing that Phillip was aboard it; they watched it all night, and Phillip stayed aboard all night—but when they got back to the office there was a complaint that he'd been out in the night cutting traps. For Phillip, that was just fine; getting blamed for what he hadn't done simply enhanced his reputation.

Also, said Fougère, the lobstermen themselves protected Phillip. A guy would call up saying that Phillip had stolen his lobsters. In one typical instance, when Fougère checked, Phillip said, "No, so-and-so gave them to me"; when Fougère asked so-and-so, he said, "Yep, I gave them." "How many?" "Oh, I don't know, I just gave him a bunch of them." Furthermore, Phillip's brother Gerard owned a lobster pound and sold lobsters to the public, which meant he could give receipts. On one occasion when Norman was questioning him, Phillip pulled a receipt out of his pocket and said, "See what I got here, just in case you catch me?"

I had heard that Phillip had once called a Fisheries officer and threatened to burn his house down. "Aw," said the officer, "I know you, you wouldn't do that." Phillip said, "Look outside your door, on the porch"—and there was a pan of gasoline sitting there.

Norman didn't comment on that story, but he did say that sometimes during questioning Phillip would pull out his lighter and started flicking it on and off.

"Are you threatening me?" Norman once demanded.

"No, no," said Phillip, smiling serenely. "I'm just . . . flickin' my Bic."

When Pierre la Moustache was a Fisheries officer, he refused to carry a sidearm even though it was supposed to be compulsory—and even though, as Pierre tells me, he was "attacked many times on the job, a couple of times with oars and twice with a knife, you know.

"But my mouth calmed them down and I got away with it. If I'd have been a Fishery officer in 2013, then Phillip'd be in jail—or I'd be in jail—because I wouldn't have let him get away with what he was doing there. I'd have been there with a patrol boat, and I'd have went after Phillip. I'd have got him arrested, took him, seized his boat and everything, called the RCMP, 'cause what he was doing comes under the Criminal Code. And the RCMP would have come there and arrested him. It would've stopped the shooting."

Even in his mid-eighties, long retired, master only of a pleasure boat, Pierre was more than a match for Phillip. One evening he came in from a little cruise, tied up his boat—and later found Phillip cutting his fenders and mooring lines, setting his boat adrift. He collared Phillip.

"I says, 'Now I got you,'" Pierre remembers. "'You're not going to get away with it this time, mister, you're going to go back in the pen where you belong. How come you do that to me? I didn't do anything wrong to you.'"

Phillip replied that someone had told him that Pierre didn't like him. But, said Phillip, "'don't you worry. I'm going to fix that fellow. I gotta go see where that fellow parks his car. I'm going to give him four flat tires. I'm going to slash his four tires.'

"He told me that outright," Pierre says. "Oh my God, the man was unreal."

In the end, Phillip promised that if Pierre didn't call the cops, he'd replace all the gear he'd damaged. Pierre agreed.

"The next day I got up and drove down the wharf," Pierre says. "I had brand-new lines, brand-new balloons. The boat was never geared that nice—and well tied, too. In the afternoon I went back. Somebody was there scratching his head and looking at my boat. He said, 'Where did you get those balloons and where did you get those lines?' Phillip went and stole that gear from somebody else and put it in my boat."

Pierre and his partner, Irene—who calls him Peter—live across the road from Craig Landry. Craig has been a very good neighbour to them, even when he was under house arrest.

"That winter Craig wasn't allowed to cross the road, Peter was outside shovelling," Irene tells me. "Craig took a chance to come over, and he shovelled for Peter. Then he went to the RCMP and said, 'Look, I went across the road. I did something I wasn't supposed to. I'm probably going to get in shit because a lot of the people around here don't like me and don't talk to me. But this man, who's a friend, is eighty-seven years old and he was shovelling outside'— and the cop said, 'That's fine. If that man needs help, you go help him at any time.' That's what the RCMP told him.

"About Phillip," Irene continues. "We went sailing one day and I never got such a fright in my life. We were going mackerel fishing, and I said to Peter, 'What are all those things over there?' He said, 'Those are all Phillip's traps that he steals from everybody and sets them after the season.'

"So I take the binoculars and I look—and when I looked I froze. There he is, Phillip, with his gun pointed right to our fucking boat. I guess he must've thought Peter was going to go over there. I got so scared I started to cry. I said to Peter, 'Get the fuck out of here, he's going to shoot us!' I don't think I went in the boat after that."

"Now I knew that was his traps, see?" says Pierre. "But anybody that would go there after the season and cut his traps, he wouldn't keep living in Petit de Grat. Phillip'd clean him. And he'd tell him to his face."

Guy Landry tells a similar story. He was coming into Petit de Grat one day in his fishing boat and saw five illegal traps that he knew were Phillip's. Someone aboard wanted to take some action—lift the traps, cut the buoys, something like that—and Guy said "No, you never know where Phillip is. Leave them be." Phillip came up to Guy afterwards and said, "Good thing you didn't fuck with my traps just then. If you had, I'd have shot you. I had a .22 loaded in the bow of the boat."

ISLAND VOICES

"The thing about Phillip is, you never knew where he'd strike next."

"If you can look at a guy you shot at, someone you know, that's begging for his life, and then go ahead and kill him, I say you got no heart, you got no soul."

"I don't care what anybody says, those guys were not murderers. They're not murderers, that's my opinion. I cried, I actually cried when they sent James to jail 'cause that is one of the nicest men I have ever met."

Nicole Gionet belongs to a very large family in Isle Madame, and has survived—by her account—an abusive marriage and a tempestuous range of family relationships. She started a blog called *Nikky's Corner: To Stop the Cycle of Domestic Abuse and Violence*, in which she slashed and skewered a wide range of neighbours and family members, generally under pseudonyms: Rambo, NoBalls, Feather Duster, Garbage Man. Members of the family were angry, hurt, and embarrassed—and sufficiently troubled that they called in Nova Scotia's CyberScan unit to see whether they could invoke the province's new anti-cyberbullying law to make her stop.

In the meantime, Nikky continued blogging, releasing more than two hundred posts by the end of 2018. One of the names she didn't disguise was Phillip Boudreau. She wrote a disturbing blog post about being attacked by a companion of Phillip's and then being raped by Phillip himself. There are people in her family who say she misconstrued the whole incident, that it didn't happen this way at all. But in a chilling post called "Another Night from Hell," she gives a graphic account of the event.

"I have the right to say no," she wrote. "I did say no in French as Buster shoved me down my hallway to my bedroom. I tried to say no, I tried to push him off. He kept telling me 'come on' as he held my shoulders down on my mattress and forced my legs apart with his. I remember that he couldn't cum and when he rolled over I jumped up and grabbed something to cover myself."

She went out to her living room, where she found Phillip going through her photo albums.

"When he sees me, he whips me around like a dishcloth and before I know it he has me down the hall, in my bedroom. Phillip talked a lot while he raped me." She vividly remembered "those evil eyes of Phillip looking back at me," and also "their scent, that smell of sweat. The sound of Phillip's voice, the pitch in his laugh when he'd make fun of how I was getting what I deserved."

Eventually, a taxi picked up the two men, and Nikky waited until it drove away. Then she came out to the kitchen "and found a note on the table thanking me for the best night he ever had. All I want at that moment is to die. Please oh please god, take me!" She desperately wanted to make sure her family didn't find out, "but as fast as they whipped out of my driveway, Midnight Ryder had to go brag about his latest catch."

"Phillip is dead now," she concluded. "I didn't want him to die the way he did, but he did make a lot of people hate him."

"And this is Nikky's Corner."

Nikky and Sara weren't the only ones Phillip attacked. "Sylvia Breau" is a false name, but everything else in her story is true.

In 1990, Sylvia was twenty-two. She had a communication disability that made it difficult for her to speak, particularly to those outside her family, and she tended to be reclusive. So when her parents and two sisters went to Port Hawkesbury on December 7 to do some Christmas shopping, Sylvia stayed home to watch movies by herself. The door was locked.

When the family returned, they found the door splintered. Phillip had broken in and stolen a hunting rifle. Over the next couple of days Sylvia told the full story to her sister, who told it to their father, who called the RCMP. Phillip hadn't merely broken in and stolen the gun: he had also raped Sylvia. Staff Sergeant Daniel Parent came to investigate, but by then two days had passed.

"We investigated the scene and found no physical evidence," Parent recalls now. "And I had difficulty communicating. I would get dribs and drabs from the sister but not from the victim. So, try to make a case out of that. But we got the psychologist to assess the victim and we also got some other people—a teacher, for one.

"Talking to the teacher reinforced my belief in the victim, that she was being truthful. So we eventually decided to go to court.

The Crown believed her, the teacher believed her, the psychologist believed her, we all did." In court, however, things did not go well. Sylvia, who couldn't appear in open court, testified through her sister via a TV link from an adjoining room. In the end, says Parent, "she failed to tell us what did happen to her. There was no way that the judge could make any finding."

But there was a second charge—break and enter with intent to commit an indictable offence—and there was solid evidence for that: Sylvia's father's gun had turned up in Phillip's brother's woodpile. On that charge the judge was able to put Phillip away for two and a half years. As Parent says, "We got rid of Phillip for a while, anyway."

After the trial, said Sylvia's sister, "I honestly never saw Phillip again. I moved to Halifax and never lived in Petit de Grat again. I was angry for a lot of years. I couldn't look at Sylvia without tearing up. She was never the same. And my mom . . . it broke her."

Aside from that rape case, says Daniel Parent, "I've never known Phillip to be actually violent. It was always by way of threats." For Parent, though, threats are worse than an assault. "So I give you a punch in the mouth? After fifteen minutes it's over." But a threat works on your mind; you never know what's going to happen. You can never relax. For Parent, a threat carries "much more weight than the actual violence."

Phillip actually threatened Parent himself—right in the police station.

"I was interviewing him on break and enters, and he changed the topic and says, 'Your daughter is pretty good looking. I met her last weekend at so-and-so's house and I think I'm going to meet her again.' It was a threat—not a direct threat but a veiled one. At that time I stopped the interview. I was going to strangle the bastard, I'm telling you. That was an indirect threat he made to me, and I can just picture him doing that to people from the area. It wasn't clean, it wasn't open, but it was a threat that he would come back at some point, harm your family, burn your property, or do whatever. It's like he has access and can do it. But he didn't actually say he was going to do anything."

I suggested to Parent that one of the key factors in this whole tragedy was Phillip's repeated threats that he would burn down Dwayne's and Carla's house with their twin eight-year-old daughters inside it. Those threats never came out in public, largely because the courts refused to hear about the long and maddening background between Phillip and his killers. This refusal is based on the notion that "we can't convict a dead man of crimes he was never charged with." Within the narrow confines of the judicial process, that's perfectly true—but it also means you fundamentally don't understand the events you're judging. That's why the glib phrase "murder for lobsters" gained such currency. Poaching was the only motivation that the courts would allow themselves to hear about.

Phillip's history with the *Twin Maggies'* crew wouldn't necessarily have served the defence well either; it would have been a mitigating factor, but it would also have provided a credible motivation for murder. Better to be misunderstood and convicted of manslaughter than correctly understood and sentenced for murder.

But Phillip's threats against James's grandchildren, Dwayne's children, were well known in the community. I heard from at least four separate sources that he had actually tried to burn down the house, though I was never able to confirm it. It's also well known that the couple repeatedly complained to the police about Phillip's threats.

"Oh, he threatened James and Dwayne's kids before he died," said Pierre la Moustache. "They were all threatened, everybody." I told Edgar Samson at Premium Seafoods that I had heard Phillip had waved a knife at James and said he was going to burn down the house with his two grandchildren in it.

"Yes, absolutely," said Edgar. "James told me that himself."

Dwayne and James would have had to assess whether Phillip's threats could safely be ignored, and whether they were willing to gamble with the lives of their children—and if not, what could be done about it. They clearly didn't set out to murder Phillip that morning—but in the heat of a largely unexpected confrontation, with the two of them wound up as taut as fiddle strings, their frustration and fury simply boiled over.

It wasn't planned, said Ronnie LeBlanc, Dwayne's brother-in-law, the man who presented the petition at Dwayne's bail hearing. "If it was planned, it was the worst-laid plan in the history of planning—having something happen in broad daylight in the middle of the harbour in Petit de Grat where all the old-time fishermen are sitting in their window with binoculars watching the boats come and go every day. They might as well have videotaped whatever happened. No, it definitely was something that just got out of hand."

After decades of investigating crimes, Daniel Parent understands.

"It could happen to anyone; enough is enough," he said, reflecting on Phillip's threats to his own daughter. "I would have felt that way. 'You would not threaten me forever, buddy.' I couldn't stand for it. 'I don't need this, you bastard, and I'm going to get you.'"

Possibly the best summary came from Lionel Boudreau, an electrician who lives in Petit de Grat: "If you've got a fellow in front of you waving a knife and saying 'I'm gonna rape your daughter and I'm gonna rape your wife, and then I'm gonna burn your house down—and what're you gonna do about it?,' well, if it was me, and I was standing there with a gun, I'd have thought, 'Well, maybe I'm gonna go to jail for a really long time—but you're *not* going to do that.'"

After Phillip disappeared, his boyhood friend Marcel Heudes spent days on the water helping in the fruitless search for his body—the same Marcel who'd given Phillip his only real break in recent years, flying him to Calgary in 2008, giving him a job and a place to live. By 2013, though, both Marcel and Phillip were living in Petit de

Grat again. Why hadn't they stayed in Calgary, where things had been working out well?

Phillip's mother had fallen ill, so Marcel had bought him a ticket home. And although Phillip later returned to Calgary, he remained worried about his mother. He wasn't alone in this; Kim Heudes also missed her mother and wanted to go home. So in 2010 the Heudes family moved home to Petit de Grat, taking their construction company with them. Phillip moved home too.

Back in Petit de Grat, Phillip worked with Marcel again for a time—but, said Marcel, "everybody was telling me, 'If you don't get rid of Phillip, you're not going to get another job around here. Nobody wants a thief on your crew.' I said, 'What the fuck? He's working now, he's not stealing. I'm paying him per week and you guys are still saying if I don't leave him go then I'm not going to get jobs. What kind of fucking community is this? What are you guys doing?'

"But in the end that's what happened. He was staying out of trouble, and he worked with me until May 2013. But then I thought, 'I better leave Phillip go, 'cause I'm not getting the work just 'cause of Phillip.' He wanted to go back to Alberta, and I told him, 'Let me see what I can do, see if my brother can get you a job off the island.' Gilles had him another job, too. He would've went back but it was a week too late. It was just before lobster season, and in June he got killed.

"If I would've kept him, it wouldn't have happened. If I would've kept him going he'd still be alive."

13

COURTROOM 3:
SENTENCING

JANUARY 29, 2015

TWO MONTHS AFTER THE VERDICT, the familiar cast reconvenes: Chief Justice Kennedy presiding, Shane Russell and Steve Drake for the prosecution, Luke Craggs for the defence, James Landry watching quietly as his fate is debated. What should James Landry's sentence be?

The Crown goes first. The difference between murder and manslaughter, Shane Russell notes, is the specific intent to murder, and the jury evidently didn't find that James had that intent. Since the jury delivered its verdict without giving reasons, it will be up to the judge to determine what the actual facts are. The Crown contends that there is extensive and logical evidence that the shooting, the repeated ramming, and the gaffing did occur, that Phillip died in the water, and that the anchor was used to dispose of the body as part of an attempted cover-up. The Crown believes that these are the facts, and that these actions amounted to "vicious manslaughter, a continued series of assaults" and "an indignity to the body."

So what should the sentence be? Russell reviews two leading cases in Nova Scotia. In both, the court found that the primary consideration is to protect the public, either by deterring others from similar actions or by reforming the convicted killer, or both. The sentence needs to send a message that "vigilante justice is never justified." James's positive pre-sentence report notes that he is a productive and respected citizen with no criminal record; on the other hand, he really hasn't accepted responsibility for killing Phillip, and he attempts to justify what he did, arguing that the authorities had failed to hold Phillip accountable.

No matter, says Russell. The law is quite clear that citizens cannot take the law into their own hands. Phillip Boudreau had some issues, but he was a person with friends and a loving family, and he was "in no way deserving of the barbaric circumstances in which he died."

Manslaughter involves a sliding scale of sentencing based on "moral blameworthiness," with the lightest sentences for actions that are little more than accidents and the heaviest sentences for actions that are "near murder." The Crown sees James as "morally blameworthy in a high degree." Yes, he's an elderly man with a clean record—but he committed a protracted assault involving a series of violent acts; he used a firearm; he had opportunities to back off and cool down, but he didn't. As for his intent and motivation, James said he wanted to kill Phillip, destroy him, get rid of him, cream him. He made efforts to thwart the investigation, notably by leading investigators to the wrong gun. His actions tore at the fabric of the community.

Russell concludes that James should receive a sentence in the vicinity of fifteen years with credit for the time he's already served. He should also provide a DNA sample and be barred for life from owning or using firearms. Furthermore, he should be ineligible for parole until he has served at least half of this sentence.

Phillip's sister, Margaret Rose, reads a compelling and eloquent victim impact statement. Phillip's family can see from their home the spot where he died, "discarded as 'old bait.'" They can see the beach where he used to walk his dog, and because the body has never been found, they have no closure. She directly addresses James, an old family friend who shattered the lives of Phillip's family and his own. The death has isolated Phillip's parents, aged seventy and eighty-eight, from the community. "To be present in court," she says, "and hear about the last moments of my brother's life, was cruel, appalling, frightening, and a damn nightmare." But, she says, "we've learned to accept what is, let go of what was, and have faith in what will be."

Speaking for the defence, Luke Craggs reminds Chief Justice Kennedy of his often-expressed high opinion of the jury. In its verdict, Craggs says, the jury "spoke loud and clear. Listening to the Crown's submission, I wonder whether the Crown heard what the jury said." The Crown's submission is just a repetition of their theory of the murder. "They're asking you to believe everything that Craig Landry said, and they're asking you to accept facts which clearly the jury did not."

Craig and James agree on a great deal, Craggs says, but their accounts diverge after the ramming. Craig's account is much more colourful. The jury accepted the testimony that was shared, but "did not accept the uncorroborated, unconfirmed, and frankly fanciful testimony that involved the gaffing or the anchoring. Had the jury accepted that testimony, then they would have convicted James Landry of murder—but they didn't."

The unlawful acts that could have led the jury to a verdict of manslaughter include firing the rifle and encouraging Dwayne Samson to run Phillip over. The ballistic evidence shows that four shots were fired, none of which seemed to have hit Phillip. All four penetrated the boat between the waterline and the rail; if one had hit Phillip it would likely have been in the lower leg, but his boots showed no bullet hole. In running over Phillip's boat, Dwayne would have committed an assault with a weapon, and in abetting that act, James would have committed another offence himself.

Pre-sentence reports, Craggs notes, often describe real criminals with terrible histories; reading them, you aren't surprised that the guy eventually killed someone. James's report, however, describes an individual who's been a productive member of his community for his entire life. He has the support of his family, who are hard-working, law-abiding people. The report includes positive comments on how well he's been doing in custody, including commentary from a supervisor at the correctional centre and from his teacher; James is a model prisoner who's been working in the kitchen and has been upgrading his education while in jail. The report is peppered with positive comments from James's previous employers and business connections.

However, says Craggs, the Crown still thinks this is murder, and is ignoring the jury's findings. But it's important not to confuse anger with intent. Other recent cases of manslaughter suggest a sentence of about seven years, and that's what the defence is proposing.

It occurs to me that the jury may have believed Craig and yet also considered the consequences of their verdict—despite Justice Kennedy's firm caution that consequences "are for me or for the courts." But the courts have limited authority over a murder sentence; the mandatory minimum sentence for second degree murder is life in prison with no parole for at least ten years and possibly twenty-five. And James was sixty-seven. As a result of "one very bad day," as Justice Kennedy put it, an otherwise productive citizen could spend every remaining day of his life behind bars. That might be sound law, but would it be justice? However it arrived at its verdict, the jury seems to have found a way to balance condemnation of James's actions with recognition of his character.

So what does Chief Justice Kennedy decide?

On the facts, he accepts Her Majesty's Story—Craig Landry's story—almost completely. He accepts that James caused Phillip's death or significantly contributed to it. He finds that James fired four shots, one of which hit Phillip; that James participated in the ramming and the attempt to tow Phillip's boat; and that James also repeatedly gaffed and towed Phillip before tying him to an anchor and sinking his body. He repeats even such details as Phillip's nakedness from the waist down when the *Twin Maggies* finally stopped.

Recognizing that the protection of the public is a major objective in sentencing, His Lordship observes that the public is best protected by citizens' respect for the rule of law. He also notes that moral blameworthiness is a key consideration, declaring that this particular homicide is on the "near-murder" end of the manslaughter spectrum. He understands that Phillip's death has had powerful effects on the families involved, and that the manner of his death will have impacts on the community for decades. He also accepts, implicitly, that "murder for lobster" is what the case is all about; he says that there are six hundred ways that James could have addressed the loss of his lobsters, and that most observers would consider that, when Phillip was in the water pleading for his life, James had certainly succeeded in scaring him.

On the other hand, James is sixty-seven, has no criminal record, and has been an exemplary prisoner, with little risk of reoffending. He'd like to fish again, "but that's not likely to happen." His Lordship will order that James give a DNA sample and be prohibited from using or possessing firearms or ammunition. He will leave the issue of parole in the hands of the parole board, and will award James 1.5 days' of credit for each day he's already served. Since James has been incarcerated for 601 days, that's a reduction of 901 days in his sentence.

And the sentence?

"Considering the moral blameworthiness of Joseph James Landry's acts, of the terrible series of assaults on Phillip Boudreau over a considerable time frame when he was vulnerable and defenceless, firstly in a small boat and then in the water, considering the message that I believe must be delivered to those who would take the law into their own hands—considering all of those factors, I sentence Joseph James Landry, on the charge of manslaughter, to a period of fourteen years in a federal institution."

ISLAND VOICES

"How much did that trial cost? Couldn't you have hired another cop for a lot less than that?"

"I don't care what anybody says, those guys were not murderers. They're not murderers, that's my opinion. I cried, I actually cried when they sent James to jail 'cause that is one of the nicest men I have ever met."

"People in Ontario think of lobster as luxury. But here lobster was always a poor man's food. A fisherman'll give you lobsters if he knows you're hungry. Nobody kills somebody for a couple of lobsters."

"There's only so much the cops and the Department of Fisheries can do, okay, I know that. But couldn't they have picked Phillip up just before the lobster season on some charge or other and kept him out of circulation just until the season was over? Lots of things they could have charged him with."

James will appeal his sentence, without success. But the case against James was the Crown's strongest case; with this outcome, there's no chance that Dwayne can now be convicted of murder, and even less chance that Carla can be convicted of anything. A few weeks later I get a phone call. There's been a deal. Dwayne will plead guilty to manslaughter and the charges against Carla will be dropped; the *Twin Maggies* will be released to her.

On May 18, 2015, Dwayne enters his plea and is released on bail to his own home in D'Escousse until his sentencing hearing, scheduled for August but later postponed to September. On June 15, charges against Carla are dismissed after Steve Drake tells Justice Simon MacDonald that the Crown has "no realistic prospect of conviction." Nash Brogan moves for dismissal, Justice MacDonald grants it, and Carla Samson turns around and walks out of the courtroom without a word.

On September 11, Craig Landry is sentenced to two years' probation. Since he was initially charged with second degree murder, Joel Pink has done a fine job for him.

The only remaining matter before the courts is Dwayne's sentencing. And so, on September 21, the parties assemble in the courtroom: Shane Russell and Steve Drake for the Crown, and Nash Brogan and his colleague T.J. McKeough for the defence, Mr. Justice Simon MacDonald presiding. The two sides have composed an agreed statement of facts that, once again, is basically Her Majesty's Story, though it doesn't include sinking the body with the anchor.

T.J. McKeough calls Carla Samson to the stand. This will be the only time Carla ever speaks at length and in public. Under McKeough's questioning, she recounts how her father asked her in 2005 if she'd be interested in the licence, because the Fisheries department's paperwork was becoming too demanding for him. She took over the licence in 2007. At first James remained as captain, but after she and Dwayne bought *Twin Maggies* in 2012, Dwayne became the captain. She wasn't fishing in 2013; she had decided to stay ashore "because of the stress that was happening on the water with Phillip Boudreau at that time." She had been aware of Phillip for many years, but had dealings with him only after she started fishing. He would threaten them on the water, cut their traps, and—

—Wait a minute. Shane Russell objects: McKeough is alleging criminal activity on the part of a man who is not here, who is not alive, and who has never been charged in this connection. None of this is contained in the agreed statement of facts, though it could have been raised when the statement was being prepared. The Crown has no way of responding to these allegations; since they're outside the statement of facts, they're irrelevant. McKeough should not be allowed outside "the four corners" of the agreed statement of facts.

Brogan rises to say that the history between Phillip and the Samsons goes right to the issue of blameworthiness. In all the many cases of manslaughter that the Crown described in its brief on sentencing, there is not a single one where the victim brought on the confrontation or acted as the catalyst for the confrontation. The typical victim did nothing to provoke the fatal attacks, which resulted from bungled robberies, home invasions, sour drug deals, and the like. But in this case, Phillip's activities set the incident in motion—

Justice MacDonald isn't buying it. Carla can talk about the impact of having her traps cut, but that's all.

So she does, describing not only the way a buoy line can be cut but also how the four sides of the trap itself can be cut so as to destroy the trap. Then you have to replace the traps, which cost about $100 each, and buy additional Fisheries Department tags for the new traps. In addition, during the four or five days you don't have those traps in the water, you're losing lobster catches averaging about five pounds per trap per day. Every year she would lose twenty to twenty-five traps, representing a loss of $5000 to $6000. The situation had been getting worse—and the only year she didn't lose traps was a year when Phillip Boudreau was in prison. Later, in cross-examination, Steve Drake suggests that although she knows the traps were cut, she doesn't actually know who cut them—to which she replies, "Phillip Boudreau told me he cut them."

She confirms that she is the sole owner of the lobster licence, and that she did indeed continue to fish the licence for the two seasons that Dwayne was away in Halifax. After Phillip's death, her traps were never cut. Because the *Twin Maggies* had been impounded as an alleged murder weapon, she used the much smaller boat that had originally been her father's. Just twenty-eight feet long, it was named *T-Buddy*, which was James's genial salutation to people he knew: "How you doin', T-buddy?" In Acadia, the short form for *petit* (little) is *ti*, so "ti-buddy" is "little buddy."

Carla herself is petite, but she's a very capable captain. On May 10, 2014—almost a year after Phillip Boudreau's death—*T-Buddy* and Carla's crew of three were plunging through heavy seas off Petit de Grat, not far from Mackerel Cove. The surface of the water was frothing with whitecaps piled up by a thirty-five-knot gale from the southwest. Looking far out into Chedabucto Bay, Carla spotted a grey rock where no rock had been before. As she drew closer, she saw something waving.

She altered course and headed for the unknown object. Soon she could make out what it was—a grey Zodiac inflatable boat, heaving sluggishly in the waves and filled with water. Manoeuvring alongside it, she saw two men in the swamped boat. One of them was a ghastly greenish white colour, barely conscious, clearly in an advanced stage of hypothermia.

While she held the *T-Buddy* up against the boat, her crew pulled the two men aboard and got a tow line on the Zodiac. With the inflatable boat wallowing heavily behind, *T-Buddy* made its slow way towards the Premium Seafoods wharf in Arichat. The crew gave what comfort they could to the men, who turned out to be divers, one of them a heavily accented European. They had gone out from Canso, on the mainland side of the bay, and their engine had failed, leaving them adrift.

Carla called ahead, and so when they finally arrived at the wharf an ambulance was waiting along with an RCMP cruiser. The two divers were taken to hospital, where the hypothermic one was put on an intravenous solution. After six hours they were released, not much the worse for what had clearly been a very close call.

"Funny thing," said the man who told me the story, "one of the Mounties said the skipper should get an award for rescuing those fellers, but then he found out who she was, and the story never even made the papers. Bad news travels fast, good news not so much."

After her own arrest, Carla was barred from any communication with Dwayne at all for seven months, and then for another six months she could talk with him only by phone. The impact on their twin girls, now ten, had been disturbing. To speak on the phone to their father, they had to go to their grandparents' home down the road. They became very worried about divorce or separation, and very concerned about security without their father at home. They cried at night for months, and "couldn't understand why I couldn't speak to Dwayne and why Dwayne couldn't speak to me." When Carla had to send them off to Halifax to visit their father, "I would have to put them in the car, screaming, because they were afraid I wouldn't be there when they got back, because of my arrest in front of them on June 7." The children, she says, "have a lot of separation anxiety over this." Getting Dwayne back after his guilty plea in May and then realizing they were about to lose him again after sentencing had been particularly painful.

"Last night they never slept a wink," she reports. "They cried all night because they knew their father was leaving."

When asked about her involvement in her community, she mentions that she teaches religious education to students in grades one to three in the church, and that she is vice-president of the Richmond County Inshore Fishermen's Association and the recognized agent for a group of crab fishermen. Carla is also a member of several local organizations, including the D'Escousse Civic Improvement Society, which operates the community hall. The community has been very supportive.

"I'm very grateful for all the support we've received," she says. "Prayers, candles, phone calls, visits, we've had quite a bit of support." And Dwayne, who's been living at home since his guilty plea in May, has been welcomed back into the community.

Next up is Dr. Peter Scott Theriault, forensic psychiatrist and associate professor at Dalhousie University. He's been asked by the defence to assess whether Dwayne Samson has a mental disorder, to comment on his mental state at the time of the offence, and to give an opinion about whether Dwayne is a risk to commit violent crimes again. Having interviewed Dwayne for two and a half hours, Dr. Theriault says that he's a low risk to reoffend, that he isn't suffering from a mental disorder, and that at the time of the attack he was apparently in a state of panic, overwhelmed by the situation and in a "mild dissociative state," feeling he was observing the situation from above. He doesn't doubt Dwayne's description of his state of mind, since it's consistent with what is known about responses to extreme stress. In his view, Dwayne wasn't truly the captain of the boat; the events were driven mainly by James Landry, and Dwayne was largely following James's lead. After the killing, for example, Dwayne felt sick and wanted to go home but James wanted to continue fishing, so that's what they did.

Steve Drake, who has spent many hours in a motel room studying Dr. Theriault's report, goes after him like a beagle running down a rabbit. The only information you had was information you got from Dwayne Samson, right? You interviewed him two years and twenty days after the event. How accurate are his memories? Are the characteristics of a state of panic difficult to discover? Can't you get that information from Google? Isn't it possible that Dwayne made up his account of his symptoms? You say he has no record of panic attacks either before or after the event, and that he displayed those symptoms for only a few moments while Phillip Boudreau was being killed. Really? Didn't he direct Craig to get the gun and load it? Didn't he ask James if he was going to shoot? Wasn't he driving the boat throughout? Was Dwayne capable of understanding what he was doing? Was he capable of understanding that he had options?

"Well, that's where things become a little more complicated," says Theriault. The question really is, Could his emotional state have caused him to have errors in judgment? Maybe: "higher-level critical thinking can become impaired in states of extreme stress, as the individual's primary motive is to escape or end the conflict in some fashion."

Drake gets Theriault to read out a passage from his report: "Mr. Samson reports that after the weapon was fired into the boat, striking Mr. Boudreau, that 'I went into a state of panic.' When asked to describe this, Mr. Samson described a state of autonomic hyperarousal with typical symptoms seen in such a state, such as profuse sweating, dry mouth, shakiness, palpitations, increased heart rate, visual changes—'everything was red'—and mild dissociative symptoms described by Mr. Samson 'like I was above and looking down' on the scene as the events transpired. He indicates that everything seemed to be happening so fast that it was like a 'whirlwind' and that he had no time to think."

Drake comments that Dwayne "didn't report these symptoms to anyone until the date of this assessment. Any red flags during your assessment that he might have been making this up?" Was there any corroborating evidence from anyone else? Theriault responds that mental states are internal and subjective and wouldn't necessarily be visible to others—and that the others weren't primarily attending to Dwayne's mental state anyway.

After lunch, both sides confirm that they are satisfied with Dwayne's pre-sentence report. Maggie Boudreau reads her victim impact statement. It's the same one she read at James's sentencing, but it seems to affect her even more this second time; her voice breaks, and she's on the verge of tears.

In his final argument, Shane Russell relies heavily on the fourteen-year sentence handed down to James Landry, noting Chief Justice Kennedy's condemnation of "vigilante justice" and his stress on respect for the rule of law, which is "absolutely basically necessary to our society. If each of us were able to exercise revenge and retribution as we alone determine our lives, it would be chaos, characterized by fear and brutality. This would be Animal Kingdom." Dwayne was just as responsible as James; the only mitigating factors are his remorse and his guilty plea. He could have stopped the attack. He had "time to call the police to seek out justice in a proper fashion." The Crown calls for a sentence of twelve years.

Nash Brogan responds that there have been two previous sentences coming out of Phillip Boudreau's death. One is fourteen years in prison, but the other—which Brogan calls "fit and proper"—is two years' probation. Craig Landry was also a party to the killing. How can the Crown accept probation for Craig and ask twelve years for Dwayne?

Brogan stresses three main points. First, the events started with Phillip, and quickly got out of control. But in no other case cited in this hearing did the victim's activities precipitate the conflict. Second, in the other cases, the killers had long criminal records, drugs and alcohol were involved, the victims were particularly vulnerable, and the attacks often involved planning. This conflict has none of those features. The Crown's own chosen cases undermine the Crown's argument. Third, these are decent, God-fearing people who've led blameless lives and have deep and demonstrated community support. Dwayne has been under house arrest for 772 days with absolutely no incidents, and he is "totally remorseful." An appropriate sentence might be six to eight years.

And at that, the court adjourns for the day.

The next morning, Justice MacDonald directs Dwayne to stand and asks if he has anything to say.

"My Lord," Dwayne responds, "I'd like to say I'm sorry for the pain and suffering I caused Phillip Boudreau and his family and his friends and my family and my friends, and every day I live with regret that this incident happened."

Justice MacDonald reviews the arguments on both sides. He places heavy weight on Maggie Boudreau's statement and on the "horrific" manner of Phillip's death. He is satisfied that James Landry was the driving force in the events, but concludes that Dwayne played a significant role by calling for the rifle and asking James if he was going to shoot. He "should have known that there was animosity and dislike between the people on his boat and Mr. Boudreau," and he "could have taken himself out of the equation." Justice MacDonald agrees with Chief Justice Kennedy's comments in the Landry sentence about the importance of the rule of law in society, and he quotes with approval the observation of Justice Ron Pugsley in *R. v. G.A.M.* (1996): "The sentence imposed by the court should reflect society's recognition of the unique gift of life, and the seriousness with which we view the actions of those who trivialize that gift by taking it from another."

Dwayne will provide a DNA sample, and is barred from owning or using firearms. He is sentenced to "ten years in jail, less credit for time served."

Before passing sentence, Justice MacDonald remarks that he "does not consider trap cutting to be provocation." He's quite right—and Dwayne Samson would probably agree with him. But in this whole marathon journey through the courts, nobody has been able to speak about the genuine provocations, about the deeper dilemma that underlies the whole Phillip Boudreau affair. Nobody has really talked about lethal threats, and how a person might handle them.

Nobody has really talked about how to deal with a man like Phillip Boudreau.

14

THE NATURE OF THE LAW

THE BOYS WERE PERHAPS twelve or thirteen years old. Lulu
and I were Mark's parents. Curtis's parents were Gordie and Jeanette
Ellis, our good friends and next-door neighbours. Jeanette was a
nurse. Gordie had been a truck driver and a hard-rock miner, but
he spent much of his life at the power-generating station in Port
Hawkesbury. They were one of the happiest couples we'd ever met.

Normally our two sons got along fine, but somehow they had
gotten into a scrap, and the village kids were putting the word around
that the two of them were going to have a big fight that everyone
should come and watch. I didn't hear about any of this, but Gordie
did. He collared the two boys, stuffed them into the cab of his little
4x4 pickup truck, and drove them out the Doyle Road, an almost-
abandoned dirt track running through the woods from D'Escousse
in the general direction of Rocky Bay. A mile or two into the bush,
he stopped the truck.

"I can't stop you from fighting," he said. "You guys have a beef
and you need to fight it out, okay. But you're gonna do it here, just

the two of you, without a crowd egging you on. Goodbye." And he turned his truck around and left them there.

As I recall Mark's account of it, he and Curtis looked at each other, tried to remember what they were so angry about, laughed, shrugged, and had a long and very pleasant walk home.

This is how you deal with conflict. This is how you teach your kids to deal with conflict.

In the British common-law tradition, that event would not count as law-making. Common law is a bit like an unchanging yardstick against which people and events are measured. If the boys had actually fought, the police might have been called and charges might have been laid—assault, mischief, uttering threats, who knows? The boys could have ended up in juvenile court and become entangled in the elaborate apparatus of juvenile supervision. Who can tell where that path might have led?

There are other legal traditions, however, and some of the most sophisticated and sensitive ones belong to the First Nations. In an Indigenous tradition, Gordie's intervention could be the kind of event that actually generates law. As the great Anishinaabe legal scholar John Borrows explains, law is "what provides guidance for people in their lives," and it is found in "the things that deserve respect in the world. So, if you see a good set of behaviours from elders, you would find law emanating from those people, because they are worthy of respect, because they have demonstrated that worthiness through their actions, the way they have talked and they've lived."

Furthermore, the sources of Indigenous law are not only human.

"If you see a bird and the way that that bird takes care of its young, and you recognize in that interaction there is something that you should be taking into your life," says Borrows, "you would find law in that source as well. So, you make a judgment about whether or not what you're seeing around you is worthy of emulating, is worthy of taking guidance from."

Looking back on the whole story of Phillip Boudreau's death—the background, the confrontation, the long legal journey, the community's reaction—one can discern two distinct systems of law. One is the formal system of prosecutors and juries and courthouses. The other one, the informal community system, is very like the Indigenous system, rooted in a community's daily life, its history, and its most cherished values. Gordie Ellis's intervention belongs to that tradition of what's sometimes called "vernacular justice." In the story of Phillip Boudreau, both systems failed—but the failure of the community system has caused its members anguish and self-criticism. The formal system, by contrast, barely even suspects that it failed.

The great irony of the Boudreau story is that the formal judicial system constantly scolded the accused for "taking the law into their own hands" without ever recognizing that the accused had repeatedly and unsuccessfully tried to persuade the authorities to deal with Phillip. The root causes of the tragedy include a systemic failure of the legal system itself.

Go back to May 2013. Phillip Boudreau is on the loose during the lobster season. Phillip is a tragic figure, and I mean that literally. On his small local stage, he is a mini-Macbeth: energetic, clever, and addicted to power, caught up in a prolonged and escalating sequence of criminal acts against innocent people, acts that his community ultimately cannot tolerate. The story moves implacably towards an explosion of violence that results in his death. Phillip has many sympathetic qualities—he's inventive, funny, courageous, proud—but, as a neighbour said, "not everything between his ears seems to be screwed down right tight," and it's hard to believe that his life can end well.

Now look at the situation from the perspective of the Samson-Landry family. James is industrious, capable, passionate, volatile—and intimidated by the bureaucratic processes that have transformed his traditional world. Carla and Dwayne are the straightest of straight arrows—law-abiding, churchgoing, hardworking parents. They are playing by all the rules and yet they are being bullied, robbed, vandalized, and threatened by an outlaw who totally ignores those rules and often gets away with it.

The outlaw is particularly hostile to Carla. Nobody quite knows why. Some sources suggest that she's fishing in territory that Phillip's brother Gerard either claims or covets, but it seems more personal than that. Other observers believe he's offended by the fact that she's a woman and a very successful fisher—and that he can't intimidate her. She doesn't fight back, but she won't back down. He's already cut a couple dozen of her traps, and now he's telling Craig Landry at the Corner Bridge store that he's going to cut her traps along the entire shoreline of Cape Auget. Worst of all, he's been threatening to burn down her house with her two children in it. The whole situation has become so tense that Carla has actually quit fishing. This season she's hired Craig to take her place, and she's staying ashore.

She has gone to the police and the Fisheries officials to complain, but the only result is that Phillip—who knows she has complained—is even more hostile. The police can't do very much. To start with, the Isle Madame detachment in Arichat is staffed by three officers, sometimes only two. Often they can't even answer the phone; incoming calls are patched through to Sydney, 125 kilometres away, and passed on to Arichat the next day. And in any case, how much can the police do about a threat? Listen to Thilmond Landry, who was sitting in his living room one day when the police arrived:

"The cop says to me, 'Get away from the window.' I said, 'Get away from the window?' I said, 'Buddy, I'm home here. What are you talking about?' He said, 'We had nine complaints that Phillip went to homes, looking for a gun to shoot you.' I said, 'Is that so.' He said, 'Yeah.' 'Well,' I said, 'if Phillip is going to shoot me, you do your job. Go look for him and arrest him.'

"Do you know what he said? I'm going to tell you what he said. 'We can't arrest him before he shoots you.' You know what I said? 'What the fuck are you doing here? Get out of my house.' And I said a lot more than that."

The police are understaffed and overloaded, and they can't mount a twenty-four-hour guard over someone who's threatened. They can't arrest Phillip pre-emptively, and if they charge him with uttering threats, he'll eventually be sentenced to five months, as he was in 2007, or three months (2009), or two months (2010). And then he'll be out.

So if Phillip threatens to burn down your house with your kids in it, what remedies does the law provide? Suppose you do get a serious hearing from the police, as a fifty-eight-year-old real estate agent named Susan Butlin did in Tatamagouche, Nova Scotia, on September 14, 2017. She pleaded with the RCMP for protection against her neighbour, Junior Duggan, who had assaulted and raped her. Butlin had told Duggan's wife about the attack, and now Duggan was threatening to kill her. The Mounties offered to help her seek a peace bond, a court order directing Duggan to keep away from her. Such an order provides no real protection, but it does allow the police to arrest someone like Duggan if he breaches it. But on September 17, before the bond had even been issued, Susan Butlin was dead and Junior Duggan was in custody after a shootout with police.

The truth is that the law enforcement system offers no effective protection for someone like Susan Butlin—or Carla Samson. None. Aside from a peace bond, all you can do is hope—hope that your tormentor doesn't act, or that he bungles his attack, or that he's prevented by some extraneous piece of good fortune like a deadly car accident or a sudden massive heart attack.

That's the real world of law enforcement, and the police know it well. They see it every day, most notably with battered wives. If you ask them privately what they recommend, or what they would do if they were seriously threatened themselves, they will tell you that the only real answer is self-defence. That may or may not work; when Susan Butlin died, she was sleeping with a baseball bat at her side.

Perhaps the most telling story I know on this point comes from the tragedy at Mayerthorpe, Alberta in 2005, when four Mounties were shot dead by James Roszko, who then committed suicide. Linden MacIntyre covered the story for *The Fifth Estate*, and in the course of his research he interviewed a long-term member of the Mayerthorpe detachment who had had many altercations with Roszko. In addition to being a bully, thief, marijuana grower, and cop hater, Roszko was into violent sexual abuse, and eventually did time for sexual assault.

He also threatened to harm the Mountie's family. In response, the Mountie taught his eleven-year-old daughter to use a rifle. Then he put a photo of Roszko on his fridge and told his daughter that if she ever saw that man in the yard, she was to shoot him.

Who can fault him? But if the only solution even a Mountie can devise is to instruct his child to shoot first, what choices do the rest of us have? The ultimate law is the law of survival, which comes down to this: if you genuinely believe that someone is going to kill you, kill him first.

I deeply believe in the importance of an independent and impartial judicial system. In 2003, my wife and I bought a Norwegian-built motorsailer which we named "Magnus" to honour Magnus VI of Norway, who ruled from 1263 to 1280. It was "Magnus the Law-Mender" who revised the laws to embody the idea that crime is an offence against the state, not the individual, and therefore is not a matter for personal vengeance. That idea is really the foundation of modern civil society. But it's an abstract idea, and sometimes the judicial system—the courts and the prosecutors—seems rather loosely tethered to the concrete, ambiguous realities of daily life. The actors in the courtroom often assume, for instance, that the enforcement system is able to do things that it patently cannot do, like provide real protection to citizens in danger of being murdered.

The gap between legal concepts and concrete experience leads judges and prosecutors to use glib, sonorous phrases like "taking the law into their own hands" to describe people like the Mayerthorpe Mountie, people who are actually protecting themselves and their families in desperate situations where the law has nothing to offer them. It leads even so intelligent and thoughtful a man as Shane Russell to contend that, in the middle of the uproar in Mackerel Cove, Dwayne Samson had "time to call the police to seek out justice in a proper fashion."

Really? *Really?* Dwayne is at sea, accompanied by a furious man with a rifle, confronting a criminal who has threatened to kill Dwayne and his whole family. He's furious himself, and deeply frustrated. He has called the authorities numerous times, without avail, to complain about Phillip. If he cries "Stop, boys, stop!" and whips out his cell phone, will they stop? Will a call to the RCMP reach an officer on Isle Madame, or will it be patched through to Sydney? And what will happen then? Do the Mounties have access to a boat, or will everyone simply hold still until an officer comes walking out over the water to handcuff Phillip? In the abstract world of the courtroom, Russell's suggestion is perfectly reasonable. Out on the water, it is absurd.

In the same way, the "agreed statements of facts" are heavy on the "agreed" and perhaps not so strong on the "facts." Dwayne signed off on such an agreement, but—I'm told—only under intense pressure from his lawyers. Since he has never spoken, we have no way of knowing why he objected, but we can speculate. The agreed statement of facts includes Craig Landry's story that Phillip was gaffed, towed, and tied to an anchor. But the members of the Landry jury did not accept that story beyond a reasonable doubt; if they had, the jury would have had to find James guilty of murder, not manslaughter. So is that story factual? Does Dwayne admit to it? Maybe, maybe not. Again, the statement accepts that James shot Phillip. But the forensic evidence shows that all four bullets hit *Midnight*

Slider at or near the waterline, which suggests that James was aiming to sink the boat and prevent Phillip from speeding away. There were no bullet holes in Phillip's boots. Phillip didn't act like a wounded man. In truth, there is no solid evidence that any shot struck him.

But if the agreed-upon story wasn't the actual story, why did Dwayne sign it?

Because it ended his ordeal. By signing it and pleading guilty to manslaughter, he guaranteed himself a moderate sentence and early parole. If he had refused, the Crown could have tried him for murder—and a murder conviction would mean a life sentence, including a minimum of ten years in prison without the possibility of parole. Why risk that? Cut your losses. Take the deal. Do your time and get back to your life.

For all its faults, the system ultimately delivered a set of judgments about as acceptable as anyone could reasonably expect. Manslaughter convictions with long sentences, combined with generous provisions for parole: some people in the community thought the sentences were too light while others thought them too heavy, which suggests they were just about right.

Much credit for that goes to the jury, who could well have found James Landry guilty of murder but instead opted for manslaughter. The jury is the humanizing feature of a rigid, self-satisfied criminal justice system that sees people as isolated individuals to be judged and either freed or punished. It is not the court's role to understand them, to heal wounds, or to resolve conflicts. The system has little capacity for self-criticism; it appraises others, not itself. It didn't even allow itself to hear the full story behind the actions it was judging, and it certainly didn't recognize that the legal system's own shortcomings were a significant contributing factor in the tragedy. At the end of the proceedings nobody looked back to say, How did that process go? Did it meet our highest expectations? Could we have done better?

No: the gavel comes down, the proceedings are over, the convicted men are packed off to prison. Next!

Chief Justice Kennedy's condemnation of "vigilante justice" and
his stress on respect for the rule of law—indeed, the whole structure
of Canada's criminal law—rest on a particular view of the human
situation. The chief justice sees the rule of law as "absolutely basically necessary to our society" because "if each of us were able to
exercise revenge and retribution as we alone determine our lives,
it would be chaos, characterized by fear and brutality. This would
be Animal Kingdom." The implication is that humans are isolated
individuals, competing viciously for advantage, restrained only by
the majestic impartiality of the law. Take away the police and the
courts and you are left with nature, red in tooth and claw—chaos,
terror, and slaughter.

If you change your view of the human situation, however, you
also change your concept of law. Indigenous thinkers would remind
us that, as humans, we are not only competitive; we are also cooperative. Why don't I murder my neighbour? Not because I'm terri-
fied of the police, but because my neighbour and I enrich each
other's lives. Humans actually *are* animals, but deeply social ones,
like bees and geese and the other species of great apes. Law is not so
much a matter of judging good and evil as it is about the shared
understandings that shape our lives together. As John Borrows says,
"Law is about how people organize their relationships in patterns."
And those patterns extend to our relationships with the beautiful
green world we have inherited. Laws are nourished, Borrows says,
"by a grandparent's teachings, a law professor's reflections, an animal's behaviour, an engraved image, and a landscape's contours."

It follows that we all make law as we learn principles of behaviour
from the world around us, from our social traditions, and from our

own experience. Law-making becomes not the province of an elite group of learned professionals but rather a thoroughly democratic endeavour involving us all. As Borrows says, "We have authority in the way that we do the work of law. Law needs love; it needs respect." And a proper use of law is "to sustain, to be healed or revitalized."

Through their centuries of isolation, the Acadian communities developed their own patterns of organized relationships—in Borrows's terms, their own laws. You belong to a community; you support it, and it sustains you. You contribute to the "day" that's held to help a family in distress. You support the cooperative enterprises on which the community depends—producer co-ops, consumer co-ops, credit unions. You derive principles of behaviour from the wise people in your life.

There is law in Gordie Ellis's intervention with our sons. There is law in Omer Boudreau's powerful story about his father giving his firewood to a poor family, a story that still shapes Omer's thought and behaviour seven decades later. We can find law in the experience of my great friend the late John Boudreau, who told me that when he was ten and his father and uncles took him fishing, they dropped him off in a small dory tied to the fairway buoy. That buoy is in the open Atlantic; it guides ships into the Strait of Canso, and the nearest port due east is Bordeaux. There the boy jigged cod while the men went on to fish farther offshore; they picked him up on the way back in. The lessons that John derived from that had to do with competence, courage, trust, and the obligation to help provide for the people who also provide for you. When I think about the man John Boudreau ultimately became—a superb leader, a fine teacher, a devoted community servant, and a delightful companion—I am tempted to collect a fleet of ten-year-old boys and tow them all offshore in dories.

In such stories, we see law merging into education in a process the Catholic Church calls "formation"—the construction not only of intellectual understanding but also of character and spiritual insight.

This is the process by which the community creates the citizens it needs to maintain its own strength and integrity.

The mainspring of Phillip Boudreau's story is the character of Phillip himself, which is fundamentally a failure of formation. So what does traditional Acadian law say about an incorrigible person? Even in the recent past, says RCMP Staff Sergeant Daniel Parent, Isle Madame and similar communities had collective methods of dealing with such people without involving the formal justice system.

"What I found from Isle Madame," he told me, "is that the real bad one, the real bad apple, the community will chase them out of there. It was more so in the 1970s when I first got there than nowadays. But the community used to clean the area on its own. You don't go and frig around because you'll be straightened out right quick. Eventually those that are troublemakers would move out, transfer out to Sydney or to Halifax or whatever, and that would give the place some peace. And the community used to do it on its own."

But not today?

"No. I think there's more tolerance than there used to be, or it could be a lack of 'enough is enough.' In the olden days, it seems to me like people would take care of their own problems. I've had those experiences in Point Aconi, on the island there and in other isolated communities. They won't take any shit. They clean out their own place. There's no point calling the cops—'It takes them forty minutes to get here, and the problem is here right now, so I'm going to get rid of it.' I've seen that in Gabarus, I've seen it in Marion Bridge. They do their own policing."

This sounds a lot like taking the law into your own hands—but ultimately, says Parent, "crime is not the police problem, it's the community problem." If the police don't have community support, they can't function. When Phillip was hiding, for instance, "those who were in the know just wouldn't tell us. So if you want it that way, okay, you live with it. When he was on the run there, when we were looking for him, we got no help from nobody. That went on for about two, three weeks, and then one person who'd had enough pointed me where he was, and that's where I went."

According to the police and the courts and the media, the killing of Phillip Boudreau split and divided the community, tore its fabric, created wounds that would take decades to heal. No, not really. One might reasonably have expected such a split, and people on the island certainly held vigorously differing opinions. But arching over the whole episode is an almost universal mood of sorrow, regret, and guilt. Phillip was an outlaw, but not an outcast. You hear it over and over: *It shouldn't have happened. Nobody deserves to die that way. Those guys aren't killers. We should have stopped it.*

A few days after the jury delivered its verdict, the CBC interviewed André LeBlanc, an Isle Madame community development worker and a contemporary of Dwayne and Phillip.

"As a community, you feel a sense of guilt that you've failed," said André. "You've failed all those involved, including Phillip's family and the Samson-Landry family. We have to ensure that it doesn't happen again. Had nobody bought the lobsters, Phillip would have had no choice but to earn a living honestly. And if the community had reached out and offered him some opportunities, perhaps none of this would ever have happened."

Yes, though even that is not so simple. People did offer Phillip opportunities, most notably Marcel and Kim Heudes, who flew him to Calgary for a complete restart—an intervention that briefly turned his life around and might have done so permanently had everyone stayed in Calgary. And Marcel wasn't the only one to offer opportunities to change. Edgar Samson of Premium Seafoods says, "I used to tell him, 'Phillip, why don't you work? I need workers, you know. Why don't you work and make a few dollars and help support your mother and father?' He said he didn't want to hear of it."

At some level, Phillip probably liked the life he'd created—his freedom from direction, for example, and his power over others who often despised him. In some respects he was a manipulative genius, like Shakespeare's Iago, bringing out the worst in people, playing on their inherent weaknesses, their cowardice and cupidity. When people say "You got better deals from Phillip than you ever got from Walmart," you can see them fertilizing the soil in which a Phillip can flourish. At one level he was a tyrant—terrorizing people, defying them to act against him—and at another level he was a tool, acting out the dark wishes of those around him, often for pay. As several people have said, "There's plenty of guilt to go around."

If we think back to John Borrows's description of the law as something from which we draw guidance, then we can see that forgiveness, rehabilitation, and self-critical reflection are also aspects of law as the Indigenous peoples understand it—and surely any robust understanding of law must include those features. This, incidentally, is how we will all benefit from the process of reconciliation between the imported cultures and the Indigenous ones; reconciliation and a deep, respectful understanding of Indigenous traditions will enlarge both our perception of our situation as humans and the scope of our moral imaginations.

This is where the story comes to rest: with a community reaching for redemption, deeply saddened and shocked, reflecting on the patterns of its relationships, trying to understand how the criminal became a victim while the victims became criminals. By the end of 2018, James and Dwayne, who had been model prisoners, were both on full parole, back in the community where they belonged, deeply regretful, picking up the threads of their lives.

Phillip Boudreau, however, would not come walking out of the sea, dripping with brine and festooned with kelp and eelgrass. His community would be reflecting on his death for a long time to come. Our way forward, its people were saying, is to learn how we failed, how we let this situation spin out into tragedy. Our way forward is to become better, braver, and smarter, so that we will not fail one another again.

ACKNOWLEDGMENTS

In December 2016 I found myself wintering in Vancouver, working on this book and needing some additional interviews. I flew home to Nova Scotia and spent two weeks moseying around Isle Madame and talking to people. One of them was Edgar Samson, who, with his late cousin Brian, has built Premium Seafoods from a small local fish plant into a successful international business headquartered in Arichat. I have known and admired Edgar since he was a very young man. He belongs to a large and brilliantly entrepreneurial family; people on the island sometimes joke that the Samson businesses actually are the economy of Isle Madame. Articulate, warm, and astute, Edgar is generally my preferred source on issues relating to the fishery, and I enjoyed my conversation with him.

I met Edgar again in the departure lounge of Stanfield International Airport in Halifax. He was heading off for a cycling vacation in Vietnam, which tells you how deeply the island has become connected with the rest of the globe. He wanted to know how my research had gone.

Well, fine, I said. I had gathered some terrific interviews—vivid, funny, thoughtful—but I had actually come to wonder if I should finish the book. Most people were eager to help and eager to read it—but a significant minority, including some people I deeply respected, felt that it was a bad idea to dredge the story up again. For them, it was time to put the whole episode behind us and move on.

Actually, Edgar, I said, I'd really like to know what you think. The last thing I want to do is give pain to people I love.

Edgar looked out over the runways for a few long moments. Then he turned back to me.

"You should finish the book," he said firmly. "You'll be fair and honest, and the book will help the island to heal."

Looking back on it, I think the fate of the book actually hung in the balance at that moment. Whenever I've had my doubts—and I've had plenty of them—I go back to that conversation. I am deeply grateful to Edgar, and through him, to the scores of people who gave me the support and insight that I needed to write this book. I really don't know where to begin thanking them. In truth, this book was nearly half a century in the making, and in expressing my gratitude to Edgar Samson, I intend for him to represent all those people, living and dead, who gave me what I needed to write it—and who gave me so much else that I needed throughout what is now a long and happy life. I am not just grateful for their help with the book. I am grateful for their tolerance, affection, and generosity on every front and at every turn.

I did not speak about Phillip's death with the four people accused of his murder, though I asked several times. They were perfectly willing to talk about other matters, but they had nothing to gain by talking about the crime, and possibly a lot to lose. Dwayne's parole doesn't completely end till 2025, and, as Carla Samson said while politely declining an interview, "Silence has served us well." Her father, James Landry, died on November 3, 2019.

I do have some specific acknowledgments to make, starting with the people in the legal system, particularly Chief Justice Joseph Kennedy, the prosecutors Dan MacRury, Stephen Drake, and Shane Russell, and the defence lawyers Luke Craggs, Joel Pink, Nash

Brogan, and T.J. McKeough. I'm grateful to Kevin Patriquin and Larry Evans for background about the legal culture of Nova Scotia, and particularly of the Strait of Canso area. Dana Hunt, the deputy prothonotary of the court in Port Hawkesbury, was unfailingly helpful in finding and providing essential CDs and transcripts.

I am extremely grateful to the people on and off Isle Madame who were willing to be quoted and named in the book, but also to the many people who were willing to share what they knew but very reluctant to see their names used. You can get some idea of the discussion from the comments on Parker Donham's blog, Contrarian. ca. I am glad those people gave me what they could, and I gladly protect their privacy.

Some of the historical material came from conversations with my great friend, the late Marshall Bourinot (1904–1991), publisher of the long-vanished *Richmond County Record*. I learned a great deal from the late Lorenzo Boudreau, who devoted much of his life to documenting the intricate genealogy of Isle Madame. I have also relied on the work of Lorenzo's son, Don Boudrot, a retired teacher who is the most active local historian in Isle Madame today. Stephen White, the legendary genealogist at the Centre d'Études Acadiennes at the Université de Moncton, was generous with his assistance, as he always is. I am deeply grateful for the help of my friends Denise Saulnier and Edwin and Joan DeWolf, and to Peter Zimmer, whose astute comments led me to find a workable structure for this complex story.

My agent, Denise Bukowski, and my publisher, Diane Turbide, provided invaluable feedback, as did my brother Kenneth and—of course—my beloved wife, the author Marjorie Simmins.

I hope I have not forgotten anyone, but with a book of this nature, I almost certainly have—and I apologize very sincerely. I am sure this book has other faults and failings as well—and as always, alas, those mistakes are all mine.